BACH'S MODAL CHORALES

To the memory of Christopher O. Lewis,
friend and mentor.

BACH'S MODAL CHORALES

By Lori Burns

HARMONOLOGIA SERIES No. 9

General Editor: Joel Lester

PENDRAGON PRESS

Stuyvesant, NY

Other titles in the Series **HARMONOLOGIA: STUDIES IN MUSIC THEORY**

No. 1 *Heinrich Schenker: Index to Analyses* by Larry Laskowski (1978) ISBN 0-918728-06-1

No. 2 *F.W. Marpurg's* Thoroughbass and Composition Handbook: *A Narrative Translation and Critical Study* by David A. Sheldon (1989) ISBN 0-918728-55-X

No. 3 *Between Modes and Keys: German Theory 1592–1802* by Joel Lester (1990) ISBN 0-918728-77-0

No. 4 *Music Theory from Zarlino to Schenker: A Bibliography and Guide* by David Damschroeder and David Russel Williams (1991) ISBN 0-918728-99-1

No. 5 *Musical Time: the Sense of Order* by Barbara Barry (1990) ISBN 0-945193-0107

No. 6 *Formalized Music: Thought and Mathematics in Composition* (revised edition) by Iannis Xenakis (1992) ISBN 0-945193-24-6

No. 7 *Esquisse de l'histoire de l'harmonie: An English-Language Translation of the François-Joseph Fétis History of Harmony* by Mary I. Arlin (1994) ISBN 0-945193-51-3

No. 8 *Analyzing Fugue: A Schenkerian Approach* by William Renwick (1995) ISBN 0-945193-52-1

Library of Congress Cataloging-in-Publication Data
Burns, Lori Anne

Bach's modal chorales / by Lori Burns

p. cm. -- (Harmonologia series ; no. 9)

Revision of author's thesis (Ph. D--Harvard, 1991) under the title: J.S. Bach's chorale harmonizations of modal cantus firmi.

Includes bibliographical references (p.) and index.

ISBN 0-945193-74-2

1. Bach, Johann Sebastian, 1685–1750. Chorales. 2. Chorales–Analysis, appreciation. 3. Bach, Johann Sebastian, 1685–1750–Harmony. I. Title. II. Series.

ML410.B13B82   1995

782.25'1264'092--dc20   95-24547

CIP

MN

Contents

Preface vii

 Analytic Methodology vii

 The Chorales viii

 Relevant Literature ix

 Acknowledgments x

Chapter 1: Introduction: The Interpretation of Modal Chorales 1

 The Modal Final as a Generative Tonic 8

 Organicism: The Modal Final as a Unifying Tonic 8

 Directionality: The Modal Final as a Goal 10

 Analytic Observations 17

 The Mixolydian Mode 17

 The Phrygian Mode 25

 The Dorian and Aeolian Modes 30

Chapter 2: An Original Analytic Model for Bach's Phrygian and Mixolydian Chorales 39

 Emphasis on the Fourth Degree 41

 The Rising Fifth-Relation (IV - I) in Phrygian 43

 The Rising Fifth-Relation (IV - I) in Mixolydian 46

 Emphasis on the Sixth Degree in Phrygian 50

 Emphasis on the Sixth Degree in Mixolydian 52

 The Phrygian Lower Neighbor and Upper Neighbor 53

 The Mixolydian Lower Neighbor 54

 Ursatz Possibilities in Phrygian 55

 Ursatz Possibilities in Mixolydian 58

Chapter 3: Bach's Chorale Harmonizations of Phrygian and Mixolydian Cantus Firmi 61

 Aus tiefer Not schrei ich zu dir 61

 Gelobet seist du, Jesu Christ 84

 Dies sind die heiligen zehn Gebot 98

 Ach Gott vom Himmel sieh darein 115

 Summary 120

Chapter 4: An Original Analytic Model for Bach's Dorian and   121
     Aeolian Chorales

     Dorian and Aeolian Cantus Firmi   124

     The Diatonic Seventh Degree in Dorian—Upper Neighbor   128
          Figure

     The Diatonic Seventh Degree in Aeolian—Upper Neigh-   130
          bor Figure

     The Diatonic Seventh Degree in Dorian—Lower Neighbor   131
          Figure

     The Diatonic Seventh Degree in Aeolian—Lower Neigh-   136
          bor Figure

     Dorian Mediant and Aeolian Mediant   138

     Subdominant-Tonic Relation in Dorian and Aeolian   141

     Ursatz Possibilities in Dorian   144

     Ursatz Possibilities in Aeolian   148

Chapter 5: Bach's Chorale Harmonizations of Dorian and   149
     Aeolian Cantus Firmi

     Christ lag in Todesbanden   149

     Was main Gott will das g'scheh allzeit   159

     Erschienen ist der herrlich Tag   170

     Von Gott will ich nicht lassen   177

     Mit Fried und Freud ich fahr dahin   182

     Summary   183

Appendix 1: Modal Cadence Systems in Historical Theory   187

Appendix 2: Dorian, Phrygian, Mixolydian and Aeolian Cantus   219
     Firmi, as Classified by 17th– and 18th–Century Theorists

Appendix 3: Index to the Chorale Examples   225

Appendix 4: Representative Modal Chorales by Bach   231

Appendix 5: Texts and Translations for Cantatas 38, 77, and 91   233

Bibliography   239

Index of Names   249

PREFACE

This study presents an original theory of modality in the chorales of Johann Sebastian Bach, a theory that entails an analytic methodology and individual analytic readings for chorales based on modal cantus firmi. In Chapter 1, I will provide the necessary background for the study by generalizing the broader issues that I have attempted to address. There, I will discuss pertinent issues confronted by the modern analyst when interpreting modal harmony; I will also analyze briefly some representative chorales, without formally defining my analytic terms.

Analytic Methodology

My analytic method is based on Schenkerian techniques, but these are extended to accommodate the individual modes. In Chapters 2 and 4, I will define and illustrate harmonic and melodic formulas peculiar to each mode and specify my symbology. Departures from Schenkerian norms will be noted and thoroughly explored. Chapter 2 explores an original analytic model for the Phrygian and Mixolydian modes; Chapter 3 then analyzes pertinent chorales by Bach. Chapters 4 and 5 do the same for Dorian and Aeolian. The modes are paired in this way since Phrygian and Mixolydian share certain common analytic issues, as do Dorian and Aeolian.

My theory of modality naturally reflects my own perceptions, but it has not arisen in isolation from other theoretical or analytical ideas. Rather, it responds to a wide range of literature, ranging at least from Zarlino through Schenker and Dahlhaus into the present. Since the present study is not offered as a historical survey, I will not provide an extensive discussion of modal theory; however, Appendix 1 investigates modal cadence systems and reproduces examples from several pertinent theorists from the sixteenth through the nineteenth centuries. Appendix 2 lists representative chorale melodies in each mode as they are identified by pertinent authors who engage the modes and the modal chorale.

The Chorales

The chorales that I have chosen for analysis are representative of Bach's modal practice. Appendix 3 lists these chorales and provides important source information for each. It would have meant little to fatigue the reader with endless sketches and analytic commentary, so I restricted the analyses to this group. A longer—albeit still incomplete—list of representative modal chorales by Bach is provided in Appendix 4. Not every chorale listed in Appendix 4 is a "pure" example of its mode: some introduce ficta unconventionally and are more "tonal" in expression, but those chorales are also interesting for comparison.

Throughout the text I will identify chorales by *Bach Werke Verzeichnis* (BWV number) and also by their assigned number in the Breitkopf and Härtel (B & H) edition.[1] For each example, I will also identify the source of the musical text. Many of Bach's chorales derive from extant larger vocal compositions—cantatas, motets, passions, oratorios—for which authoritative sources have been received; in such cases, the score will be based on the *Neue Bach-Ausgabe* or, if that is still unavailable, the *Bach Gesellschaft* edition. Although I do not offer my analyses as studies in text/music relations, I will occasionally refer to the text of a given cantata. For these discussions, I have provided the complete text and a translation in Appendix 5.

A large number of Bach's chorales have been singly transmitted through chorale collections organized in manuscripts and posthumously published editions. For this group of chorales, a possible larger work context cannot be identified. They may derive from cyclic compositions which were not preserved, but it is also possible that they were intended as independent compositions. Not only can we not place these singly transmitted chorales, neither can we be confident that the musical texts, as they have been transmitted in the manuscript collections and editions, are reliable. The degree to which collectors and editors may have altered these chorales cannot be precisely determined. In my examples, the musical texts of the singly transmitted chorales will be based on the *Bach Gesellschaft* edition or, if possible, on Ms. R 18, a gathering of 149 chorales in a manuscript prepared by Bach's assistant, Johann Ludwig Dietel, around 1735. Appendix 3 dis-

---

[1]Once again, I will refer the reader to Appendix 3, which provides source information on the chorales.

cusses this manuscript as well as the historical editions of Bach's chorales in greater detail.

Not all of Bach's modal chorales are at the transposition level of the "white-note" modes. Some Phrygian chorales, for instance, have an F rather than an E-Phrygian final. In certain cases, I have found it useful to transpose a given chorale to the corresponding white-note mode. This makes it easier to compare, for instance, one Phrygian chorale to another, examining in particular different harmonizations of the same cantus firmus, which Bach may set at different pitch levels. The white-note transposition level also helps us to relate the chorale settings to the abstract theoretical formulas and principles defined for the individual modes.

However, there are also clear disadvantages to transposing the chorales. Such transpositions disengage the chorale from its original context. For instance, if the chorale is part of a larger vocal work, then its function within the original tonal plan is suppressed. The transposition is also problematic with respect to instrumental and vocal tessitura. For instance, it is common for "Hypodorian" melodies to have a final of G so that the ambitus of the melody fits more comfortably within the range of the voice. When such a melody is transposed down to D, the tessitura is altered significantly. My global transpositions are thus offered for the purposes of our theoretical study, and are not to be imagined as the compositions themselves. Those chorales which have been transposed will be clearly marked for the reader.

Relevant Literature

The Bibliography lists the materials that I have found to be particularly useful in this investigation. It is not by any means intended as a complete bibliography for the study of modal theory, nor for the study of Bach's chorales. The bibliographic entries are organized according to three main topics: "Bach References," "Hymnological References," and "Theory and Analysis."[2]

---

[2]Within these larger fields, I have made further subdivisions. In the larger category of Bach References I have listed 1) General References, 2) Editions and Manuscript Sources for the Chorales, 3) Chorale Studies and Analytical Studies. Under the topic of Hymnological References I have listed 1) Sources for the Texts and Cantus Firmi and 2) Historical Chorale Works. The Theory and Analysis listings are entered under 1) Historical Theory, 2) Schenkerian Theory and 3) Analytical Writings.

Acknowledgments

The present study is a revision of my dissertation, "J. S. Bach's Chorale Harmonizations of Modal Cantus Firmi," Harvard, 1991. I owe a serious debt of thanks to the people who assisted me in that initial exploration of this subject—my readers, David Lewin, Lee Rothfarb, Christoph Wolff, and members of the Eda Kuhn Loeb library staff, Nym Cooke, John Howard, and Millard Irion.

I wish to thank the University of Ottawa's Research and Publications Committee, which granted me a publication subvention in 1994. While on faculty at The Ohio State University during 1992–93, I was awarded a University Seed Grant, which funded my work on this project. I am grateful to Edward Klonoski for his assistance during that year.

Passages in Part I appeared in my article: "J. S. Bach's Mixolydian Chorale Harmonizations," *Music Theory Spectrum* 15/2 (Fall, 1993), 144–172. The present study provides a broader context for the theoretical work and analyses demonstrated in that article. I am grateful to the editor of the journal, Joel Lester, for allowing me unrestricted use of the earlier study.

I also wish to thank Joel Lester for the painstaking care with which he read this manuscript and for asking me challenging questions, both speculative and analytical. To David Lewin, who has read the work in its many stages, I express my deepest appreciation. I would also like to thank Robert Kessler of Pendragon Press for his interest in and efforts toward publishing this study and Kristina Kwacz for her careful preparation of the manuscript. And finally, to my husband John Armstrong, a special word of thanks for providing compositional insights, for preparing the musical examples, and for his unlimited patience.

Lori Burns
Ottawa, July 1995

CHAPTER 1

Introduction: The Interpretation of Modal Chorales

J. S. Bach's chorale settings of modal cantus firmi pose an interesting problem for the modern analyst: What assumptions—modal or tonal—does one bring to the music and what analytic techniques does one use? Are conventional tonal theories adequate to represent the harmonic techniques used in this repertoire? Are conventional modal theories adequate? The implications of the analyst's bias—modal versus tonal—are serious; indeed, for the Mixolydian and the Phrygian modes, the degree of the scale which is heard as modal final or modern tonic is itself at the center of debate. In this introduction I will examine representative Mixolydian, Phrygian, Dorian and Aeolian chorales in order to illustrate some of the interpretive difficulties that arise in their analysis. Before turning to the musical examples, however, I would like to explore some of the theoretical assumptions that underlie a harmonic analysis. The discussions in this chapter are not intended as formal theoretical and analytical essays; rather, such formalism will be delayed until Chapters 2 through 5. Here I wish only to comment upon some of the critical issues which spark the "modal versus tonal" debate.

What do we mean when we say that a piece is tonal? Theorists have meant different things by this statement, drawing upon various metaphors to define tonal function. Such metaphors include a definition of the tonic as a generator of harmonic activity, the tonic as a goal of directed melodic and harmonic motion, and the tonic as a unifying harmony throughout all levels of composition.[1] In the following discussion I will review a few such definitions of tonality and consider their general pertinence for constructing a definition of modality.

---

[1]Here I would like to give credit to David Lewin for his thoughts on how the tonic was defined in historical theory. His seminar on the development of tonal theory from Zarlino to Schenker was invaluable in this regard.

1

One may challenge this line of investigation and assert that modal music should only be analyzed using the theoretical premises of the period in which the music was composed. At the other end of the spectrum would be the analyst who unconditionally judges modal music by the modern standards of tonal music. Even if an analyst wished to do so, it is difficult to put oneself into the historical position of being able to analyze music from a purely contemporaneous perspective. Once influenced by later musical practice, how are we to rid ourselves of modern influences? Daniel Leech-Wilkinson challenges the notion that analysis must always be based on contemporary historical theory:

> Even on historical grounds it must be clear that there is no possibility of adequately reconstructing such a view of a musical work as might have been held by the most educated and perceptive musician of its time. Such a view, were it available, might still be open to substantial amplification by a similarly expert musician of a succeeding generation, able to see the period in question in its larger context. And ultimately, however much we may be able to recapture of a period view—using such evidence as notation, theory treatises, literary sources and archives—*what we then see in the music has still to be expressed in terms which make sense to us.* Thus analyses of surviving works, while taking careful account of what we know of period techniques, have to proceed from, and to seek to explain, what we currently see and hear in the music. There is no other view available to us.[2]

I believe Leech-Wilkinson is suggesting that we find a balance between the two extremes: while it is important not to ignore the period view, it is equally important to express the music in terms which make sense to us. Yet I would submit that the modern analyst must proceed cautiously in order not simply to dismiss or overlook features of the music which are distinctly modal.

A purely historical approach can also be restrictive to the modern music theorist. My musical/theoretical imagination embraces definitions of tonality that were developed from the eighteenth through the twentieth century. While it is interesting to consider historical discussions of the modal chorale repertoire, these discussions do not always explain the musical language in a way that is comparable to the explanation of tonal music advanced, for example, by Schenker. I have certainly been influenced by earlier theorists in my analysis, but have not found any one

---

[2]Daniel Leech-Wilkinson, "Machaut's *Rose, Lis* and the Problem of Early Music Analysis," *Music Analysis* 3/1 (1984), p. 9 (my emphasis).

particular contemporary approach that explores and defines the musical language to the extent that I would like. Kirnberger, for instance, offers some interesting observations on the subject of his teacher's modal chorales, focusing on intervallic structure, degree emphasis, cadential paradigms and musica ficta. Kirnberger's discussion is valuable to anyone studying Bach's chorales, but it cannot be viewed as a comprehensive theory of modal harmony.[3] Saul Novack expresses his frustration with the limits of a purely historical analytic approach in his article "On the Analysis of Pre-Baroque Music":

> As musicians, theorists, and musicologists, we have a great desire to understand the history of musical structure. If we are to concern ourselves with the evolution and history of triadic tonality from the earliest prolongations of simple tones, which tools are we to employ? What has traditional musicology offered us? Shall we depend on descriptions of modes, sometimes several operating simultaneously in accordance with the limited views of contemporaneous theorists? Shall we count the cadences and their various ways as the basis for determining the sense of "key"? Shall we yield to the computer to enumerate a statistical status of chords as a determinant of "style"? Shall we be content to talk about the obvious so-called stylistic features that are in effect the small details of the foreground? Etc., etc.
>
> . . . We could not begin to understand the historical process without a Schenkerian approach to triadic tonality. This is the only way we can cut across the boundaries of eras of style that have distorted much of our understanding of the history of the art of music. . . . We have no other recourse for understanding the music of the past but to rely upon what Schenker has taught us. Its validity is unquestionable; its limitations, none.[4]

Perhaps given that the particular repertoire under consideration here was composed by Bach, the appeal of tonal theory is even greater. It does not seem unreasonable to bring tonal expectations to the analysis of his music. Yet I do not mean to suggest that the tonal system is a standard

---

[3]Johann Philipp Kirnberger discusses the modes in his treatise *Die Kunst des reinen Satzes in der Musik*, vol. 2, part 1 (Berlin-Königsberg: G. J. Decker and G. L Hartung, 1776; facs. ed., Hildesheim: Georg Olms Verlag, 1988); trans. David Beach and Jürgen Thym, *The Art of Strict Musical Composition* (New Haven: Yale University Press, 1982). The relevant passage on the modes is found in part 1, chapter 2 of vol. II, pp. 314–335 of the translation, pp. 41–67 of the German original. I will say more about Kirnberger in this chapter; in addition, his proposed cadence systems for the modes are discussed in Appendix 1, along with those of several other theorists who engage modal degree emphasis in their writings.

[4]Saul Novack, "The Analysis of Pre-Baroque Music," *Aspects of Schenkerian Theory*, ed. David Beach (New Haven: Yale University Press, 1980), pp. 132–33.

to which modal music must comply. Indeed, it is that very instinct which I
mean to question here—there are certain chorales for which a traditional
tonal analysis is inadequate. From a simple Roman-Numeral analysis to a
detailed Schenkerian sketch, any *strict* tonal analysis will not be sufficient
to reveal the modal features of Bach's chorales. Thus the challenge lies in
defining an analytic system which will address the same questions as do
our modern definitions of key, but which will also accommodate the
idioms and higher-level structures that underlie these modal chorales. So
I return to the original questions posed: What do we mean when we say
that a composition is tonal? And can theories of modern tonality serve as
a model for constructing a definition of modality?

An important theoretical concept developed to explain common-practice tonal language is that of the tonic as a generator of harmonic content. Rameau, in his *Traité de l'harmonie*, relies on string
divisions to explain how a root generates its upper fifth. The fifth
progression from tonic to dominant is then expressed as the most perfect fundamental bass movement.[5] In *Der freie Satz*, Schenker similarly
cites the overtone series in order to generate his chord of nature, a
major triad.[6] This is then transformed into the arpeggiation of the fundamental structure (I - V - I) and developed at the middleground level
into a contrapuntal voice-leading event.

The derivation of harmonic content from a natural source has
strong implications for developing a tension/resolution model of harmonic progression. Rameau's most perfect progression from tonic to
dominant creates the expectation that the fifth must return to its source.[7]
In addition to this method of accounting for directed motion in harmony,
Rameau also identifies dissonance as a requirement to make one desire
repose. It is not enough that the dominant must return to its source (the
generating tonic); in addition, the dominant must resolve to the tonic because it is dissonant and the tonic is consonant. To distinguish the two
perfect chords, Rameau makes the dominant less perfect (that is, dissonant) by including its seventh.[8] Rameau also classifies the intervals

[5]Jean Philipp Rameau discusses the fundamental bass progressions and their relation
to the natural division of the string in his *Traité de l'harmonie* (Paris, 1722), trans.
Philip Gossett, *Treatise on Harmony* (New York: Dover Publications, 1971), Book II,
Chapter 1, pp. 59–60.

[6]Heinrich Schenker, *Der freie Satz* (Vienna: Universal Edition, 1935); trans., ed. Ernst
Oster, *Free Composition* (New York: Schirmer, 1979), Chapter 2, Section 1, §1.

[7]Rameau, *Treatise on Harmony*, Book II, Chapter 18, Article 1, p. 143.

[8]Ibid., Book II, Chapter 2, pp. 61–62.

within the cadential V₇- I progression in order to rationalize further the tension/resolution model: the major third of the dominant is lively and must rise while the minor third above the fifth (the seventh of the chord) must fall because it is sad.[9]

In the same spirit, Fétis explores interval classifications when he defines tonality. Intervals and scale degrees are classified according to their relative degree of repose and harmonic directionality is created through the required resolution of non-reposeful scale degrees and intervals. The intervals and scale degrees are classified so as to define the tonic as the reposeful goal of directed motion.[10]

Schenker's theory of tonality also engages the metaphor of directionality. The fundamental line, supported by the arpeggiation I - V - I is described in the following way: "To man is given the experience of ending, the cessation of all tensions and efforts. In this sense, we feel by nature that the fundamental line must lead downward until it reaches $\hat{1}$, and that the bass must fall back to the fundamental. With $\hat{1}$ [supported by] I all tensions in a musical work cease."[11] He is quite specific that directionality is created only by the ascending arpeggiation which is logically followed by its return through the descending arpeggiation, citing the overtone series once again as the theoretical validation for this preference. Other fifth progressions, such as the descending arpeggiation I - IV - I, "express no motion whatsoever and thus do not signify an artistic realization of a chord." [12]

For Schenker, directionality is also created through the composing out of the tonic triad in the vertical dimension: ". . . Nature as well as art is satisfied if the course of a melody offers to our ear the possibility of connecting with a certain tone its fifth and third. . . ."[13] According to Schenker, the clarity of harmonic content through the linear dimension is

[9]Ibid., Book II, Chapter 5, p. 64. Rameau cites Zarlino on this subject, who attributes such directional implications to major and minor thirds in his *Istitutione harmoniche*, Part III, Chapter 10, p. 182, and Chapter 38, pp. 219–220.

[10]François-Joseph Fétis, *Traité complet de la théorie et de la pratique de l'harmonie contenant la doctrine de la science et de l'art* (Paris, 1844). Fétis classifies diatonic intervals in Book I, Chapter 2.

[11]Schenker, *Free Composition*, p. 13.

[12]Ibid., p. 14.

[13]Heinrich Schenker, *Harmonielehre* (Stuttgart: Cotta, 1906); trans. Elisabeth Mann Borgese, *Harmony*, ed. Oswald Jonas (Chicago: University of Chicago Press, 1954), p. 133.

a feature of tonal music and something that is lacking in mode-based melodies.[14] Plain chant, he says, "is particularly instructive if we want to demonstrate how musical instinct, to begin with, was totally inartistic and only very gradually condensed and rose from a chaos of fog to a principle of art."[15] He criticizes a number of modal chant melodies for their irrational harmonic unfolding. For instance, the second Credo of the *Liber Gradualis*, reproduced here as Example 1, is criticized for its lack of tonal organization.[16] Schenker does not know whether to attach tonic status to G or E, since neither is properly prolonged by its dominant—if G is the tonic, then its dominant, D, should receive greater emphasis, and if E is the tonic, then the notes F and D are illogically placed.[17] At the root of Schenker's criticisms is his basic tenet that the harmonic relationship needed to define tonality is that of tonic to dominant; when that relationship does not emerge, the music lacks coherence.[18]

Example 1: Credo, cantus firmus incipit

Cre-do in u-num De-um

Schenker engages another definition of tonic—his tonic is not only the generator of harmonic content and the goal of directed harmonic motion, but also the unifying harmony in tonal music. In the opening of *Der freie Satz*, he states that his approach explores the concept of organic coherence in free composition as it is revealed in the fundamental structure and in the subsequent levels. The organic coherence he describes is based on the prolongation of the chord of nature.

A far-reaching implication of Schenker's theory of organicism is that there is a link connecting all tonal music—every tonal composition is based on the chord of nature expressed in the commonly shared fundamental structure, which differs only in the scale degree that initiates the melodic descent ($\hat{3}$, $\hat{5}$, or $\hat{8}$). By comparison, according to Schenker, the modes simply cannot generate a uniform harmonic language that would

[14]Ibid., "Note"at the end of §76, "The Realization of the Triad," pp. 134–137.

[15]Ibid., p. 134.

[16]Ibid., Example 104, p. 135 (Example 138 in the German original).

[17]Ibid., p. 135.

[18]Ibid., p. 137.

bind the repertoire together. Their irregularity of structure is one of Schenker's main criticisms—the chords on the tonic, subdominant and dominant degrees do not reflect harmonic consistency. Whereas the minor (Aeolian) and major (Ionian) modes have minor and major chords respectively on each of these primary degrees, the Dorian, Phrygian, Lydian and Mixolydian modes display irregular triadic configurations on these degrees. Further, the Phrygian and Lydian modes have diminished triads on the dominant and subdominant degrees, respectively.[19]

The issue of uniformity versus plurality is present not only in Schenker's distinction between modes and keys, but also within his own tonal theoretical system. He assigns the major mode its "natural" primacy and considers the minor mode to be artificially derived from the major.[20] Tonality is thus a fixed system at the highest or "primordial" level. And Schenker's carefully defined norms of tonal progression assume the primacy of this "natural" major mode.[21]

---

[19]According to Schenker, such harmonic inconsistency is "most inappropriate for the development of motivic intentions. . . ."(Ibid., p. 55.) He finds it to be particularly problematic in the composition of fugue. If, for example, the subject were introduced on the tonic in the Mixolydian mode, then an answer on the minor dominant would not permit true motivic parallelism. In choosing this particular example, Schenker reveals his inclination to apply tonal logic and compositional expectations to the modal system. He assumes that all subject/answer pairs will be based upon tonic - dominant thematic relations. In the Mixolydian literature, however, the conventional answer to a tonic subject would be on the subdominant, not the dominant.

[20]In the first section of *Harmony* Schenker discusses "The Origin of Tonal Systems," defining the major mode as the natural tonal system (pp. 3–44) and the minor mode as the artificial tonal system (pp. 45–54).

[21]In *Free Composition*, Figure 1 illustrates "the *fundamental structure*" as a major phenomenon. Figure 2 illustrates "arpeggiation as an outgrowth of the harmonic series"; this of course is a major phenomenon. Figure 3 illustrates how both the *Baßbrechung* and the *Urlinie* derive from the major arpeggiation of Figure 2. All of the abstract theoretical Figures continue to be given in C major up until Figure 26, which gives an abstract schema for an interruption-form "in minor." The theoretical figures, beyond Figures 1–2–3, are specifically Figures 4–7 (first part), 8–11, 14–19, 21, and 23–25. The intervening Figures, namely 7a–b, 12–13, 20, and 22, are all analytic illustrations. Figures 7a, 12, 20.1, and 20.2 analyze minor compositions. Figure 13 analyzes Chopin's "B-flat minor" Scherzo, which Schenker hears in D-flat major. Schenker's footnote on the "Scherzo in B-flat minor" seems to be only the second place the word "minor" appears in the treatise; it appears only to identify the usual title of Chopin's composition (*Free Composition*, p. 26; there is a reference to "the major-minor system" on p. 8.) By this time, Schenker has finished Part I, on the Background. Figure 26, "in minor," draws some discussion of the minor mode from Jonas (p. 39, footnote 10), but not from Schenker himself. The reference to Figure 26, on p. 39, is 11 pages into the discussion of the First Level in the Middleground.

A great deal more has been written on the subject of tonal theory, but let us stop here and consider how the principles of tonality just reviewed might be transferred to a definition of harmonic modality. Before I launch into this discussion, however, I need to make some comments on terminology. I have not found a solution to the problems created by borrowing tonal descriptors in a modal context. For instance, as I have just attempted to demonstrate, "tonic" is a loaded term, with many important associations for analysis. Yet it is the only term I know for clearly identifying the chord on the first degree of the scale or mode. It is sometimes possible to use modal "final," but one cannot consistently use "final"; for example a "final" cadence might mean a "tonic" cadence or the last cadence in a composition. "Dominant" and "subdominant" are also problematic, for their associations with common-practice tonality. Yet for the purposes of analyzing harmony, in a modal or a tonal context, I see no other solution but to use these terms. Now I would like to return to the subject at hand—the relevance of tonal metaphors for modal theory.

The Modal Final as a Generative Tonic

The assumption that the overtone series generates the triad, which in turn generates the most fundamental progression from tonic to dominant simply cannot be transferred to modal harmony. Not all modes emphasize the harmony on the fifth as a structural dissonance. Compositions in the Phrygian mode, for instance, cannot explore tonic-dominant relationships, given the quality of harmony on the fifth degree. In a Phrygian composition, which may have a structural bass arpeggiation of I - IV - I, it is simply not possible, nor theoretically valuable, to identify a "natural" source for the harmony.

Organicism: The Modal Final as a Unifying Tonic

Related to the problem of attaching generative significance to the modal final is the problem of hearing the modal tonic triad prolonged at higher levels of structure. That is, the underlying structure of a given mode-based composition does not always reduce to the same "primordial state" of Schenker's system, a triadic unfolding of the "sound in nature." A given mode might be expressed by means of a triadic structure, with emphasis on $\hat{1}$, $\hat{3}$ and $\hat{5}$, but it might also be expressed by means of other structures, emphasizing different degrees of the scale, such as $\hat{4}$ and $\hat{6}$. Furthermore, in the analytic model proposed in this study, I not only admit different fundamental structures for each individual mode, but I also recognize different structures within a single mode.

This is not to say that organicism is absent from modal harmony. On the contrary, modal compositions can present cogent background structures that relate organically to other levels of composition. What is lacking is a connection among all modal pieces—since modal music is not based on the unfolding of the chord of nature, there is no common thread that connects Phrygian structures to Mixolydian structures to Dorian structures, etc.

On the subject of organicism, let us consider the views of Carl Dahlhaus, a modern theorist who attempts to develop a historically sensitive theory of modality. Dahlhaus finds modal harmony to be independent from an organic hierarchical structure, citing the disposition of cadential degrees as support for his argument. He draws a comparison between the abstract schema of cadential degrees and the harmonic progressions that express these cadential degrees. Dahlhaus points out that in the tonal system, the relationship of dominant key to tonic key is expressed locally in the V - I cadential progression; in the modal system, however, the relationship between the secondary cadential degree to the final is not similarly expressed in a local cadential structure. For example, in the Phrygian mode, the harmonic relationship between the commonly stressed secondary degree C and the final E is nowhere expressed as a local harmonic progression C - E.[22] In other words, Dahlhaus asserts that modal harmonic relationships are not reflected at different levels of structure, whereas tonal relationships are.

This distinction between modality and tonality is, however, debatable. The emphasis on the secondary degrees A in Phrygian and C in Mixolydian is reflected in the plagal harmonic progressions A - E and C - G, which are, respectively, the common final cadential progressions in these modes. The relation between C and E is also expressed harmonically in the Phrygian mode, through the idiomatic cadential progression VI - vii - I (C - D - E).

---

[22]Carl Dahlhaus, *Untersuchungen über die Entstehung der harmonischen Tonalität* (Kassel: Bärenreiter, 1968), trans. Robert O. Gjerdingen, *Studies on the Origin of Harmonic Tonality* (Princeton, 1990), p. 221.

Directionality: The Modal Final as a Goal

Directionality is perhaps the most provocative and challenging metaphor to apply to modal harmonic progressions. Since theories of tonal directionality are so uniformly dependent on the resolution of the dissonant dominant to the reposeful tonic, one has to be careful not simply to search for a comparable V - I progression in modal harmony. Indeed, such a fifth progression may or may not be present, depending on the mode and on the composition. Furthermore, if a fifth relation is present, it may not represent a tonic-dominant, but rather a subdominant-tonic relationship.

The problem of the fifth relation is thus a serious one, as it affects modal identity. If a composition does not define its tonic through the tonal V - I progression, then Schenkerian theorists claim that the mode is not adequately defined, that a sense of harmonic direction and resolution is absent. In his study of some Bach organ preludes, William Renwick makes the following statement:

> Among the modes, Phrygian is the most highly-resistant to a common-practice harmonic treatment. There is no functional dominant chord because of the lowered second degree. This means that it is impossible to set up E as a point of resolution in a traditional tonal sense through a perfect cadence without at the same time denying the fundamental character of the mode. To be entirely faithful to the mode, one must give up principles of fundamental harmony and accept a modal harmonization which is not based on the usual tonic-dominant relationship: in forming the dominant of E, F would have to give way to F-sharp. To be faithful to the principles of functional harmony, on the other hand, one must abandon the centrality of the mode: the so-called Phrygian cadence (IV - V in minor) can provide an effective cadential harmonization of the melodic pattern F - E, but in the key of A minor.[23]

Renwick suggests here that the Phrygian mode does not measure up to the standard of harmonic logic found in the major and minor modes of tonality. In Renwick's description, no matter how we handle this mode, we face a losing proposition: the addition of F-sharp would make possible a tonic-defining V - I progression, but then the mode would be lost; or F-natural could be harmonized diatonically in Phrygian, but then it would be interpreted in A minor. Renwick raises an interesting question here about modal identity and harmonic directionality—how is the centrality of the Phrygian mode expressed? He is certainly correct that a harmonic syntax

---

[23]William Renwick, "Modality, Imitation and Structural Levels: Bach's *Manualiter Kyries* from *Clavierübung III*," *Music Analysis* 11/1 (1992), p. 58.

which defines Phrygian centrality is not synonymous with that which defines tonal centrality. Perhaps we simply have to measure modal centrality by a different yardstick. For instance, Renwick's suggested harmonization of a descent from F to E by D minor - E major is indeed a definitive Phrygian progression.

Certain historical tonal theorists also evaluated modal harmonic relations in terms of the modern scales. Georg Andreas Sorge, for instance, in the *Anleitung zur Fantasie* of 1767, adopts a tonal stance when he evaluates the modes. The Phrygian mode is equated with Aeolian and the Mixolydian mode with Ionian:

> Phrygian is no other mode than our A minor, only with the distinction that the dominant harmony e g-sharp b begins and ends, as the chorale "Ach Gott vom Himmel sieh' darein" illustrates.
>
> . . This type of close [A to E] arouses a desire to hear more. It is called in Printz's *Satyrischen Componisten clausula desiderans.* . . . .
>
> Mixolydian, g a b c d e f g, is no other mode than our modern C major, when we begin and end with the dominant harmony g b d. An example is the chorale "Komm Gott Schöpfer heiliger Geist," if the F-sharp is avoided.[24]

Although earlier, in the *Vorgemach der Musikalischen Composition* (1745), Sorge had recognized the plagal cadence in the Phrygian and Mixolydian modes as a characteristic expression of the modal final, he now explicitly interprets these progressions tonally.[25] The Phrygian final is functionally equivalent to the dominant of A minor and the Mixolydian final to the dominant of C major.

---

[24][Der *Phrygius* ist keine andere Tonart als unser A moll, nur mit dem Unterscheid, daß der herrschende Accord e gis h anfängt und endiget, wie der Choral: Ach Gott vom Himmel sieh' darein, bezeuget. . . . Diese Art zu schliessen erwecket ein Verlangen ein mehrers zu hören. Sie heißt in Printzens Satyrischen Componisten *clausula desiderans.* . . . Der *Mixolydius*, g a h c d e f g ist nichts anders als unser heutiges C dur, wenn wir mit dessen herrschendem Accorde g h d anfangen und endigen. Ein Beyspiel giebt der Choral: Komm Gott Schöpfer heiliger Geist, wenn das fis vermieden wird.] Georg Andreas Sorge, *Anleitung zur Fantasie oder zu der schönen Kunst, das Clavier, wie auch andere Instrumente, aus dem Kopfe zu spielen* (Lobenstein, 1767), p. 42.

[25]Sorge, *Vorgemach der Musikalischen Composition* (Lobenstein, 1745); trans. Allyn Dixon Reilly in "Georg Andreas Sorge's 'Vorgemach der Musikalischen Composition'; A Translation and Commentary," Ph.D. dissertation, Northwestern University, 1980, Chapter 11.

In his closing chapter of *Between Modes and Keys*, Joel Lester addresses this question with respect to the Phrygian mode. He reproduces the opening and closing passages from Bach's chorale "Ach Gott vom Himmel sieh darein," BWV 153/1 (B & H, Nr. 3), which is given here in its entirety as Example 2.[26] Lester questions the validity of the traditional interpretation for the fifth relation A - E as tonic-dominant, and suggests a different kind of dynamic interpretation:

> In this chorale, whose melody is Phrygian . . . Bach's harmonizations seem at first to begin on the dominant chord of a minor key. The first two phrases appear to rhyme harmonically, with open and closed cadences. But Bach concludes the final cadence of the melody on the apparent dominant of the key. Perhaps instead of thinking of the opening harmony as a dominant, he conceived of the opening and concluding harmonies as being the conclusive chords of the Phrygian mode. After all, many theorists had regarded the cadence on the fourth degree of the Phrygian scale as a final cadence. . . . *Are the norms of harmonic directionality leading from dominant to tonic reversed here? That is, does the "minor tonic" chord drive toward the "major dominant" rather than the other way around?* The question is inescapable here, for these chorales are the presumably conclusive finales of multi-movement cantatas, not internal movements followed by other music. . . .[27]

Indeed, the Phrygian mode demands a different approach to the interpretation of fifth-relations and dissonance resolution. If the only fifth-relation evident in a composition is that of E major to A minor, and if one analyzes that relationship as dominant to tonic, then all Phrygian compositions will be interpreted in A minor, with the final harmony on E functioning as an unresolved dominant. Such an interpretation neither does justice to the individual character of the Phrygian mode, nor to the harmonic integrity of Phrygian compositions.

My theoretic objective with this study will be to identify the thematic and dynamic harmonic relations that are characteristic to the individual modes. This demands an analytical system which does not rely upon the uniform hearing of a harmonic relation, as for example, the fifth-relation, but rather which allows for a multiplicity of har-

---

[26]Joel Lester, *Between Modes and Keys: German Theory, 1592–1802* (New York: Pendragon Press, 1989), p. 157, Example 9.4. He also gives the comparable passages from another setting of this chorale by Bach, BWV 2 (B & H, Nr. 262). The chorale in Example 2 (BWV 153/1) will be discussed in Chapter 3. The musical text in Example 2 is based on *NBA* I/4, p. 201.

[27]Ibid., p. 158 (emphasis is mine).

Example 2: "Ach Gott, vom Himmel sieh darein," BWV 153/1 (B & H, Nr. 3)

monic and melodic relations. It is difficult, however, to assign dynamic or directional significance to these characteristic modal progressions. In tonal music, we have been conditioned to hear the tendency of the dissonant $V(_7)$ chord to resolve to the reposeful tonic. Since it is not possible to identify a single progression that will invoke dynamic resolution in modal harmony, how are we to understand the role of directional or functional hearing in modal music? For the Phrygian mode, the resolution from A minor to E major might be heard as conclusive; for the Mixolydian mode, from C major to G major; for Dorian, from A major to D minor, etc. We must shift our expectations from one mode to the next. The perception that certain tones must absolutely resolve a particular way, *independent of context* (as in the V_7 - I progression), is simply absent from modal hearing.

Dahlhaus assumes a self-reflective stance on the topic of functional hearing; he is extremely careful not to interpret the modes as he would interpret the modern keys. He suggests that the listener must abandon

tonally conditioned responses and develop a different kind of ear for listening to the modal repertoire. Whereas in tonal theory, harmonic directionality is defined by invoking the tonic as a goal that is approached by its
naturally generated upper fifth or by classifying the reposeful nature of
scale steps in relation to a central tonic, Dahlhaus asserts that modal harmony is not based on such harmonic tension and dynamic relationships.
The modal fifth-relation is quite distinct from the tonal:

> In the harmonically tonal fifth-relation, two features are intertwined: first,
> the fifth-relation as a two-sided, "bilateral" relation without a sense of a
> particular alignment, and second, the "tendency" of the one degree
> toward the other. In contrast, only the first factor is operative in the
> modal fifth-relation. There is a relationship between a and e, but it does
> not include a dependence of one degree upon the other. The fifth-rela-
> tion is nothing but a bilateral relation, and it was perceived as such
> without e being related to a as a dominant or a to e as a subdominant. A
> listener who has grown up in the tradition of major-minor tonality may
> find it difficult to discontinue hearing a sense of alignment in degree
> relationships, but to do so is not impossible.[28]

Dahlhaus explains the bilateral fifth-relation as one in which a connection
between A and E, for example, is established, without necessitating a
choice between A as final and E as repercussion, or vice versa. Neither
degree is subordinate to the other. The meaning of the relation between
A and E is not affected by certainty concerning the final.[29] The fifth-relation is self-contained; it does not suggest anything beyond itself. In that
sense, it is lacking in tendency.[30]

Also "self-contained" is the modal step progression, to which
Dahlhaus refers as a "contrasting" chord progression.[31] The theorist
distinguishes the step relation in modal harmony from that in tonal
harmony. In the tonal progression I - ii - V - I, the step progression I -
ii creates a tension that is resolved by the dominant. In the modal system step-progressions can occur, such as G - F or F - E, which do not
require such resolution. As with the fifth relation, the step progression is asserted as a "self-contained event from which no consequen-
ces need be drawn."[32]

---

[28]Dahlhaus, *Studies on the Origin of Harmonic Tonality*, p. 223.

[29]Ibid., pp. 223–24; see also p. 241.

[30]Ibid., p. 245.

[31]Ibid., p. 241.

[32]Ibid., p. 245.

Although this might suggest that modal harmony is "devoid of tension," Dahlhaus asserts that tension is created through the articulation and resolution of imperfect sonorities. As an example he cites the Phrygian cadence vii$_6$ - I in E, in which the imperfect major sixth $\frac{D}{F}$, resolves into the perfect octave $\frac{E}{E}$. Dahlhaus cautions against hearing this progression in functional A minor. It is a "self-contained progression, not a fragment of an A-minor cadence."[33]

In this view of modal chord relations, cadential progressions stand independent of tonal function. The modal "clausula" is not the result of harmonic progression as is the tonal cadence. Although the clausula degrees are in themselves mode-defining features, the clausula "forms neither the center around which the sonorities group themselves nor the goal toward which they strive. . . . In modal polyphony, unlike tonal harmony, it is seldom possible to predict on which clausula degree a series of sonorities will end."[34] Dahlhaus still maintains that there are primary and secondary clausula degrees, in other words, degrees which are prominent as cadence points, but they are not prepared by the harmonic progressions.

Dahlhaus's suspicion of reading tonal function into modal harmonic events is warranted. His approach to modal harmonic analysis, while extreme, might well be adopted, especially in the interpretation of fifth relations. However, it distorts modal practice to deny completely the existence of goal-oriented expectations which may or may not correspond to those of the tonal practice. Instead of understanding modal harmonic relations as "self-contained," perhaps it is better to hear them as context-dependent. In the case of the Phrygian mode, for example, is it not possible to understand that a concluding IV - I progression could resolve tensions that were established through the harmonic and melodic fabric of the composition? That is, can we understand structural dissonance as being based on the particular features of a given chorale in a given mode, rather than based on an assumed hierarchy such as the tonal relationship of dominant to tonic?

In a recent discussion of a Phrygian chorale by Bach, David Neumeyer and Susan Tepping reveal how reluctant modern theorists are to hear harmonic directionality in modal music. The underlying harmonic progression of the chorale is identified as I - iv - VI - vii - I,

[33]Ibid., p. 240.
[34]Ibid., p. 243.

a common Phrygian structure. Borrowing terminology developed by Felix Salzer, the authors identify this as a "completely contrapuntal structure" as opposed to a "functional harmonic structure" such as I - V - I or I - ii - V - I.[35] Salzer's terminology here is telling of a tonal bias—only those progressions which include the I - V - I arpeggiation are functional; other progressions are merely contrapuntal.

In my own analysis of the modal repertoire, I have been aware of the ways in which I am influenced by tonal common practice, but have been interested in challenging my tonal expectations and in developing a sympathetic ear for modal harmony. This requires a different approach to analysis, especially to reductive analysis. Schenkerian methodology plays an important role in my analyses, yet in order to integrate modal patterns into a reductive sketch, I have avoided the Schenkerian tendency to justify them somehow in tonal/functional terms. Rather, I have attempted to retain the distinctly modal patterns and, where Schenkerian analysis cannot accommodate them, to develop a new reductive symbology. My results indicate that each mode requires a different interpretation of melodic and harmonic relationships. There exist characteristic Mixolydian, Phrygian, Dorian, and Aeolian relationships that unify compositional structure at all levels.

While my definition of modal organicism may not be identical to Schenker's definition of tonal organicism, it is not so far removed from his meaning. Nicholas Cook aptly describes Schenkerian analysis as "a kind of metaphor according to which a composition is seen as the large-scale embellishment of a simple underlying harmonic progression, or even as a massively-expanded cadence; a metaphor according to which the same analytical principles that apply to cadences in strict counterpoint can be applied, *mutatis mutandis*, to the large-scale harmonic structures of complete pieces."[36] Cook's interpretation of Schenkerian analysis relates well to my analytic solutions for the modal chorales: I attempt to show an organic connection between foreground gestures (such as cadential progressions) and deeper-level harmonic structures, a connection that lends a sense of organicism to the musical work.

---

[35]David Neumeyer and Susan Tepping, *A Guide to Schenkerian Analysis* (New Jersey: Prentice Hall, 1992), p. 113. Salzer developed these terms in *Structural Hearing*, 2 vols. (New York: Charles Boni, 1952).

[36]Nicholas Cook, *A Guide to Musical Analysis* (London: J. M. Dent and Sons, Ltd., 1987), p. 36.

Analytic Observations

I would like now to turn to some representative chorales, for a brief exploration of the interpretive difficulties associated with their analysis. With these chorales, I hope to raise some of the questions that will be answered by the original theoretical model and the formal analyses presented in Chapters 2 through 5.

The Mixolydian Mode

I will begin with a traditional Mixolydian chorale melody, "Gelobet seist du, Jesu Christ." Schenker's discussion of the melody in *Kontrapunkt I* (1910) illuminates an important problem which arises when the tonal analyst confronts the Mixolydian mode.[37] Schenker's clearly articulated opposition to a G-Mixolydian interpretation, in favor of a C-major tonal reading, is precisely the perspective on modal analysis which I would like to challenge.

Schenker's purpose in the pertinent section of *Kontrapunkt* is to clarify the structure and function of the cantus firmus. Citing the "old rules" of counterpoint, he asserts that the first and final notes of a cantus should be treated as the tonic. Schenker claims that this rule obtains only in the harmonization of the cantus firmus as an exercise; in the harmonization of a chorale melody in free composition the rule does not obtain since the melody is, at that stage, part of an "artwork." His reason for making such a distinction between exercise and free composition becomes clear, he asserts, if we look at the Mixolydian melody and some harmonizations of it by Bach and Bellermann, given as Example 3.[38] If one harmonizes the tune according to the contrapuntal rule, then one must begin and end on G, giving the tune a Mixolydian final. Since Schenker does not recognize the viability of a modal setting, he cannot allow this rule to obtain. Accordingly, he proposes the rule that the final note can be something other than the tonic so that he can make a tonal (that is, C major) setting of this tune, expressing—so he claims—the melody's "natural"

---

[37]Heinrich Schenker, *Kontrapunkt*, 2 vols. (Vienna: Universal Edition, 1910, 1922); trans. John Rothgeb and Jürgen Thym as *Counterpoint*, 2 vols. (New York: Schirmer Books, 1987), vol. I, pp. 33–40. Schenker's interpretation of modal harmony here is consistent with his historical view that modality was "corrected" by tonality. In this context, he discusses the modes extensively in *Harmony*, pp. 55–69, 110–115, 134–37, 163–73.

[38]Example 3 reproduces Schenker's examples in *Counterpoint*, vol. 1, pp. 34–37. (©1987 Schirmer Books, a division of MacMillan. Used by permission.)

tendencies. His setting, in which he limits himself to root-position triads, is also provided in Example 3.

Example 3: "Gelobet seist du, Jesu Christ" (Reprinted with permission of
Schirmer Books, an imprint of Simon & Schuster MacMillan, from
Counterpoint, vol. I, by Heinrich Schenker, translated by John Rothgeb and
Jurgen Thym, copyright © 1987 by Schirmer Books.)

J.S. Bach, BWV 91/6

Example 3, cont.

J.S. Bach, BWV 64/2

Bellermann

Example 3, cont.

Schenker's version

    In order to analyze the cantus firmus, Schenker advises us to "abandon all prejudice of earlier theory and use our unbiased ear to the fullest by simply following in the horizontal melodic direction the fifths, which help to establish the content so beautifully. . . ."[39] The theoretical biases that he wants us to shed are those of the modal system. According to his "unbiased" ear—that is, according to the "natural" laws of melody and harmony—the fifth-relation G - C, which dominates the melodic content, is not a tonic-subdominant relation in G-Mixolydian, but a dominant-tonic relation in the key of C major. He criticizes the modal settings of Bach and Bellermann because the "forced" Mixolydian features distort the internal relationships of the melody. Schenker accuses the composers of ignoring these relationships in order to adhere to an "alleged" system, a "theoretical" system.

    The strong articulation of the subdominant harmony in the Mixolydian mode is thus a critical issue in the modal versus tonal debate. It is that emphasis which leads Schenker to interpret "Gelobet seist du, Jesu Christ" in a functional C-major tonality. A C-major interpretation, however, does not yield a fair analytic or compositional solution for this Mixolydian chorale. It undervalues the cantus firmus, which does end with a complete Mixolydian descent to

[39]Schenker, *Counterpoint*, vol. I, p. 36.

G. A C-major analysis would also suggest that the chorale is harmonically incomplete, unable to stand on its own, which has serious implications for the larger work context of a chorale, especially when it is used as a final movement to a cantata, as is the case of BWV 91/6.

While Schenker seems to focus his comments on the emphasized relation between C and G, there are other ways in which the Mixolydian mode asserts itself in these chorales. A distinguishing feature of the Mixolydian scale is the minor seventh above the tonic—F-natural as opposed to the F-sharp of G major. Bach's and Bellermann's settings offer different solutions to the treatment of the seventh degree. Bach's BWV 91/6 opens with a one-sharp key signature, which suggests a more modern G-major treatment. Bach does, however, allow the diatonic Mixolydian mode to assert its identity in the final cadence—F-sharp is transformed into F-natural immediately before the plagal resolution. Bach's BWV 64/2 and Bellermann's setting do not have key signatures and are, in general, more diatonic than BWV 91/6. Indeed, BWV 64/2 seems to play on the treatment of the seventh degree: in the third phrase, D is first heard as a minor harmony (m. 5), but is then altered to become major at the cadence in m. 6; during mm. 7–9, the seventh degree is raised when it resolves up to G, but lowered when it falls to E. Bellermann consistently uses F-sharp only at cadence points in clear dominant-tonic or tonic-dominant resolutions (m. 4 and mm. 8–9), while he uses F-natural elsewhere to maintain the diatonic mode. It is noteworthy that during his prolongation of D in mm. 5–7, it is a D-minor rather than a D-major harmony.

From our brief look at these chorales, two important issues emerge concerning the treatment of chromaticisms in the Mixolydian mode: 1) the use of F-sharp in local chord connections, and 2) the use of F-sharp when the dominant *Stufe* is prolonged. Historical theorists address both of these issues, and their comments are worth consideration here.

J. G. Walther and J. P. Kirnberger were sensitive to the issue of ficta since they were trying to preserve the modes—especially for chorale composition—as distinct from the modern keys. Writing at a time when the major and minor keys were beginning to be defined, Walther's views reflect a changing perspective on modal harmony. In his *Praecepta der musicalischen Composition* (1708), Walther provides the V - I progression with ficta F-sharp as the perfect cadence in

Mixolydian.[40] In the later *Lexicon* (1732), he takes a more rigorous approach to modal diatonicism; he is specific on the issue of modal ficta and how it affects harmonic process:

> [The Mixolydian mode] . . . makes its cadence on G, but in such a manner that no f-sharp enters in another voice. In order to avoid this the bass concludes not from d to G but from c to G. Since it also does not admit the cadence on B for the same reason, but prefers the C cadence, it also cadences on f—from which it probably received its name, since the just-mentioned cadence is characteristic of the Lydian mode in the diatonic genus.[41]

The *Lexicon* thus rejects the dominant-tonic progression as the primary cadence because of the foreign note F-sharp. The appropriate bass progression that allows modal diatonicism is the plagal gesture from C to G.

Kirnberger has a similar interest in maintaining modal integrity for chorale harmonization. His discussion of the Mixolydian mode also focuses on the restricted use of F-sharp, which, according to Kirnberger, is not suitable for a dominant-tonic close in the Mixolydian mode. Although he advocates the leading tone for dominant cadences in Dorian and Aeolian, he does not support its application in Mixolydian:

> If one were to use the dominant with the major third throughout the Mixolydian mode, the mode would instantly become Ionian. However, the major third can be added to the dominants in the Dorian and Aeolian modes even though they are not contained in their scales, because they would still be entirely distinct from the other modes.[42]

Because F-sharp must be avoided, Kirnberger recommends a plagal close with the bass progression G - C - G.[43]

The harmonic quality of the dominant when it is prolonged or tonicized is another important mode-defining feature for Mixolydian. Kirnberger specifies the nature of the primary and secondary mode relationship: "In the case of modulations, the tonic of the new key

---

[40]Walther, Johann Gottfried, *Praecepta der musicalischen Composition* (Ms., 1708), ed. P. Benary (Leipzig: Breitkopf und Härtel, 1960). Appendix 1 reviews Walther's discussion of the modes in the *Praecepta*.

[41]Walther, *Musicaliches Lexicon oder Musicalische Bibliothek* (Leipzig, 1732), article "Modus musicus," trans. Lester, *Between Modes and Keys,* p. 223. As mentioned in footnote 40, Walther's modal cadence systems are discussed more thoroughly in Appendix 1.

[42]Kirnberger, *The Art of Strict Musical Composition*, p. 329.

[43]Appendix 1 reproduces Kirnberger's cadence systems in their entirety.

must retain the third that the scale of the main key indicates."[44] Thus, when D is prolonged in Mixolydian, it should be a D-minor (D-Dorian) rather than a D-major harmony.

While Walther and Kirnberger are theoretically clear on the subject of ficta, it is not always easy to sort out the role that chromatic alterations play in practice. Such historical theoretical views are certainly useful, as *generalizations* about practice, but as with any theory, the music itself presents a more complex treatment of the given issue. There are Mixolydian compositions which close with perfect cadences without thwarting their Mixolydian identity. Walther's and Kirnberger's approach here might be explained as a conservative view of an older compositional practice; that is, in the interest of preserving the era of modal chorale composition, Walther and Kirnberger advocate a strict diatonic style, a usage which may not reflect actual practice. Indeed, as is evident in Bach's settings of "Gelobet," the use of F-sharp versus F-natural was not nearly so consistent as the theorists might like.

To demonstrate strict Mixolydian writing, Kirnberger provides Bach's setting of "Komm, Gott Schöpfer, heiliger Geist," BWV 370 (B & H, Nr. 187). The chorale, as it appears in Kirnberger's text, is reproduced as my Example 4.[45] Kirnberger does not explain why he chooses this particular chorale as an example of strict Mixolydian writing; I think his choice was based on the diatonic nature of the setting, and on the cadential progressions. There are only two chromaticisms to be found in Kirnberger's reproduction of Bach's setting.[46] In m. 4, F-sharp is introduced as a local lower neighbor to the G; the cadential progression is from C to G and the unaccented F-sharp is not part of the harmony. In m. 6, the secondary leading tone C-sharp is introduced in a local cadence on the minor dominant. Otherwise, the chorale is diatonic. In particular, the dominant appears in its unaltered form, D minor, in m. 1, m. 6 (tonicized), and m. 7.

In addition to the diatonicism, the cadential structure probably attracted Kirnberger to this chorale. The opening phrase cadences from G to C, the second and final phrases from C to G and the third phrase, after a strong emphasis on C, closes with a brief tonicization

---

[44]Kirnberger,*The Art of Strict Musical Composition*, p. 330.

[45]Ibid., Example 2.13, pp. 332–333 (p. 63 of the German original). Example 4 differs from the *BG* edition (volume 39, Nr. 117) in one respect: in the penultimate measure of the *BG* edition, the tenor has a B-flat instead of a B-natural.

[46]In the *BG* edition, however, there are three: as discussed in footnote 45, the penultimate measure has a B-flat.

Example 4: "Komm, Gott Schöpfer, heiliger Geist," BWV 370 (B & H, Nr. 187)

of the minor dominant. The Mixolydian subdominant-tonic relationship is thus a vital feature of the composition. That the opening two phrases are to be heard in the larger context of G and not C is supported in a subtle way by the F-sharp in m. 4: although the note is incidental to the plagal progression, it nudges the ear towards G.

Thus far I have identified plagal emphasis and the use of the diatonic seventh degree as distinct features of the Mixolydian mode. There are other harmonic relationships, which characterize Mixolydian chorales, but which are not so easily classified. Chapter 2 will deal with such relationships in a formal way; for now, suffice it to say that there are certain progressions which do not make sense in tonal functional terms. As a brief example, let us consider the opening five chords in Bach's harmonization of "Komm, Gott Schöpfer." How do we hear the bass succession G - F - C - D - E? Is the progression heard as V - IV - I - ii - iii in C, or perhaps as I - VII - IV - v - vi in G? In either key, the opening descending step progression from G to F is not in keeping with directional tonal harmony, nor are the subsequent ascending step progressions from C through d to e. Although such step progressions are unusual for tonal harmony, they are not uncommon to the modes. In particular, the C - D - E gesture is an idiomatic Phrygian pattern which usually supports a descending third-progression G - F - E. Here, rather than the melodic third-progression, the Mixolydian final is prolonged through its diatonic lower neighbor in the pattern G - F - G. In the context of the Mixolydian mode, the opening phrase makes sense as an elaboration of a middleground-level descending arpeggiation G - E - C, a progression that is idiomatic in Mixolydian.

The Phrygian Mode

The interpretive issues that are encountered in the Phrygian mode are similar to those in Mixolydian: the treatment of chromaticisms and their effect on modal identity, the strong sub-dominant emphasis, and individual chord successions which deny tonal logic but which are characteristic for the mode.

In Phrygian, the diatonic second degree (F-natural) poses unique harmonic problems. While historical theorists are willing to allow the ficta F-sharp under certain circumstances in the Mixolydian mode, they are much stricter about its use in Phrygian. Similarly, the raised seventh in Phrygian, D-sharp, is prohibited. For instance, Walther illustrates his disapproval of chromatic alteration in his discussion of the chorale "Es woll uns Gott genädig sein," reproduced as Example 5a.[47] The fifth phrase introduces an F-sharp before the cadence on E. Walther criticizes the single occurrence of F-sharp in the melody, but remarks that it is outnumbered by three occurrences of F-natural. The frequency of the diatonic degree seems to lessen the seriousness of the corruption, but Walther is still not entirely satisfied with the chorale setting. He offers an alternate solution to the "offensive" phrase; the solution is reproduced in Example 5b.[48] He restores the characteristic F-natural and substitutes the bass progression C - D - E for the problematic E - B - E.

Since the dominant *Stufe* in Phrygian must be avoided, it is common for the subdominant to receive local as well as structural emphasis. In *Der vollkommene Capellmeister* (1739) Johann Mattheson explores Phrygian degree emphasis as heard during fugal imitation.[49] His topic is the appropriate subject/answer pair for the chorale "Christus, der uns selig macht." He is concerned about organists who

---

[47]Walther, *Lexicon*, Table XV, F1.

[48]Ibid., Table XV, F2.

[49]Johann Mattheson, *Der vollkommene Capellmeister* (1739); facs. *Documenta Musicologica* V, ed. Margarete Reimann (Kassel and Basel: Bärenreiter, 1954); trans. Ernest C. Harriss, *Johann Mattheson's Der vollkommene Capellmeister* (Ann Arbor: UMI Research Press, 1981). The Chapter in question is in Part III, Chapter 20 "On Simple Fugues," pp. 693ff in the English translation.

Example 5 : "Es woll uns Gott genädig sein," in Walther (1732)

Example 6: Soprano from Bach, "Christus, der uns selig macht," BWV 245/21 (B & H, Nr. 81))

do not know how to answer the chorale incipit. The entire tune, as it appears in a setting by Bach, BWV 245/21 (B & H, Nr. 81), is reproduced in Example 6. Before Mattheson suggests a fugal response to the incipit he discusses the modality of the tune:

> This song appears to be in the Phrygian mode at the end; however in the course of the melody it is so strongly in the Aeolian plagal mode that the majority of the pitches rightly name the mode. Now the b occurs seven times; the a however is there thirteen times; indeed, there is even a full cadence made on the last, and it almost always precedes in it as in *quarta modi*. Nevertheless it is not to be denied that three cadences do occur, just as they are, on b.[50]

Mattheson explores different possibilities for the fugal answer. The first, given in Example 7a, is not a good solution, because of the false fifth relation, B - F. Example 7b proposes an antecedent/consequent relation on tonic and dominant in which the F-sharp corrects the false fifth, but since F-sharp is foreign to the Phrygian mode, it is not a proper answer.

---

[50]Mattheson, *Der vollkommene Capellmeister*, trans. Harriss, p. 711. He discusses "Christus, der uns selig macht" on pp. 710–712.

Example 7: Phrygian Imitation, Mattheson (1739)

a)

b) antecedent   consequent

c)

Example 7c is an answer which is faithful to the mode and ends on E as the final; it is therefore accepted as the appropriate solution. Mattheson's theoretical justification for the subject/answer pair leans heavily on an ascribed relationship between Phrygian and Hypoaeolian—he has demonstrated that the division of the Phrygian octave E - E at the fifth B, is not the basis for the fugal response, but rather the division of the Hypoaeolian octave E - E at the fourth A. Although Mattheson is willing to refer to E as the final, he can only justify the emphasis on A in this way, thus mixing Phrygian with Hypoaeolian.[51]

The chorale melody (Example 6) incorporates the *dux/comes* relationship suggested by Mattheson with Example 7c. The registral span of the cantus firmus E^5 to E^4 subdivides into two "Phrygian" tetrachords, E - D - C - B and A - G - F - E; that is, the melody parses motivically into two descending fourth spans, each of which has the same interval content—the descending pattern tone - tone - semitone. Indeed, seven of the eight phrases conclude with either the "tonic" form of the motive (E - D - C - B) or the "subdominant" form (A - G - F - E).

Bach's setting of "Christus," BWV 245/21 appears in Example 8.[52] The contrast between tonic and subdominant in the motivic melodic fourth spans is reflected in an opposition between tonic and subdominant in the harmonic framework of the chorale. The plagal emphasis manifests itself at the lower levels of structure through local I - IV - I progressions as well as through prolongations of the subdominant *Stufe*. In the first half of the chorale, the "tonic" forms of

[51]Mattheson inherits this theoretical tradition from Gioseffo Zarlino, whose account of "mixture" is discussed in Appendix 1.

[52]The musical text in Example 8 is based on *NBA* II/4, p. 51. (© 1973 Bärenreiter. Used by permission.)

Example 8: "Christus, der uns selig macht," BWV 245/21 (B & H, Nr. 81)

the subject (the E - B spans) are harmonized to close on the Phrygian final (mm. 1–4) and the "subdominant" forms (the A - E spans) are harmonized in comparable progressions to close on the fourth degree.

At the end of the chorale, however, the situation is different. The final gesture is a "subdominant" statement of the motive (A - G - F - E), but it is not harmonized in A. Rather, the harmonic setting creates closure in E. The last two phrases in the cantus firmus (mm. 13–17) repeat phrases 3 and 4 (mm. 5–8). Whereas the A - E fourth span is harmonized in both phrases 3 and 4 to emphasize the subdominant harmony, the final two phrases recast the same material to close ultimately on the modal final. Indeed, after repeating the cadence from m. 6 in m. 14, the bass continues (in m. 15) to imitate the bass progression of m. 7 through the gesture D - C - F, but then breaks off to move towards a cadence on E rather than a cadence on A. In this final cadence Bach allows both fourth-spans to emerge: the alto voice during mm. 16–17 articulates the "tonic" version of the fourth span (E - D - C - B) as a counterpoint to the structural soprano voice. Thus, within the context of this Phrygian chorale, there is a dynamic conflict between the modal final and its fourth degree that is developed motivically and ultimately resolved in favor of the modal final. An E-Phrygian interpretation allows this conflict and Bach's sophisticated handling of the motivic material to emerge clearly.

The Dorian and Aeolian Modes

The Dorian and Aeolian modes will also receive my close attention in this study. The actual modal finals of Dorian and Aeolian are themselves never in question, whereas the Mixolydian and Phrygian modal finals can be challenged, in theory, by the modern tonics C major and A minor respectively. Even though there is no such debate about Dorian or Aeolian finals, I shall nevertheless argue that Dorian and Aeolian modalities are manifest beyond their finals, in harmonic and melodic structures that are distinctly modal rather than tonal.

An important issue that emerges in historical discussions of Dorian and Aeolian is their close connection with modern minor. Knecht, for instance, directly compares modal versus tonal harmonic practice by studying a chorale melody harmonized in D Dorian as well as D minor. The Dorian and D-minor settings are reproduced in Example 9a. Knecht is particularly interested in the harmonic diversity of the Dorian setting: where the D-minor harmonization modulates only to the mediant (F major), the Dorian setting introduces other secondary degrees.

> In the lower melody, no other modulation is perceived than to the tonic of the mediant and ... [then] ... to its dominant, which is much too feeble for church writing. Because of this, the melody at its repetition will be dragging and tedious. In contrast, the upper melody charms our perception at every repetition, through its modulation: the first phrase turns away from the final toward C major, the second toward G major, the third toward A minor, the fourth toward F major, and the last returns again to the final as is seen in [Example 9a]. This is sufficient to prove the value and necessity of the old modes, particularly in setting chorales.[53]

[53][Statt daß der untersten Melodie keine andere Modulation als in dem Hauptone seiner Mediante, und bei dem zweiten Satze (oder Perioden) einer halber Schluß in der Dominante derselben, der doch viel zu unkräftig in der Kirche ist, vernommen wird, wodurch die Melodie bei der ersten Wiederholung schleppend und langweilig wird, reizt der obere Gesang die Aufmerksamkeit bei jeder Wiederholung durch die

I would like to consider the secondary degrees that are tonicized and the chromaticisms that are inflected in Knecht's Dorian setting. How do these secondary degrees contribute to a Dorian modal identity?

Middleground analytic sketches of the two settings are provided in Example 9b. The Dorian sketch presents a diatonic octave descent in the structural soprano line from D^5 to D^4. The descent $\hat{7}$ - $\hat{6}$ - $\hat{5}$ is heard in the larger context of an A-minor or A-Aeolian prolongation. $\hat{7}$ is first supported by A minor. A minor gives way to its mediant, C major, which is then prolonged in a I - V - I_6 progression. The middleground sketch provides an alto-voice G throughout the prolongation of C major. This G is analyzed as a lower neighbor to A: it is approached from A and returns to A while E is held in the bass and the harmony changes from I_6 of C to V of A and the structural $\hat{7}$ descends to $\hat{6}$. $\hat{6}$, in turn, falls to $\hat{5}$ as the dominant of A resolves to its tonic.

For comparison, Example 9b also provides an analysis of the D-minor setting. The opening prolongation of the tonic already signals a different approach. The leading tone C-sharp is introduced as a chromatically altered neighboring pitch in the cantus firmus, supported by dominant harmony. Where the Dorian sketch moves away from D-minor harmony towards A minor in m. 2, the D-minor sketch prolongs and reinforces D minor in m. 2. At m. 4, the natural seventh degree does appear in the D-minor octave descent, but its harmonic context is very unlike the Dorian analog. In m. 4 of the D-minor sketch, $\hat{7}$ (C^5) is harmonized by F-major rather than A-minor harmony, and the continuation from $\hat{7}$ indicates that the C^5 is heard as the fifth degree of F major—C^5 descends to B-flat which becomes the minor seventh (dominant seventh) of F major and resolves to A as the harmony returns to F major. Thus, the descent $\hat{7}$ - $\hat{6}$ - $\hat{5}$ is heard as $\hat{5}$ - $\hat{4}$ - $\hat{3}$ in F. Whereas the Dorian harmonization retains the diatonic sixth degree, B-natural, in its octave descent, the D-minor harmonization uses B-flat in its octave descent.

---

reiche Modulation, indem der erste Satz desselben gleich von dem Haupttone nach C dur ausweicht, der zweite nach G dur, der dritte nach A moll, der wierte nach F dur, und der letzte wider in den Haupton zurückkehrt, wie aus folgendem zu sehen ist: [Example 9b]. Dieses kann hinlänglich seyn, den Werth und die Nothwendigkeit der alten Tonarten vornehmlich in dem Choralgesange zu erweisen.] Knecht, *Vollständige Orgelschule für Anfänger und Geübtere*, vol. 3 (Leipzig, 1798), p. 43.

Example 9: Dorian versus D minor chorale writing, Knecht (1798)

The descent from $\hat{5}$ to $\hat{3}$ in the Dorian and D-minor settings also provides an interesting comparison of tonal versus modal harmonic practice. In the Dorian middleground sketch, $\hat{5}$ is first supported by A-minor, then by F-major harmony. F major moves to C major as $\hat{5}$ descends to $\hat{4}$; C major then resolves directly to D minor, while $\hat{4}$ resolves to $\hat{3}$ in the structural line. The beamed bass pattern in the Dorian sketch thus far is D - A - F - *C* - D, a pattern which prolongs the Dorian final by means of a triadic arpeggiation, but in which the presence of C-natural suggests a Dorian tonic rather than a traditional D-minor tonic.

In contrast, the D-minor sketch clarifies the tonic as a modern tonic during the descent from $\hat{5}$ to $\hat{1}$. As $\hat{5}$ is held, the harmony changes from F major to D minor. $\hat{5}$ is prolonged further as D minor moves to its dominant in first inversion, with C-sharp in the bass; then $\hat{5}$ descends to $\hat{4}$ over this C-sharp, creating a dominant seventh harmony as support for $\hat{4}$ which can resolve conventionally to tonic as support for $\hat{3}$.

In summary, the Dorian and D-minor settings differ in how the D-minor tonic is prolonged through secondary degrees and the introduction of chromaticisms. The D-minor setting introduces B-flat and C-sharp in contexts which prolong the tonic conventionally, whereas the Dorian setting is primarily diatonic, using both B-natural and C-natural as essential elements of its *Außensatz*; this forces harmonic contexts that are unconventional in tonal terms.

During the eighteenth century, the Aeolian mode gradually came to be considered the modal equivalent of the modern natural minor scale. This is clearly articulated in some theoretical writings, and more or less suggested in others. In Walther's case (*Lexicon*, 1732), it is reflected more by what he does not say, than by what he does. He reveals a different attitude towards Aeolian through his simplified treatment of the mode. When discussing the Dorian, Phrygian, Lydian and Mixolydian modes, Walther introduces problems of modal identity and ficta application, but he does not bother to do so for the Aeolian and Ionian modes. He provides the requisite information about these modes (range, final, transposition levels, a list of cantus firmi), but does not feel the need to go any further. Although he does not explicitly identify these modes with their modern counterparts, his approach implies that they require less attention, presumably due to their familiarity.

Sorge does explicitly equate Ionian with modern C major and Aeolian with modern A minor. Concerning the A modes, he makes a distinction: "The eleventh [mode], Aeolian, goes from A through B C D E F G to A, like our present A minor in descending form. But since no G-sharp can be used in the scale, this does not ascend without modal force."[54] Sorge's mention of the natural seventh degree is of particular import. In my study of Bach's Aeolian chorales I have found that the natural seventh degree plays a significant role in distinguishing Aeolian from modern A minor.

Knecht also explicitly compares the Aeolian and Ionian modes to modern minor and major keys, and he gives voice to the sentiment that these modes do not demand the same degree of theoretical attention that must be granted the other modes:

> Since the Aeolian and Hypoaeolian modes match perfectly modern A minor, of which the remaining modern minor keys are merely transpositions, and the Ionian and Hypoionian match perfectly modern C major, of which all other major keys similarly are only transpositions, there is a similar harmonic treatment of such accordingly set melodies, which is in no way subject to such difficulties as the preceding old modes. Consequently, no special remarks are necessary concerning the two foregoing or the two following chorale examples, since we wish to spare room for other materials yet to be treated.[55]

Knecht thus downplays any possible distinction between Aeolian and A minor. The topic does not deserve his theoretical effort when other issues are more pressing. Despite such authority, I shall argue that Aeolian is manifest in structures that are discretely modal, rather than tonal. A brief discussion of Bach's chorale "Meine Seel erhebt

---

[54]Sorge, *Vorgemach*, trans. Reilly, p. 203.

[55][Da die aeolische und hypoaeolische Tonart dem heutigen A moll, von welchem die übrigen heutigen Moll-tonarten nur Uebersetzungen sind, und die ionische und hypoionische Tonart dem heutigen C dur, nach welchem alle andere Durtonarten ebenfalls nichts als Transpositionen genennet werden können, vollkommen gleich kömmt: so findet auch eine gleiche harmonische Behandlung solcher darnach gesetzen Melodien statt, welche keineswegs solchen Schwierigkeiten, wie die vorigen alte Tonarten, unterworfen ist. Folglich sind keine besondere Anmerkungen weder über die zwei vorhergehende, noch über die zwei nachfolgende Choralbeispiele zu machen nöthig, wenn wir anders das Raum auf andere noch abzuhandelnde Materien sparen wollen.] Knecht, *Vollständige Orgelschule*, vol. 3, p. 73.

Example 10: "Meine Seel erhebt den Herren," BWV 10/7 (B & H, Nr. 358)

den Herren," BWV 10/7 (B & H, Nr. 358), which is reproduced in Example 10, will bring to light some of these mode-defining idioms.[56] In this harmonization, the chorale melody is given a G-Aeolian final, with a two-flat key signature.

This melody is the ninth psalm tone, or *Tonus peregrinus*; nevertheless its identity with Aeolian is clear and it was classified as such by several seventeenth- and eighteenth-century theorists.[57] The cantus firmus is strongly characterized by its emphasis on scale degrees $\hat{5}$ and $\hat{7}$. The first phrase begins with the melodic skip D^5 - F^5 - D^5, which is followed by a gradual descent to B-flat^5 at the cadence in m. 5. The second phrase begins again with the ascending skip from D^5 to F^5, but

---

[56]The musical text in Example 10 is based on *BG* 1, p. 303. This is the final chorale of cantata "Meine Seel erhebt den Herren."

[57]The tune appears in the Aeolian lists of Matthaei, Walther, Knecht, given in Appendix 2.

continues with a leap down to C^5 and a gradual descent to G^4 for the second cadence. Phrases 3 and 4 repeat phrases 1 and 2 respectively, so that we hear a total of four phrases, which alternate cadences on B-flat and G, and each of which begins with the thematic skip from D^5 to F^5. The melody thus occupies the registral space from high F^5 down to G^4—the F^5 remains as a natural seventh degree which is always introduced in its motivic melodic relation to scale degree $\hat{5}$, which never resolves (as one might expect in modern G minor) up through a possible leading tone F-sharp to G, and—even more significantly— which never resolves unequivocally down to $\hat{6}$. That is obviously the case in the second and fourth (final) phrases; even in the first and third phrases, the melodic E-flat^5 appears as a neighbor to D^5 only well after the F^5 has returned, neighbor-fashion, to D^5.

In his setting, Bach develops the melodic gesture F - D as a harmonic construct that contributes to the Aeolian character of the work. A harmonic tension exists between G and its third degree B-flat and this tension is played out to explore the function of F; that is, sometimes it is heard as the natural seventh degree of G and sometimes as the fifth of B-flat.

The melodic skip from D up to F begins each phrase of the cantus firmus. In mm. 1–2, the F is harmonized by a first-inversion F-major triad that resolves to B-flat major as the melodic F returns to D. This progression might be heard as V_6 - I in B-flat. B-flat major then returns to G minor through a passing V_3^4. Already in these opening few chords, the harmonic tension between G and B-flat is apparent. The harmonic emphasis on B-flat originates very naturally from the melodic D - F - D incipit. The emphasis on B-flat continues as the first phrase closes through an authentic dominant-tonic cadence in B-flat. On hearing the chorale for the first time, this cadential gesture might suggest that the chorale is in B-flat. Despite its status as the first chord of the chorale, G has not been firmly established at this point.

The second phrase explores the thematic D - F incipit further. In m. 5, the soprano's D is supported by a B-flat major triad. D skips up to F as the harmony maintains B-flat major. In this phrase the melodic F does not return to D but rather leaps to C, supported by F major. Following the V - I cadence in B-flat at m. 5, it is easy to hear the movement from B-flat to F in mm. 6–7 as I to V in B-flat. But the F-major chord in m. 7 does not resolve conventionally as the dominant of B-flat. Indeed, the F-major chord resolves quite unconventionally as it moves through a first-inversion C-minor triad to the cadential six-four in G on the downbeat of m. 8. How should the F-major chord be analyzed in this context? The soprano is clear in its gradual melodic descent from D to G. But as support for that descent the bass moves from I to V in B-flat and then from V to i in G, without a logical "tonal" connection between the dominant of B-flat (F) and the cadential six-four of G. Indeed, as one hears the chorale for the first time, one might expect the bass D and soprano B-flat in m. 8 to support a first-inversion B-flat major harmony as the resolution of the F dominant in m. 7. Instead, the bass D and soprano B-flat support the six-four in G, initiating the cadential resolution that ultimately confirms G as the modal final. The connection from V of B-flat (F) to V of G (D) may be difficult to explain in terms of modern tonal language, but it can be understood to be logical within the "modal" context of the Aeolian chorale harmonization. In Bach's Aeolian chorale practice, the F - D pattern is idiomatic, not only as a melodic construct as it appears in this chorale incipit, but also as a thematic harmonic construct. As modern analysts, we are tempted to hear the F as a dominant of B-flat, but in the G-Aeolian mode, F can relate directly to the Aeolian tonic or dominant.

The question of a tonal versus a modal interpretation is not as threatening for the Aeolian as it is for the Mixolydian or Phrygian modes. The modal final itself is never challenged, but there are subtle details of melodic and harmonic structure that would be lost if this chorale were subjected to a traditional Schenkerian analysis. For instance, if one were to analyze this chorale without regard for its Aeolian identity, how would one justify the described tension between B-flat and G, and how would one account for the melodic D - F - D gesture that is thematic to the melody? An Aeolian analysis, rather than a modern G-minor analysis, is better adapted to illustrate such unique characteristics.

These brief analytic sketches demonstrate the interpretive values and problems associated with modal chorale analysis. I have attempted to bring out specific features that are difficult for traditional analysis, but that contribute to the modal character of the individual works. Chapters 2 and 4 will define precisely how these harmonic and melodic features are to be understood as distinctly modal. There I will take greater care to define the modal formulas and explore the theoretical implications for a Schenker-based analytic methodology.

As a modern analyst who appreciates Schenkerian analysis for its encoding of sophisticated tonal harmonic procedures, I cannot help but wish to develop a comparable linear analytic technique for modal harmony. The analytic system that I will define in this study might be described as a synthesis of historical analytic approaches and Schenkerian linear techniques. The historical theorists were particularly sensitive to issues of modal ficta and degree emphasis; their discussions and examples offer valuable insights into modal harmonic procedure.[58] Yet my analyses are neither an accurate contemporaneous understanding of modal chorale practice, nor an accurate application of Schenkerian linear graphing techniques. Rather, they are an account of the music that makes sense to *me*, a modern analyst grappling with a specific repertoire that exists in a historical framework.

---

[58]I will refer the reader once again to the discussion of historical modal cadence systems in Appendix 1.

CHAPTER 2

An Original Analytic Model for Bach's Phrygian and Mixolydian Chorales

In the Introduction, I explored interpretive problems associated with Bach's modal chorales without explicitly developing the theoretical issues. In the chapters to follow, I will develop in greater detail the theoretical and analytical methodology adopted for this study. I will define unique formulas for the Phrygian, Mixolydian, Dorian and Aeolian modes and show precisely how these idioms relate to or diverge from traditional tonal progressions.

Schenker's ideas about reductive analysis play a significant role in my analytic method. My graphic representation of structural levels in the chorales exhibits a Schenkerian hierarchic approach. I also borrow from Schenker many principles and techniques of prolongational analysis, often using his vocabulary. I adhere to Schenker's principle that there are "norms" of harmonic progression, and that these progressions exist at all levels of composition to create a unified organic structure. It is in the precise definition of the norms that I depart most drastically from Schenker. The paradigmatic progressions that I admit for modal harmony diverge in many respects from Schenker's tonal models. Certain harmonic and melodic relationships in the modal system do not conform to Schenkerian models, and need to be defined and clarified with new analytic symbology.

Although Schenker himself did not analyze modal music, some of his students and followers have attempted to find meaningful applications of his theories to the pre-tonal repertoire. In applying Schenkerian techniques to the modal repertoire, the analyst must choose one of two approaches: 1) an analytic study that extends Schenker's linear analytic technique to accommodate the modes and thus departs from the original scope of the analytic system; or 2) an analytic study that upholds Schenker's view that modal relationships must be interpreted within the context of the modern keys. David Neumeyer expresses the methodological dilemma in the following way:

> But modal compositions force the analyst to make a decision: Should one follow the characteristics of the modes, even if that means reading the most basic events of the background and first middleground differently, or should one apply Schenker's method more or less as is?[1]

My analytic approach falls into the former category. That is, rather than engaging tonal analytic values (traditional Schenkerian values) to mode-based compositions, I have been interested in challenging my tonal expectations and in developing a "sympathetic ear" for modal harmony, even if this means having to redefine and extend Schenkerian analytic methodology.

It is important to stress that my ideas about modal harmony are based on my own experience with the Bach chorales, as affected by historical readings, and as influenced by Schenkerian models. I believe that Schenker's prolongational outlook, and many of his analytic procedures, are highly pertinent to Bach's modal chorale harmonizations. But I do not wish to criticize those works, explicitly or implicitly, as if they were imperfect modern tonal compositions. Such a criticism negates the rich historical tradition of the modal chorale, a tradition in which Bach was thoroughly engaged. Accordingly, my own theoretical approach replaces characteristic tonal paradigms, to some extent, with characteristic modal paradigms. It is important to emphasize that the abstract theory relies upon the specific analyses for its justification. Reciprocally, the analyses depend for their clarification on the abstract theoretical presentation.

The Phrygian and Mixolydian modes will be discussed conjointly here and in Chapter 3, not because they form a coordinated system, but because they share certain theoretical problems from a Schenkerian viewpoint. Similarly, the Dorian and Aeolian modes will be discussed together in Chapters 4 and 5.

---

[1]Neumeyer and Tepping, *A Guide to Schenkerian Analysis*, p. 113.

Emphasis on the Fourth Degree

One of the most striking features in a Phrygian or Mixolydian chorale is the emphasis on the fourth degree or subdominant. Indeed, this is the feature that influenced Schenker to identify a Mixolydian chorale in C major rather than G.[2] He interpreted the rising fifth-relation from C to G as tonic to dominant, whereas a Mixolydian interpretation would analyze C as the fourth degree and G as the final. In my proposed analytic model for the modal chorales, it will be necessary to distinguish the rising fifth-relation that functions as I to V from the rising fifth-relation that functions as IV to I.

Schenkerian analyst David Stern explores the function of fifth-relations in large-scale modal organization in his study of Renaissance music. Stern identifies three main types of tonal organization which result from the large-scale use of the fifth in modal polyphony:

1) I - V - I arpeggiations, at the structural or local level;

2) I - V progressions, in which the dominant may or may not be tonicized;

3) I - IV - I progressions, also at the structural or local level.[3]

Stern's practical treatment of the rising fifth-progression deserves our close attention. Although he differentiates abstractly between the I - V progression and the IV - I progression, nevertheless the functional distinction between these two becomes blurred in his analyses. In some of these, the subdominant-tonic relation is reinterpreted as an incomplete harmonic progression, and described as tonic-dominant.[4] This is evident in Stern's treatment of the Phrygian and Mixolydian modes. He assigns tonic function to the subdominant in each of these modes, drawing theoretical support from Zarlino. Because his modal theory relies on an abstract schema of cadential emphasis on $\hat{1}$, $\hat{5}$ and $\hat{3}$ for every mode, Zarlino has to ex-

---

[2] Schenker, *Counterpoint*, vol. 1, pp. 34–37. I discussed his interpretation of the Mixolydian chorales in the Introduction.

[3] David Stern, "Tonal Organization in Modal Polyphony," *Theory and Practice* 6.2 (1981), pp. 6–8.

[4] Stern does admit the I - IV - I structure in one of his Phrygian analyses—Tallis's setting of Psalm 2 (p. 23).

plain why $\hat{4}$ is emphasized in Phrygian and Mixolydian. He thus identifies the cadential emphasis on A in Phrygian as "mixture" with Aeolian, and on C in Mixolydian as "mixture" with Ionian.[5]

Stern carries the concept of mixture, influenced by a dynamic interpretation of fifth-relations, to the extreme of hearing A as the tonic in the Phrygian mode and C as the tonic in the Mixolydian mode. For example, Stern examines an A-Phrygian piece, Josquin's *Nymphes des bois*, which closes with a plagal cadence (D - A), and interprets this cadence as I - V in the tonality of D minor. He seems willing to pay homage to the A-Phrygian mode, by referring to A as the finalis, but he maintains a tonal interpretation of the piece and analyzes it in D minor. Example 11 demonstrates how he interprets the harmonic functions of D and A in the A-Phrygian mode. The Roman-Numeral V is associated with the harmony on A, and I with the harmony on D. A is thus clearly assigned a dominant function; the notated reference "A = finalis" seems to be no more than an academic reference to the mode.[6]

Example 11: Phrygian harmonic interpretation, David Stern (1981)

Nymphes de bois (D minor; A= finalis)

A	D	A
V	I	V

In addition to this type of I - V structure, in which the functional dominant of the analysis is actually the final of the mode, Stern also describes a I - V structure in which the functional tonic is the final of the mode. That is, Stern examines a Josquin piece, *Memor esto verbi tui*, which is in the Dorian mode, but closes on the confinal.[7] Stern's distinction between the two structures is, however, merely theoretical, since in his practical analyses, both pieces are effectively understood to be in D minor, ending on the dominant.

---

[5]For the interested reader, Zarlino's theory of modal cadences is discussed more thoroughly in Appendix 1.

[6]Example 11 is based upon Stern's example (p. 37). Stern discusses the piece on pp. 23 and 28, and provides his analysis of the *secunda pars* on pp. 26–27.

[7]Stern discusses the piece on p. 20, and provides an analysis on pp. 21–22.

Stern's identification of three abstract fifth-related structures in the modal system—I - V - I, I - V and I - IV - I—is convincing, but his interpretation of these structures seems to me less convincing. Whereas Stern generally interprets the progressions IV - I in Phrygian and Mixolydian as I - V in A minor and C major, respectively, I would preserve the plagal relationship and thus allow the Phrygian and Mixolydian finals to maintain their tonic status. I agree with Stern that large-scale I - V modal structures exist. Indeed, this is discussed in theory and realized in practice during the Renaissance and early Baroque periods.[8] However, it seems to me that there is a clear distinction in this context between the rising fifth progressions I - V and IV - I and that this distinction should be reflected in the analytic system.

The Rising Fifth-Relation (IV - I) in Phrygian

The subdominant side of the tonal spectrum is very strong in Phrygian chorales at all levels of structure. The subdominant emphasis generates two characteristic harmonic progressions that I will define as the Phrygian arpeggiation (PH-ARP) and the Phrygian subdominant-tonic relation (PH-IV). Example 12a illustrates a descending Phrygian arpeggiation, E - C - A - E; here, the submediant C acts as a divider (*Teiler*) between the modal final, E, and the subdominant A. In Example 12b, the final moves immediately to the subdominant, A, then arpeggiates up through the dividing submediant in approach to the modal final, E.

Example 12: Phrygian arpeggiations (PH-ARP)

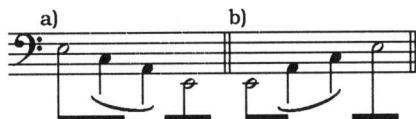

---

[8]My article "Irregular Endings in Two Chorale Harmonizations by J. S. Bach," *JMT* 38/1 (Spring, 1994), pp. 43–77, explores such confinal endings in Bach's chorale practice. I will analyze a chorale with an irregular ending later in Chapter 3.

Example 13: Phrygian subdominant-tonic relation (PH-IV)

Example 14: Contexts for PH-IV

Example 13 demonstrates the abstract I - iv - I progression, labeled PH-IV, and Example 14 provides various contrapuntal settings for the progression in linear notation. First, in Example 14a, the *Kopfton* $\hat{5}$ (B^4) is embellished by its upper neighbor C^5 as the bass articulates the PH-IV progression. In Example 14b, the *Kopfton* $\hat{3}$ (G^4) is embellished by its upper neighbor A^4 in a similar progression. Example 14c expands the harmony of A within the PH-IV progression: C^5, as neighbor to the *Kopfton*, is prolonged in a descending 3-*Zug* C - B - A as the bass arpeggiates a fifth-progression, A - E - A. The bass in Example 14c illustrates how E assumes a dual harmonic role in the Phrygian mode—first it is the final, then it is the dominant in a tonicization of A, and ultimately it returns as the Phrygian final. In the analytic discussions later on, I shall have much to say about this double function of E in Phrygian. In Example 14d, A is prolonged in its own plagal progression. C^5 is once again established as a neighbor to the *Kopfton* (B^4), prolonged now by its upper neighbor D^5, as the bass arpeggiates a descending fifth progression, A - D - A. Here, D is assigned a plagal function in A, just as A is assigned a plagal function within E.

A chorale which illustrates the plagal and nested plagal relations is Bach's "Christus, der uns selig macht," BWV 245/21 (B & H, Nr. 81); mm. 1–6 are reproduced in Example 15.[9] Phrase 1 prolongs the

---

[9]This chorale was discussed in Chapter 1 and reproduced in its entirety as Example 8. The musical text in Example 15 is based on *NBA* II/4, p. 51. (©1973 Bärenreiter. Used by permission.)

Example 15: "Christus, der uns selig macht," BMV 245/21 (B & H, Nr. 81), mm. 1–6.

Example 16: Phrygian plagal cadence (PH-P)

Phrygian final through the progression E - A - D - E. The second phrase begins on A minor and after tonicizing D minor returns to A as the penultimate harmony in a plagal cadence to E. These first two phrases clearly establish the Phrygian final. The third phrase moves away from the final (E) to prolong the subdominant (A), in a plagal harmonic progression A - D - A. Thus, the prolonging harmony in the PH-IV gesture is itself prolonged in a subdominant-tonic harmonic relation.

Example 16 provides a Phrygian cadence formula that is related to the PH-ARP and PH-IV progressions. In this Phrygian plagal cadence, labeled PH-P, the bass arpeggiation C - A - E is counterpointed against the structural descent $\hat{3}$ - $\hat{2}$ - $\hat{1}$. Scale degree $\hat{3}$ is supported by C in the bass; $\hat{2}$ descends to $\hat{1}$ over the A in a $^{6-5}_{4-3}$ resolution; A ultimately resolves to E, completing the descending arpeggiation, C - A - E.

The PH-ARP, PH-IV, and PH-P progressions described above are problematic within a Schenker-influenced analytic system. The root of the methodological problem (and thus the focus of any orthodox Schenkerian criticism) will certainly be grounded in the assumption that the *Ursatz* can be reduced further to a simple triadic expression. I have already asserted that I cannot take that final reductive step; my structural bass elaborations of the Phrygian final do not prolong the tonic by unfolding its triad, as in Example 17a, but rather by unfolding a descending fifth progression, as in Example 17b. The

Brechungen of Example 17a express a single vertical consonance, an $\frac{8}{5}$ or $\frac{5}{3}$ that projects a tonic sonority over E. Those of Example 17b, however, express a dissonant vertical sonority, a six-four triad on E, signifying neither consonant E harmony ("key of E") nor consonant A harmony ("key of A"). For certain compositions, however, the structures in Example 17b are appropriate for the purpose of asserting Phrygian analyses that have the following properties:

1) They do not depreciate the structural import of the subdominant in the Phrygian mode.

2) They do not depreciate the structural import of the final tonic cadence.

3) They do not have to assert that the pieces "are in A, but end on the dominant."

4) They do not have to assert that the pieces "modulate" from one key (A) to another (E).

5) They assert fundamental structures which relate audibly and logically to the foreground structures of the final plagal cadences.

Example 17: E-minor arpeggiations (a) versus Phrygian arpeggiations (b)

The Rising Fifth-Relation (IV - I) in Mixolydian

The Mixolydian final is also characteristically elaborated by its fourth degree, giving the descending plagal arpeggiation G - E - C - G and ascending plagal arpeggiation G - C - E - G shown in Example 18. I will refer to these as Mixolydian arpeggiations (MX-ARP).

Bach's chorale "Komm, Gott Schöpfer," BWV 370 (B & H, Nr. 187), provides an interesting context for the abstract MX-ARP formulas in Example 18. mm. 1–4 are reproduced in Example 19, with middleground and background sketches.[10] The background sketch indicates a descending arpeggiation G - E - C - G in the bass as support

---

[10]This chorale was discussed in Chapter 1 and reproduced in its entirety in Example 4. The musical text in Example 19 is based on *BG* 39, Nr. 117.

Example 18: Mixolydian Arpeggiations (MX-ARP)

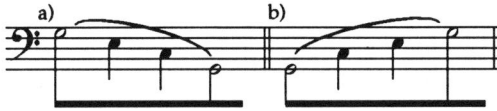

Example 19: "Komm, Gott Schöpfer, heiliger Geist," 370 (B & H, Nr. 187), mm. 1–4 and sketch

for an ascending arpeggiation G - C - E in the soprano, which leads to the *Kopfton* D. At the middleground level, the bass's E and C of the descending arpeggiation are each prolonged in progressions that continue to emphasize the harmonies of E and C. That is, following the opening tonic triad on G, the submediant E is approached in a progression (to be discussed in more detail later on) that derives from the Phrygian mode, C - D - E. Once C is confirmed at the cadence in m. 2, it is then prolonged in a progression in which the earlier bass gesture (C - D - E) is reversed to become E - D - C. C major then moves to G at the cadence in m. 4.

Example 20: Mixolydian subdominant-tonic relation (MX-IV)

Example 21: "Komm, Gott Schöpfer, heiliger Geist," BWV 370 (B & H, Nr. 187), mm. 4–6 and sketch

My symbol for structural bass progressions involving the Mixolydian subdominant-tonic relation is MX-IV. Example 20 demonstrates the abstract MX-IV progression, I - IV - I and Example 21 provides a possible context for it in mm. 4–6 of "Komm, Gott Schöpfer," BWV 370.[11] Here, MX-IV supports a local 3-*Zug* from the *Kopfton* $\hat{5}$ to $\hat{3}$; in this I - IV - I progression, IV is itself prolonged by its fourth degree (F).

In my discussion of the PH-IV relation I described a context in which E assumes a dual harmonic role: at a higher level, E is tonic and A subdominant, but when A is itself tonicized, E can assume the function of dominant. In the MX-IV relation, a similar duality exists: within a higher-level MX-IV progression (G - C - G), the C can be tonicized, in which case G will assume a dominant role to the local tonic C. This duality of function sometimes poses interpretive problems, which I will explore later when I analyze the pertinent chorales.

---

[11]The musical text in Example 21 is based on *BG* 39, Nr. 117.

Example 22: Mixolydian plagal cadences (MX-P1 and MX-P2)

Even though a ficta F-sharp makes possible a dominant-tonic close, the Mixolydian mode usually closes through the subdominant. The common cadential formulas in the Mixolydian mode which harmonize $\hat{2}$ and $\hat{1}$ in a final cadence are given in Example 22. As shown in Example 22a and b, $\hat{2}$ can be harmonized by the dominant in its minor (a) or major (b) form, but that dominant does not resolve immediately to the tonic; rather, $\hat{2}$ moves to $\hat{1}$, the dominant moves to the tonic *through* the progression V_5^6/IV - IV - I. My symbol for this Mixolydian plagal formula is MX-P1. The MX-P1 progression is slightly altered in Example 22b, in order to accommodate the ficta F-sharp. The major dominant moves through a first inversion of the tonic, to a root-position chord which has G in the bass, but which functions, because of its minor seventh, F-natural, not as a tonic of G, but as a secondary dominant seventh of C. The final close then occurs through the subdominant to the tonic. Examples 22c and d give another Mixolydian plagal formula. The dominant again appears in either its minor (c) or major (d) form. This time it moves through a Mixolydian arpeggiation, E - C - G. My symbol for this pattern is MX-P2. In both instances of the formula given in Example 22c and d, the seventh degree, F-natural or F-sharp, descends through E to D.

It is not immediately clear from the abstract structures of Examples 22 why the plagal paradigms are appropriate, since one could abstractly imagine an authentic cadence in G major, such as Example 22e, where the final tonic was elaborated through a preceding $^6_4$. Example 22e ascribes the plagal gesture a lower-level elaborative function as opposed to Examples 22a through d which allow the plagal formulas to emerge at a higher level.[12] The decision to stress the plagal formulas should be justified by their contextual analytic pertinence, not by any abstract structural features. Again, I shall have more to say on this in connection with specific analyses later on.

---

[12]Indeed, as I shall discuss presently, the plagal formulas can function at the *Ursatz* level.

For Schenkerian analysis, the same theoretical problem emerges in the Mixolydian mode as in the Phrygian mode: a plagal arpeggiation does not unfold the tonic through its own triad; therefore, it cannot be argued that the analysis has been generated from a single triadic expression. In these Mixolydian plagal patterns, not only is the final prolonged by the lower fifth, but also the progression is too "complex" a contrapuntal structure—the MX-P1 and MX-P2 plagal progressions introduce both the fifth degree and the fourth degree in the tonic elaborations; the resulting *Baßbrechung* does not express a simple ascending arpeggiation of the tonic triad $(\hat{1} - \hat{5} - \hat{1})$, nor even a simple descending arpeggiation of the tonic triad $(\hat{1} - \hat{4} - \hat{1})$. However, once again I believe that the analytic gains outweigh this theoretical drawback. An analysis that admits structural subdominant emphasis in Mixolydian will not have to assert that the piece "is in C, but closes on the dominant," or that the piece "modulates from one key to another (C to G)." Such an analysis will assert a fundamental structure which relates audibly and logically to the foreground structure of the final plagal cadence.

Emphasis on the Sixth Degree in Phrygian

In the Phrygian mode, the sixth scale degree often prolongs the final in a cadential formula which I will label as PH-VI. In Example 23, the bass line C - D - E accompanies the soprano gesture G - F - E, in the harmonic progression VI - vii - I. The progression also features a descending 4-*Zug* in the alto, E - D - C - B. Thus, while the final, E, is prolonged in the bass through a rising third progression from $\hat{6}$, the soprano and alto articulate linear progressions which clearly define the E-minor triad ($\hat{3}$ to $\hat{1}$ and $\hat{1}$ to $\hat{5}$). Again, the progression cannot be reduced further to a simple expression of the triad—the initial note of the bass (C) is dissonant with the higher-level E-minor harmony.

Example 24 provides a context for the PH-VI progression in mm. 14–17 of Bach's "Christus, der uns selig macht," BWV 245/21 (B & H, Nr. 81).[13] The fourth degree, A, is prolonged in a plagal progression at the cadence in m. 14. The structural $\hat{3}$ (G⁴) is established in m. 15, supported by C major; C is then prolonged by its lower fifth, F, while $\hat{3}$ is embellished in the upper-neighbor pattern G - A - G. In the final cadence, G descends stepwise to E, supported by a PH-VI progression.

---

[13]The musical text in Example 24 is based on *NBA* II/4, p. 51. (©1973 Bärenreiter. Used by permission.)

Example 23: Phrygian submediant-tonic cadence (PH-VI)

Example 24: "Christus, der uns selig macht," 245/21 (B & H, Nr. 81), mm. 14–17 and sketch

Emphasis on the Sixth Degree in Mixolydian

The Mixolydian final can also be prolonged by its lower third in a progression that I will identify as a Mixolydian submediant-tonic relation, labeled MX-VI. G is prolonged in the bass progression G - E - G; the E supports a root-position E-minor chord in Example 25a and a first-inversion C-major chord in Example 25b. The latter progression will be referred to as MX-VI ($^6_3$).

Example 25: Mixolydian submediant-tonic relation

Example 26 provides various contrapuntal contexts for the MX-VI progression. In Example 26a, the *Kopfton* B^4 ($\hat{3}$) ascends to E^5 as the supporting harmony moves from G major to E minor; the E^5 then steps down to B^4 as the harmony returns to G. The linear progressions in the soprano (B^4 - E^5, E^5 - B^4) suggest the harmony of E minor yet the prolonged harmony is that of G. Similarly, the movement in the bass G - E - G might suggest a prolongation of E-minor. In Example 26b, G is again embellished by an MX-VI pattern—the bass articulates G - E - G against a sustained G in the soprano; as E minor returns to G major, the alto articulates a stepwise descent from E^4 to B^3. As in Example 26a, the bass movement combined with the alto's linear progression might be interpreted as a prolongation of E minor; however, G major is the overriding harmony. The tendency to interpret these progressions as E-minor prolongations should be recognized as a response conditioned by the tonal practice in which harmonies are prolonged by the upper third and fifth. In the modal practice, a triad can be prolonged by its lower third, as in the MX-VI progression.

Example 26: Contexts for MX-VI

In Example 26c, an MX-VI ($\substack{6\\5}$) progression prolongs the tonic as the *Kopfton* D^5 descends in a local 3-*Zug* to B^4. The MX-VI ($\substack{6\\3}$) returns to the tonic through an F-major chord. The diatonic seventh degree of the Mixolydian scale, F-natural, occurs in ascent from E to G; it is a harmonized passing tone in the progression C$_6$ - F$\substack{5\\3}$ - G$\substack{5\\3}$.

The Phrygian Lower Neighbor and Upper Neighbor

A common elaboration of the Phrygian final is the "Phrygian" cadence, vii - I, in which the outer voices embellish the final by diatonic upper and lower neighbors around E. (In Chapter 1, I cited Renwick's discussion of the final two chords in this progression, D minor to E major, which he analyzed as iv - V in A minor.) For our analytic purposes, the whole-step lower neighbor E - D - E will be referred to as the Phrygian lower neighbor (PH-LN) and the half-step upper neighbor E - F - E will be labeled the Phrygian upper neighbor (PH-UN). Example 27 gives various possible contrapuntal settings of the PH-LN and PH-UN.

Example 27: Phrygian lower neighbor and upper neighbor (PH-LN and PH-UN)

Bach's harmonization of the Phrygian cantus firmus "Befiehl du deine Wege," BWV 161/6 (B & H, Nr. 270), begins with a striking composing-out of the PH-LN and PH-UN constructs. MM. 1–2 are provided in Example 28.[14] The first cadence in m. 2 is a vii$_6$ - I progression in which the bass falls F - E against the soprano's rising D - E gesture. The foreground sketch in Example 28 indicates how the penultimate harmony of the cadence, D minor, is prolonged from the beginning of the phrase: after the initial tonic E, the soprano prolongs

[14]The musical text in Example 28 is based on *NBA* I/23, pp. 63–64. The score is reduced to a four–voice texture plus an obligato line (played by transverse flutes). (©1982 Bärenreiter. Used by permission.)

Example 28: "Befiehl du deine Wege," BWV 161/6 (B & H, Nr. 270), mm. 1–2 and sketch

D in a descending fifth progression, A - D; the bass moves immediately from the opening E to the PH-UN, F, and returns to E for the cadence. The bass line is interpreted in the foreground sketch as a rising sixth progression F^2 - D^3; this requires one to hear a continuation from the bass C at the end of m. 1 into the tenor voice D in m. 2, beneath which F returns in the bass.

The Mixolydian Lower Neighbor

Although it can be raised through a ficta F-sharp, the seventh degree in Mixolydian often occurs in its natural form, F-natural. Example 29 presents some instances of the diatonic seventh degree in rising resolution. Here it functions as a Mixolydian lower neighbor (MX-LN), in the melodic pattern G - F - G. In Example 29a, the MX-LN is harmonized by the minor dominant and resolves to G, supported by the tonic. In Example 29b, the MX-LN resolves to G as the minor dominant resolves deceptively to vi (E minor).

A chorale that features the MX-LN is "Der du bist drei in Einigkeit," BWV 293 (B & H, Nr. 154). The opening two measures are

Example 29: Mixolydian lower neighbor (MX-LN)

Example 30: "Der du bist drei in Einigkeit," BWV 293 (B & H, Nr. 154), mm. 1–2 and sketch

reproduced in Example 30.[15] The F-natural - G resolution occurs in the cantus firmus itself, harmonized on the last two beats of m. 1 by the progression v - vi. Bach treats this pattern motivically, opening the chorale with the same progression, and placing the F - G resolution in the tenor voice. The dominant with raised third (F-sharp) is saved for the cadence at the end of the phrase in m. 2.

Ursatz Possibilities in Phrygian

My analytic method does admit an *Ursatz* level, that is, a fundamental structure in which a melodic stepwise descent to the tonic note (*Urlinie*) is counterpointed and harmonically supported by a characteristic

---

[15]The musical text in Example 30 is based on *BG* 39, Nr. 40.

arpeggiated bass structure (*Baßbrechung*). The following text discusses *Ursatz* formations which I have found particularly characteristic for Bach's Phrygian chorales. These are not intellectual fabrications; rather, they represent aspects of what I consider, after detailed study, the most convincing analyses of certain chorales. For each structure, I have identified the chorale that demonstrates the formula.

Phrygian background structures do not share much in common with modern E minor. The chromatic alteration that would be necessary to "correct" E-Phrygian into E minor would not be applied only to an inner voice, but would affect the *Urlinie*, specifically the Phrygian $\hat{2}$. Such an alteration would contradict the Phrygian identity in the fundamental outer-voice structure itself. Thus, Phrygian *Urlinien* are commonly descents from $\hat{5}$ or $\hat{3}$ in which the Phrygian $\hat{2}$ acts as a descending leading tone into the final and Phrygian *Baßbrechungen* emphasize the lower third and fifth to create complex contrapuntal structures that incorporate the PH-IV, PH-VI and PH-P formulas.

The Phrygian *Ursätze* in Example 31 incorporate the PH-VI progression as support for the descent from $\hat{3}$ to $\hat{1}$. In the resulting contrapuntal structures the outer voices approach the Phrygian final in contrary motion. Example 31a is a simple structure which incorporates the PH-VI formula—a *Kopfton* $\hat{3}$ is supported first by E, then by C, which initiates the PH-VI progression as support for the final descent from $\hat{2}$ to $\hat{1}$. The bass thus prolongs E through its lower third C. The double beam highlights the PH-VI cadential formula within the structural bass. Since this gesture departs from traditional Schenkerian paradigms, it is underscored with this unique notation.

The *Ursatz* in Example 31b presents an *Urlinie* descent from $\hat{5}$. The *Kopfton* is supported by E in the bass; $\hat{5}$ descends to $\hat{4}$ as the bass falls a fifth to A; the return to E is mediated by C which initiates a PH-VI progression as support for the $\hat{3}$ - $\hat{2}$ - $\hat{1}$ descent. Here the bass prolongs the Phrygian final by an arpeggiation from its lower fifth, A - C - (D) - E.

Example 31c is another $\hat{5}$-line which closes with a PH-VI progression. This *Ursatz* differs from the structure of Example 31b in the bass support for $\hat{4}$. Here $\hat{4}$ is supported not by A, but by F—the bass rises from E to F in contrary motion with the soprano descent from $\hat{5}$ to $\hat{4}$. F then moves directly to C which initiates the PH-VI progression. Thus F exists in a plagal relation to C.

Example 31:

a) "Erbarm dich mein, o Herre Gott,"
   BWV 305 (B & H, Nr. 34)

b) "Christus, der uns selig macht,"
   BWV 245/21 (B & H, Nr. 81)

c) "Herr, nun laß in Friede," BWV 337
   (B & H, Nr. 270)

Example 32: "Befiehl du deine Wege," BWV 161/6 (B & H, Nr. 270)

Example 32 introduces the PH-LN pattern E - D - E into the structural bass progression. The *Kopfton* $\hat{5}$ descends through $\hat{4}$ to $\hat{3}$ as the bass articulates a PH-IV progression E - A - E; then E in the bass is elaborated by its PH-LN as $\hat{3}$ descends through $\hat{2}$ to $\hat{1}$.

Example 33: "Aus tiefer Not schrei ich zu dir," BWV 38/6 (B & H, Nr. 10)

The structure in Example 33 incorporates the Phrygian plagal formula (PH-P) as the final cadential progression. The descent from $\hat{5}$ to $\hat{4}$ is accompanied by a PH-IV progression. The A in the bass moves to C as support for $\hat{3}$. From there, the bass arpeggiates down through the subdominant to the tonic, C - A - E and the resolution from $\hat{2}$ to $\hat{1}$ is treated as a $^{6\text{-}5}_{4\text{-}3}$ resolution over A in the bass. This final cadence is identified as a PH-P progression, defined earlier; again, the double beam underscores the PH-P gesture as a non-traditional paradigm.

Ursatz Possibilities in Mixolydian

Whereas Phrygian background structures are clearly distinguished from modern minor, the Mixolydian mode sometimes admits of an overlap with modern G major through fundamental structures which do not deviate from tonal norms. The ficta F-sharp in an inner voice makes possible a prolongation of the Mixolydian final through its upper fifth. The *Ursatz* of a Mixolydian composition might then be a conventional structure, with Mixolydian characteristics appearing at the background or even lower levels of structure. For instance, the *Ursätze* in Example 34 appear as fairly conventional Schenkerian paradigms. In Example 34a, the descent from $\hat{3}$ is supported by a simple I - V - I arpeggiation. In Example 34b, the descent from $\hat{5}$ is supported by the progression I - IV$_6$ - V $^{6\text{-}5}_{4\text{-}3}$ - I. One may wonder why these tonally acceptable *Ursätze* appear as possible Mixolydian formulas. The problem is apparent, not real; the background of a Mixolydian composition may project an *Ursatz* compatible with tonality, while the other levels of the same composition may have aspects that are inexplicable in tonal terms. Or, one may put the matter this way: the models of Example 34 are broad enough, as background structures, to subsume both traditional G-major and modal G-Mixolydian compositions as possible foregrounds. It is perfectly reasonable for the two systems to share a certain amount of overlap, after all.

Example 34:

a) "Gelobet seist du, Jesu Christ,"
   BWV 91/6 (B & H, Nr. 51)

b) "Die Nacht ist kommen," BWV 296
   (B & H, Nr. 231)

By contrast, it is certainly possible for a Mixolydian composition to have an *Ursatz* which is distinctly Mixolydian by design. In Example 35a, $\hat{3}$, supported by the tonic, descends to $\hat{1}$, in a cadential formula that was defined previously as MX-P2. The dominant, in its major or minor form, moves to the Mixolydian final through an arpeggiation E - C - G, which might be identified as an MX-ARP. As an abstract proposition, the Mixolydian background structure of Example 35a may seem forced, when there lies ready at hand the perfectly traditional background structure of Example 35b, in which the Mixolydian formula is interpreted as a $^6_4 \text{-} ^5_3$ resolution over the final tonic. However, the pertinence of Example 35a will be urged in connection with the compositional structure of specific chorales.

Example 35: "Gelobet seist du, Jesu Christ," BWV 314 (B & H, Nr. 288)

In Example 36, the bass features a different Mixolydian plagal formula, defined previously as MX-P1. In the final descent, the dominant moves to the Mixolydian final through a prolongation of the subdominant. Example 36 also features an MX-IV progression as support for the descent from $\hat{5}$ to $\hat{3}$.

Example 36: "Komm, Gott Schöpfer, heiliger Geist," BWV 370 (B & H, Nr. 187)

There are certain Mixolydian chorales for which a traditional *Urlinie* descent from $\hat{3}$ or $\hat{5}$ is problematic. Example 37a is quite unconventional in its descent from $\hat{4}$. Here, the subdominant harmony is established as support for $\hat{4}$, and is in the relation MX-IV to the tonic which follows as support for $\hat{3}$. Thereafter, the progression follows the MX-P1 formula. I wish to distinguish Example 37a from Example 37b. In the former, C^4, supported by C harmony, appears at the level of the *Ursatz*. In the latter, C^4 is subordinated as a neighbor to the *Kopfton* $\hat{3}$; its harmonic support, C, is likewise subordinated to the initial tonic of the *Baßbrechung*. The choice between 37a and b would have to be made, in a specific analytic situation, after carefully considering the particulars of the given composition. I shall once more have to postpone further explanation until the chorales in question are introduced.

Example 37: "Dies sind die heiligen Zehn Gebot," BWV 298 (B & H, Nr. 127)

CHAPTER 3

Bach's Chorale Harmonizations of Phrygian and Mixolydian Cantus Firmi

Here I will analyze representative Phrygian and Mixolydian chorales by Bach, and apply the formal theoretical model proposed above. With these analyses I will engage in the interpretive debate that plagues most analysts when considering these chorales—the potential finality of cadences from subdominant to tonic. In Chapter 1, I explored how Schenker attributed a dominant function to the Mixolydian final because of the emphasis on C throughout the work, and similar interpretations have been suggested for the Phrygian mode. However, a dominant ending neither admits closure for the individual chorale, nor—in the case of a cantata's final chorale— for the larger work. Where it is possible, I will consider how the chorale is integrated into the larger harmonic plan of the cantata and indeed how the modality of the chorale shapes that structure. Unfortunately, many of Bach's chorales have been received as singly-transmitted works, with no extant larger-work context. In such cases, it is sometimes possible to enhance our understanding of Bach's practice by examining other settings of the same melody.

Aus tiefer Not schrei ich zu dir

The Phrygian chorale "Aus tiefer Not schrei ich zu dir," BWV 38/6 (B & H, Nr. 10) is a particularly interesting harmonization with which to explore Phrygian modal identity and the dynamic relationship that arises between the Phrygian final and its fourth degree. This chorale concludes a cantata that uses the cantus firmus "Aus tiefer Not" in the first, fourth and final movements, each time in a different compositional texture and thus within a different harmonic/contrapuntal idiom. In the following discussion, I will begin with an analysis of the cantus firmus and the chorale setting; I will then

Example 38: Soprano from "Aus tiefer Not," BWV 38/6 (B & H, Nr. 10)

broaden the analytic scope by considering the other movements and the overall modal/tonal scheme of the cantata.

The cantus firmus, given in Example 38, has a strong Phrygian identity.[1] This diatonic melody spans the registral space between E^4 and D^5, introduces cadences on B, E, A, G and E (in that order) and articulates an overall melodic descent from scale degree $\hat{5}$ to $\hat{1}$. The staff below the melody copies only the initial note and closing three-note gesture of each phrase. Beneath the melody, slurs indicate the third-progressions G - A - B/B - A - G and G - F - E that compose-out the tonic triad. The first phrase begins on B and cadences with a rising third-progression G - A - B; the second phrase begins again on B, and this time cadences on the descending third-progression G - F - E; the third phrase emphasizes the fourth degree, A, and closes with the third-progression C - B - A; the fourth phrase begins on C, creating a link with the third phrase, but then resolves C to scale degree $\hat{5}$ (B) and cadences with the descending third-progression B - A - G. The final phrase continues from that G and cadences G - F - E. The composing-out of the third-span C - B - A in phrase 3 is thematically connected to the C - B - A third-spans that are incorporated

---

[1] The musical text in Example 38 is based on *BG* 7, p. 300.

into phrases 1, 2, and 5 of the cantus firmus. These instances are marked above the melody with square brackets.

The melody thus has a strong emphasis on the degrees of the tonic triad as well as the fourth degree, A. In Bach's setting, this melodic organization is developed harmonically into an opposition between the harmonies on E and A, a relation that grows quite naturally from the inherent properties of the distinctly Phrygian melody.

Bach's setting, given in Example 39, explores the inherent opposition between A and E in the cantus firmus.[2] Upon listening to the chorale for the first time, the opening four chords appear to present A as a tonic, in the progression V - i_6 - vii°$_6$ - i.[3] M. 2 then prolongs the A-minor triad by its upper third, C major, with the bass moving A - B - C - B - A. The first phrase closes in the bass from A to E, which might be heard as tonic - dominant in A, given the harmonic succession so far. However, the middleground sketch of mm. 1–3 asserts that E is the tonic and A the subdominant in a PH-IV relationship. This analytic reading is based on the larger context of the piece as a whole, which assumes an E tonic. The interpretation is supported by the melodic structure of the cantus firmus in phrase 1: the cantus clarifies the modal center as E (and works against an A tonic) through the incipit B - E - B gesture and the cadential G - A - B third-span; the C and A in m. 2 are ascribed neighbor functions—C is an upper neighbor to the *Kopton* B and A is a neighbor to the inner voice G-sharp. The sketch thus asserts E as the structural tonic, despite the interpretive difficulties that one encounters upon hearing the opening phrase for the first time.

The second phrase begins with the harmonic fifth-progression from E to A, which perpetuates the tension that existed between those harmonies in the first phrase. Immediately thereafter the emphasis on A disappears: the melodic pattern C - B - A in m. 4 is harmonized by C_6 - F and the Phrygian descent G - F - E in m. 5 is harmonized by the PH-VI cadential formula C - D - E. By the end of the second phrase the perception that A might be tonic and E dominant is dispelled; the Phrygian tonic has been defined by the idiomatic Phrygian cadence and by the clear Phrygian identity of the cantus firmus which has resolved to scale degree $\hat{1}$.

---

[2]The musical text in Example 39 is based on *BG* 7, p. 300. The notes in parentheses in the bass are played by the continuo; otherwise the continuo doubles the bass voice.

[3]The bass D in m. 1 is interesting as it appears as D in the cantata, where it can be heard as a connection from the previous movement's final cadence on D, but as E in Ms. R 18.

The third and fourth phrases comprise the harmonic digression of the chorale. These phrases prolong A in the context of the Aeolian mode, a context that was suggested in the first phrase. That is, when A is prolonged in m. 2, it is through an Aeolian gesture: in the foreground sketch of m. 2, the progression A - C - A provides harmonic support for a characteristic Aeolian melodic pattern A - G - A, which features the diatonic seventh degree of the Aeolian mode as a lower neighbor to the final. This G-natural is marked as an Aeolian lower neighbor (AOL-LN) in the sketch.[4] The AOL-LN figure is then composed-out in phrases 3 and 4 of the chorale: the third phrase begins, as shown in the foreground sketch of m. 6, with another AOL-LN gesture, supported by the bass line C - B - A; this phrase then moves towards a ii°$_6$ - V - i cadence in A. The fourth phrase modulates from A to cadence on G major in m. 10. The final phrase returns to A before ultimately cadencing on the Phrygian final. G major is thus prolonged within a higher-level prolongation of A minor. One might be tempted to treat G as the dominant of C major, since it is approached and followed by C harmony. But the G-major triad of m. 10 does not seem to "resolve" to a tonic C-major triad in m. 11. For one thing, the alto's B-natural is not resolved as leading tone to C. More importantly, a dominant function of G is never subsequently confirmed through a clear V - I cadence in C. It appears that G is not nested within a C-major prolongation, but rather within an A-minor prolongation. The middleground sketch analyzes G in the bass as an AOL-LN to A: the melody over mm. 8–12 is analyzed as a prolongation of A through the 3-*Zug* C - B - A[4], supported in the bass by the harmonic progression A - C - G - A.[5]

After this lengthy prolongation of an Aeolian A (mm. 6–11), the final phrase returns to cadence on the Phrygian final. The middleground sketch analyzes the final cadence as a Phrygian plagal formula (PH-P) in which the melodic descent G - F - E is harmonized by the progression C - A ($^{6-5}_{4-3}$) - E. At the foreground level, the bass A is

---

[4]The Aeolian lower neighbor will be discussed thoroughly in Chapter 4.

[5]Saul Novack analyzes this chorale in his article "The Significance of the Phrygian Mode in the History of Tonality," *Miscellanea Musicologica* 9 (1977), pp. 82–127. His *Ursatz* differs from the one proposed here only in how the structural $\hat{3}$ is established. He hears the descent to $\hat{3}$ in m. 10 at the G–major cadence, whereas my sketch prolongs $\hat{3}$ through m. 12. A serious problem with any descent to $\hat{3}$ in m. 10 is the resulting intervallic structure—parallel octaves are exposed when $\hat{4}$ supported by A moves to $\hat{3}$ supported by G.

decorated by upper and lower chromatic neighbors, B-flat and G-sharp: the B-flat - A gesture transfers the idiomatic Phrygian $\hat{2}$ - $\hat{1}$ gesture to the fourth degree, A.

The *Ursatz* level of Example 39 reflects the tension between E and A throughout the chorale. While the *Urlinie* descends through the Phrygian $\hat{5}$ -*Zug*, the bass supports that descent with the PH-IV progression E - a, followed by the PH-P progression C - A - E. I have already discussed the conceptual dissonance created by this structure: the *Ursatz* does not and cannot reduce to a simple triadic prolongation. But this is the structure that best reflects the compositional features of the chorale, illuminating at a deep structural level the motivic opposition between A and E, and also the melodic emphasis on C and A that is heard throughout the cantus firmus and its harmonization. Indeed, the *Baßbrechung* E - A - C - A - E is organically connected to the material of the opening phrase: the foreground sketch of that phrase projects the same progression over mm. 1–3.

For the tonal analyst, the final three chords of this chorale (E_3^6 - A - E) once again create the perceptive difficulties that were felt at the opening of the chorale. Is the A - E cadence tonic - dominant in A minor or subdominant - tonic in E Phrygian? My interpretation asserts that E is the tonic and A the subdominant, but this requires hearing a different kind of harmonic directionality. Given the development of the Phrygian harmonic idiom in this particular chorale, I hear the final movement to E as a tonic resolution. The clear Phrygian identity of the cantus firmus as well as the strong harmonic cadences on E in mm. 3, 5 and 13 lead me to hear this chorale as Phrygian, and not "A-minor, with a dominant ending." The implications of the latter interpretation are serious: this is the closing chorale of a cantata; there is no subsequent movement to resolve the putative dominant at the end of the chorale.[6]

The larger context of the cantata will help us to sort out the functions of E and A in this chorale. In particular, the fourth movement demonstrates that Bach is quite capable of treating the cantus firmus as if it were in A minor, with a dominant ending. But based on this fourth movement, it is quite clear that he did not wish to suggest an A-minor tonic in the closing chorale. In order to pursue that line of thought, I

---

[6]A dominant ending is not impossible, as I shall demonstrate in another analysis, yet I would only offer such an interpretation if it were required by the melody and the remaining context (of the individual chorale and of the larger work).

Example 39: "Aus tiefer Not schrei ich zu dir," BWV 38/6 (B & H, Nr. 10) and sketch

Example 39, cont.

would like to turn to the cantata, to investigate the use of the cantus firmus throughout, the larger tonal organization, and the function of the
final chorale within that organization.

The first movement of the cantata is a four-voice polyphonic setting of the cantus firmus in the style of a motet. The imitative entries
and the cadence structure maintain the diatonic Phrygian mode
throughout. The second movement is a recitative that begins on a C-
major triad and ends with a Phrygian cadence on E, with a bass
progression from F to E. Although the cadence on E at the end of the
second movement might be heard in the Phrygian mode, it might also
be heard "tonally," as a dominant preparation for the A-minor aria to
follow. The fourth movement is a recitative that places the Phrygian
cantus firmus "Aus tiefer Not" into the continuo bass. The final
cadence of this recitative is a Phrygian cadence on D, with a bass
progression from E-flat to D. The function of the D harmony at the
end of this recitative is ambiguous and will receive my attention
below—that is, is it the D-Phrygian final, the dominant of G minor, or
the tonic of D, as a preparation for the fifth movement in D minor?
The sixth movement is the final chorale in E Phrygian, already discussed.

Example 40 illustrates the tonal organization of the six-move-
ment work. The movements that are based on the "Aus tiefer Not"
cantus firmus are marked (c. f.). The lowest line in Example 40 summarizes the larger tonal plan of the work: E - A - D - E. Within this
tonal scheme, there is a departure from the tonal center, E, by means
of the falling-fifth sequence E - A - D, followed by a return to E. In
my analysis of the individual movements to follow, I will discuss how
this larger progression emerges at lower levels of structure and how
this scheme reflects the Phrygian mode.

Example 40: Tonal Plan, BWV 38

1	2	3	4	5	6
CHOR. (c.f.)	REC.	ARIA	REC. (c.f.)	ARIA	CHORALE (c.f.)
E-PH	ends on E	A	ends on D	D	E-PH
E		A		D	E

A detailed analysis of the first movement is beyond the scope of this study, but our brief consideration of the following questions will deepen our understanding of Phrygian harmonic procedures: What harmonic relations are explored during the opening motet and how do they relate to the final chorale? Does the harmonic design of the first movement influence our evaluation of the final chorale movement as a closed harmonic structure?

The cantus firmus dominates the contrapuntal and formal organization of the opening movement: each phrase of the melody is presented in imitative entries in the alto, tenor and bass voices that lead to an entry in the soprano in rhythmic augmentation. MM. 1 through 40 of the first movement, given in Example 41, comprise imitative entries on the first two phrases of the cantus; the *dux* and *comes* entries are marked on the example.[7]

The harmonic scheme that is explored throughout the cantata derives from the cantus firmus itself and its imitative treatment in the first movement. That is, in mm. 1–9 of Example 41, the characteristic falling fifth from B to E at the beginning of the E-Phrygian *dux* is harmonized by a progression from E to A. The A-Phrygian *comes*, which begins with its characteristic falling fifth from E to A, is harmonized first to prolong D (m. 7) and then E at the cadence in m. 9. Thus, the harmonic progression during mm. 1–9 might be understood as E - A - D - E, which is the cantata's overall tonal scheme.

The harmonic tension between E and A that was evident in the final chorale movement is developed throughout this passage. It is immediately present in the *dux/comes* relationship of the opening phrase: the tonic fifth B - E in the *dux* is answered by the subdominant fifth E - A in the *comes*. Although this is a "real" answer in intervallic structure, it is not the real answer that would be expected in common-practice counterpoint—the *comes* is heard at the interval of a fourth above the *dux* rather than a fifth.[8]

---

[7]The musical text in Example 41 is based on *BG* 7, pp. 285–86.

[8]In Chapter 1, I discussed Mattheson's solution to fugal imitation in the Phrygian mode: for the theme incipit E - D - C - B, he identified the answer A - G - F - E, as the answer that would be appropriate in Phrygian. This subject-answer relationship is also "real" in its intervallic structure, but at the interval of a fourth rather than a fifth above the *dux*.

The E/A tension is also evident in the continuo line of m. 2. While the tenor introduces the theme incipit, B - E - B - C, the continuo bass provides the counterpoint E^2 - F - G - G-sharp - A. This line is neither unequivocally in Phrygian, nor in modern A minor. The ascending diatonic gesture E - F - G suggests a Phrygian scale, but the chromatic continuation G-sharp - A suggests A minor. As the bass returns in descent from C^3, the G-sharp does not resolve as a leading tone to A, but rather continues (as it was approached earlier) through the diatonic gesture G-natural - F - E^2.

The bass line G - F - E in mm. 5–6 is not presented as a cadence on E, but rather is heard on the way down to D^2, as part of the counterpoint to the comes entry in the alto voice. It is when this alto entry concludes with the ascending melodic third-progression C - D - E in mm. 8–9 that the bass line cadences: from the earlier low D^2, the bass leaps an octave and then descends diatonically (avoiding G-sharp this time) to the low E^2 with which the line began. The alto line C - D - E and the bass descent A - G - F - E create an idiomatic Phrygian cadence.

I thus hear a Phrygian cadence at m. 9, although one might argue instead for a V- i cadence in A minor at m. 10. While the alto and bass are moving into their Phrygian resolution, the tenor introduces a cadential suspension figure A - G-sharp - A; its resolution at the barline of m. 10 might compel one to hear the bass gesture E^2 - E^3 - A^2 as a cadential V - i progression. However, I believe there are thematic features which contradict this A-minor interpretation. I have already mentioned the closure of the alto's *comes* entry in m. 9, clearly marking a melodic cadence. I have also described the dynamic shape of the bass line which sets up E^2 as the goal in m. 9: the bass ascends from E^2 up to C^3, then seems to return, but overshoots the mark by one note, arriving on D^2, from which an octave leap creates a new possibility for descent, this time reaching the goal E^2 through a diatonic descent. When the bass continues with the octave leap to E^3 and descent to A^2, this is not articulated thematically as a cadential ending, but rather as the beginning of the bass's *comes* entry. It is hard for me to hear a cadential interruption in the middle of this thematic entry.

Although I hear this first clausula in E, the next clausula does resolve harmonically in favor of A. The soprano introduces the *dux* in augmentation in m. 13 and reaches the cadential B^4 in m. 20. Against this entry, the bass repeats its opening stepwise ascent (an octave higher this time) from E up to C, including the distinctive G-sharp chromaticism, and then begins its descent from C in m. 18. This time the bass's descent is altered significantly, to create a stronger emphasis on A: from C^4, the bass descends once again to A, which is now suspended into m. 20, heightening the resolution down to G-sharp; the G-sharp of the suspension resolution is prolonged in an ornamental figure G-sharp - F-sharp - G-sharp before resolving up to A in m. 22. From A, the line skips down to F (avoiding the G of the earlier descent) and then moves into a cadential E^3 - E^2 - A^2 resolution.

The cadence in m. 24 marks the end of the imitative entries on the first phrase of the cantus. The second phrase of the cantus begins on the B^3 of the tenor voice in m. 23.[9] The tenor, alto, and bass voices present the second phrase of the cantus in imitation, leading to an augmented soprano statement in m. 31–39 and a iv - I Phrygian cadence in mm. 39–40. The close on E in m. 40 is immediately followed by a return to the material of the opening for a repetition of those 40 measures, set to the third and fourth lines of the chorale text. During the first statement of this material, the cadence on E in m. 40 is followed by a continuation on E, which reinforces an E tonic. When the second statement reaches its close in m. 80, the harmony continues to A minor. At the end of m. 80, shown in Example 41, the continuo adds a seventh to the E harmony, which resolves immediately to A minor. This connection raises a question over the function of the vocal cadence on the E-major triad in m. 80: is it a Phrygian tonic, or the dominant of A?

Thus, in the contrapuntal setting of the cantus firmus, a tension between E and A develops out of the imitative treatment of the cantus firmus, the accompanying counterpoint, and the clausula structure. The clausula structure clearly presents E and A in opposition: the cadence in m. 9 suggests an E-Phrygian resolution, but is ambiguous because of the continuation to A; the next cadence is approached similarly with an arrival on E in m. 23, but this time certain revisions (for instance, the treatment of G-sharp in mm. 20–21) predict a resolution to A in m. 24; the

---

[9]In this reading, the first two notes of the tenor entry (B – C) are heard as part of the A cadence. Perhaps this exposes a methodological inconsistency on my part. When I analyzed the cadence of m. 9, I did not want to hear the first two notes of the bass entry as part of the cadence, since that would interrupt the thematic entry. In defense of my position, I hear the entry in the bass voice—the lowest acoustical voice and the voice that directs the harmony—quite differently than the entry in the tenor. The thematic contour of the bass entry in m. 9 is very striking with its incipit fifth outline; it is also familiar, since we have heard the *dux* and *comes* entries in mm. 1–8. In comparison, the tenor entry in m. 23 does not have a distinctive melodic incipit—the opening two–note figure B – C is not enough to distinguish the gesture as the beginning of a new *dux* entry; it is only after the voices have cadenced in m. 24 and the tenor voice is left alone in mm. 24–25 that we identify this as the second phrase of the cantus firmus.

cadence in m. 40 resolves A to E as iv to I and the tonic E is prolonged
into m. 41, but when that material is repeated, the cadential E in m. 80 is
altered to become a seventh chord and continues in m. 81 to A minor. In
each of these cadences, Bach manipulates a relationship between E and
A that is idiomatic to the Phrygian mode: When E is prolonged in
Phrygian, the harmony on A is commonly invoked as the structural dissonance; in this context, A - E functions as iv - I. When A is itself
prolonged, as a secondary degree in the Phrygian mode, it is elaborated in
V - i progressions; in this context, E - A functions as V - i. To put the matter simply, the same two chords prolong the tonic E and the secondary
degree A.

Example 41: "Aus tiefer Not," BWV 38/1, mm. 1–40 and 79–81

Example 41, cont.

Example 41, cont.

Kirnberger symbolizes this relationship when he demonstrates the primary and secondary cadences expected in the Phrygian mode; his table of Phrygian cadences is reproduced in Example 42. The first cadence gives the primary close on E as a I - iv - I progression (E - A - E). The next cadence tonicizes A in the progression i - V - i (A - E - A).[10] It is this double function of the harmonies on E and A that causes interpretive difficulties for the tonal analyst. The functional duality of the tonic and its structurally dissonant secondary degree has no equivalence in common-practice tonal music. That is, when a tonal composition is in the "key" of E, the prolongations of E are based on the fifth-relation B - E; when the secondary degree, B, is then prolonged, it is through the fifth-relation F-sharp - B. In this scenario, the higher-level identity of the tonic E is never threatened. In the structural PH-IV relationship, however, the analyst is forced to distinguish the different functions of E and A, depending on their local context.

Example 42: Phrygian Cadences in Kirnberger (1776)

The tonal theorist must also resist the tendency to look for further "resolution" after a progression from A to E. That is, in the

---

[10]Kirnberger, *The Art of Strict Musical Composition.* Example 42 is based on Kirnberger's original 1776 edition (pp. 60–61), since Beach and Thym's version of the table (p. 331) deviates from Kirnberger's original in the presentation of note values. Appendix 1 discusses this example in greater detail, but I will point out here that it is meant to demonstrate, in hierarchical order, the frequency of repose on primary and secondary degrees. The use of breves, whole notes, half notes, and quarter notes symbolize the frequency of repose.

Phrygian mode, a cadential progression from A to E can stand as the ultimate cadence and does not require resolution to a putative A. Indeed, the final progression from A to E should be considered a resolution of the structural dissonance to the tonic consonance. For the tonal analyst, one's sense of harmonic directionality is very much challenged by the notion that a rising-fifth progression can be conclusive. But to assume that the final gesture is inconclusive does not do justice to the finality of the cantus firmus, nor to the thematic treatment of harmonic relations within the composition.

The closing cadence of BWV 38/1 is such a conclusive iv - I progression. The preparation for this cadence is similar to the cadential preparations in mm. 9 and 24, but now the earlier tension is clearly resolved in favor of E. Example 43 reproduces the final phrase of the cantus firmus in the soprano (mm. 127–141).[11] The soprano descends to the ultimate E in m. 134 and holds it until the end of the movement. Against the sustained E, the bass repeats the rising line from E^2 (m. 133) to C that was heard in the opening measures of the movement. During the first statement of this material, beginning in m. 1, the line returned from C^3 to cadence eventually on the low E^2 in stepwise descent. In the second statement beginning in m. 14, the phrase began the descent from C^3, but then emphasized A and cadenced on A in m. 24. In the final cadence, Bach incorporates features from both of the earlier passages: after the arrival on C in m. 136 the line descends to A and emphasizes that pitch through the descending fifth-progression from E^3 to A^2; however, the phrase ultimately resolves to the final harmony on E.

Although different in texture, the first movement and the final chorale share a common harmonic treatment of this Phrygian cantus firmus. And through the connection from the first movement to the last, closure is articulated over the course of the cantata. The final movement recalls the harmonic structure of the opening movement, and both are harmonically-closed E-Phrygian structures.

By contrast, the internal movements of the cantata are not distinctly modal; this large-scale work thus integrates tonal and modal idioms. The merging of tonal and modal languages does not merely happen at that broad level; rather, given the context of the Phrygian mode established in the first movement, Bach then plays on our Phrygian harmonic expectations in the two recitative movements. Each recitative closes with a cadence that evokes two possible interpretations—Phrygian closure and/or the dominant ending.

[11]The musical text in Example 43 is based on *BG* 7, pp. 289–90.

Example 43: "Aus tiefer Not," BWV 38/1, mm.127–41

The second movement is reproduced in Example 44a, and a harmonic reduction of it in Example 44b.[12] At some level, the final progression might be identified as a Phrygian cadence, with F falling to E in the continuo and A moving up to B in the voice; but otherwise the recitative is not based on the Phrygian mode. Another interpretation of the final cadence is that of a dominant ending in A minor; but otherwise the recitative is not clearly in A minor. The recitative begins in C, then suggests D, G and A on the way to a clearly defined cadence in E minor (mm. 6–7). The tonicized degrees D, G, and A are suggested through their dominant functions only; that is, the resolution that is expected is substituted by a dominant function in yet another key. The implied resolutions are written in parentheses in the reduction.   For instance, the fourth chord is analyzed as vii$^{o4}_3$ of D, but instead of resolving to i_6 of D, the subsequent harmony is V$^6_5$ of G. Once E is established through a cadence, the harmonic focus dissolves again, with local tonicizations of D and then A. Given the tonicization of A, the final cadence might be heard as an arrival on V of A. However, it seems curious to assign A such tonal weight when otherwise it has not been well-defined as a tonic during the movement. The next movement is in the key of A minor, for which one can understand the recitative as a preparation. However, on its own terms, the recitative seems to be more "in E" than "in A." The only strong cadence with V - I motion is the one in E minor in mm. 6–7. In fact, the attempt to arrive on A in m. 5 is thwarted in favor of the tonicization and confirmation of E. The avoided resolution to A is more strongly felt than the avoided resolutions to D and G in the previous measures because of the voice leading: stepwise connections are made between the dominant-function harmonies of D, G, and A; but from the dominant of A, the bass abruptly skips from G-sharp to D-sharp, making the avoidance of the expected resolution even more pronounced.

The point I wish to make here is that the recitative plays upon the harmonic functions of A and E: which harmony do we hear as tonic? I am not saying that the movement is Phrygian—with the possible exception of the final cadence, the harmonic progressions appear to be tonal. Yet it is possible to understand that Bach continues in this movement to explore the tension between E and A that was established in the opening Phrygian movement. Despite the tonal chord connections, the harmonic relation between E and A is not simply defined as dominant and tonic; indeed, the identity of tonic is brought

---

[12]The musical text in Example 44 is based on *BG* 7, p. 290.

Example 44: BWV 38/2, recitative score and reduction

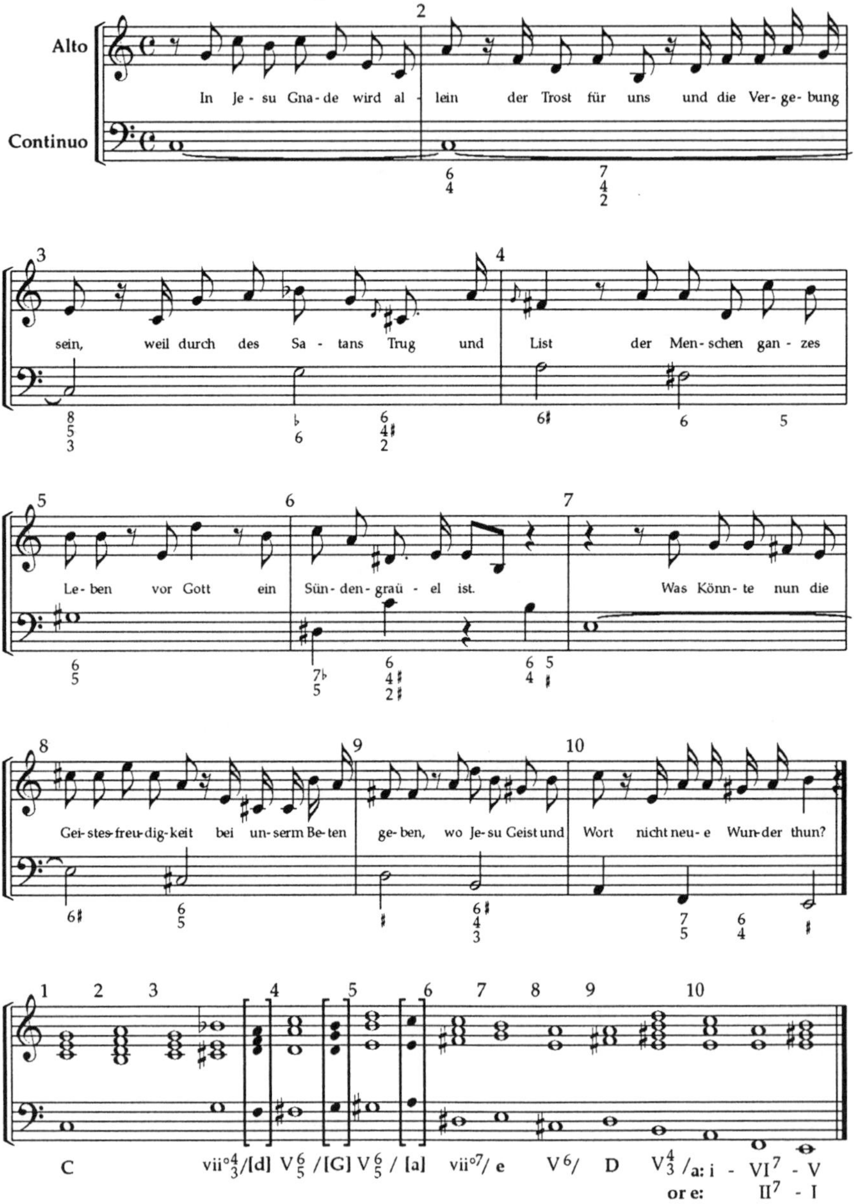

into question. Also, at the larger level, this movement participates in the Phrygian identity of the cantata by projecting over the course of mm. 7–10 the harmonic scheme E - D - A - E, which is a reversal of the cantata's design E - A - D - E.

The fourth movement, reproduced in Example 45, also plays upon the listener's harmonic expectations.[13] In this recitative Bach manipulates the Phrygian cantus firmus to create a tonal, rather than modal, harmonization. The tune appears in the continuo bass, beginning with a statement of the first two phrases transposed to A Phrygian, followed by a complete statement of the entire cantus firmus in D Phrygian. There are several aspects of Bach's setting that call for a tonal interpretation, including chromatic alterations, the harmonic treatment and the manipulation of the cantus firmus's phrase structure. Yet the ultimate tonality of this movement is not unambiguous: the final chord progression brings into question the functions of tonic and dominant within the movement.

The first phrase of the tune is altered chromatically, both in the A-Phrygian and then in the D-Phrygian statements: in m. 2, the cantus firmus's C-natural is replaced by C-sharp and in m. 6, F-sharp is similarly substituted for F-natural. This chromatic change has a striking impact upon the harmonic development of the phrase: the chromatically altered note is treated as a leading tone and is harmonized by a dominant-function chord; in m. 2, the C-sharp supports vii°7 in D, and in m. 6, the F-sharp supports vii°7 in G. Whereas the first phrase of the final chorale movement creates some confusion over modal identity (A minor versus E Phrygian), there is no such confusion here: it would not be possible to hear the passage in mm. 1–2 in A Phrygian, since there are no statements of a stable triad on A, and since the diminished seventh chord on C-sharp lies outside the diatonic realm of the A-Phrygian mode. Whereas a Phrygian setting that would be comparable to the final movement would present the harmonies of A and D in opposition, here the harmonies used are C-sharp °7 and D. Thus, it is not only the chromatically altered note (C-sharp) in the melody that works against the A-Phrygian hearing, but the harmonization of the entire first phrase using the C-sharp°7 chord as a dominant-function harmony in D. This trend continues into the second phrase. For example, the cadence at the end of the second phrase of the cantus (mm. 4–5) features the distinctly Phrygian

---

[13]The musical text in Example 45 is based on *BG* 7, p. 295.

Example 45: BWV 38/4, recitative

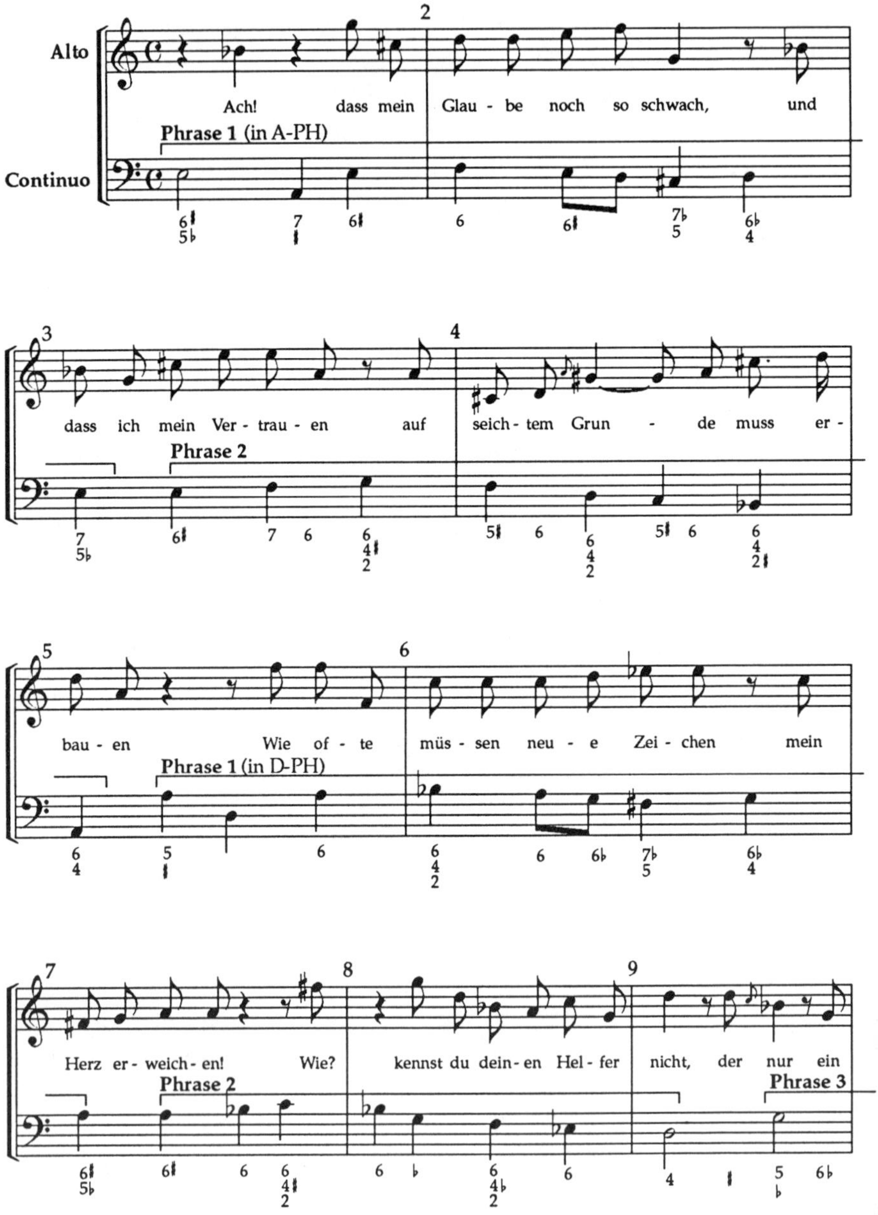

Example 45, cont.

melodic gesture $\hat{2}$ - $\hat{1}$ (here, B-flat - A), but this is harmonized to avoid its modal implications, substituting instead the strong tonal progression vii°$^4_2$ - V [$^6_4$].

The harmonization of the D-Phrygian cantus firmus statement in mm. 5–16 also contradicts a modal interpretation. To begin, Bach treats the first two notes of the cantus (A - D in m. 5) as part of a cadential pattern to conclude the preceding phrase in D minor. The final two notes of the A-Phrygian statement (B-flat - A) are harmonized as vii°$^4_2$ moving to a cadential $^6_4$. This progression is not conclusive, but must continue to the A $^5_3$; the dominant then resolves to tonic as A falls to D in the bass. Thus, Bach alters the phrase structure of the cantus firmus: in order to execute the perfect cadence A - D, the end of the second phrase in A Phrygian is elided with the beginning of the first phrase in D Phrygian.

Another instance of such rephrasing is evident in m. 9. The cantus phrase moves toward the D-Phrygian cadence, F - E-flat - D, in mm. 8–9. This is harmonized in G minor, a key that was prepared in mm. 6–8 through dominant-function and tonic harmonies. The E-flat - D bass gesture in mm. 8–9 is harmonized as iv$_6$ - V$_{4\text{-}3}$ which then resolves to tonic as the next phrase of the cantus begins on G. As was the case in the first two phrases of the recitative, it is not possible to hear m. 9 as a D-Phrygian tonic cadence, since the stable triad on D was completely avoided in mm. 6–8; instead of the triad on D, Bach uses an F-sharp diminished harmony or a dominant seventh on D wherever possible.

In this recitative, Bach harmonizes the A-Phrygian cantus phrases in D and the D-Phrygian cantus in G, thus thwarting the modal implications of the melody in favor of the tonal possibilities. In the final phrase of the D-Phrygian tune, the stage has been set for a final phrase in G minor, with the last cadence from E-flat to D harmonized as iv$_6$ - V. In the final measure, however, the voice suggests D as a tonic through the melodic gesture C-sharp - D - A; the C-sharp sounds as leading tone and the final leap from D to A as tonic to dominant. With this final measure, Bach exploits the potential of the cantus to close on a tonic, rather than a dominant harmony. As with the earlier recitative, I am not arguing that the harmony of this movement is modal; although it would be possible to hear the E-flat - D gesture in D Phrygian, the C-sharp in the final measure contradicts that mode; also, the remainder of the movement has explored tonal, instead of modal, harmony. Rather, I am saying that with this final gesture Bach causes us to reevaluate our perceptions of harmonic finality and directionality. In m. 5 we perceive a D tonic, in m. 9 we perceive a G tonic, and at the end of the movement, we can hear both implications at once: the final chord on D is prepared as V of G, but the ultimate vocal gesture stabilizes that harmony as a possible tonic, and the next movement in D minor confirms that interpretation. Bach also demonstrates quite clearly that he is capable of exploiting the tonal potential of the Phrygian cantus firmus when he wishes to do so. This treatment in the fourth movement stands in striking contrast to his modal settings in the first and final movements.

The falling-fifth tonal scheme of the cantata, E - A - D - E, can be related to the cantata text. The cantata is based on Psalm 130, which Luther conceived as the cry of a "truly penitent heart that is most deeply moved in its distress."[14] The first movement, in E-Phrygian, is the cry of distress, asking God for forgiveness despite humankind's sins. The falling fifth at the opening of the cantus firmus is a musical representation of the text incipit, "Aus tiefer Not." The falling fifth in the *dux* is then imitated by the falling fifth in the *comes* E - A, which continues the descending fifth chain. The next two movements explore the E - A relationship established at the beginning of the first movement. The recitative begins by identifying Jesus' mercy as a source of comfort and forgiveness; this opening statement is set in C major. As Satan's influence is then identified as the origin of humankind's sin, the harmony is unsettled, hinting at, but avoiding clear resolution in D, G, and A, before cadencing in E. The last line of text reflects on the positive influence of Jesus, set to a harmonic progression which is more stable than the previous one, but which is still transitory as it briefly tonicizes D, then A, and then finally E. The aria that follows this recitative presents a strong A-minor tonic and a more positive text, in which Jesus assures us that God will indeed be forgiving. (Interestingly, in the recitative the mention of Jesus' spirit and word coincided with the resolution to A.) The fourth and fifth movements explore the next harmony in the descending fifth chain, D. The fourth-movement recitative is an expression of the frailness of faith, with a harmonic setting that focuses on D, at first as a tonic and then as a dominant of G which is never resolved.[15] The fifth move-

---

[14]Martin Luther, "Commentary on Psalm 130." trans. Arnold Gübert, in vol. 14 of *Luther's Works,* ed. Jaroslav Pelikan (St. Louis, 1958), p. 189. A complete copy of the text and a translation by Z. Philip Ambrose is provided in Appendix 5.

[15]Bach halts the descending fifth chain to avoid G, perhaps because G minor would contradict the E–Phrygian mode.

ment, an aria, continues to invoke despair and sorrow, in the key of D minor. (Again, it is interesting that in the second recitative, the reference to Satan was in D). Thus, in the internal movements of the cantata, there is a symbolic association between the key of A minor and hope, and between the key of D minor and despair. The final movement arrives at the knowledge that God is full of mercy; this movement is in E-Phrygian, which is a return to the modal center that initiated the cantata, and a resolution of the tonal conflict.

Gelobet seist du, Jesu Christ

In his cantata "Gelobet seist du, Jesu Christ," BWV 91, Bach creates harmonic/contrapuntal contexts for the G-Mixolydian cantus firmus which conflate tonal and modal idioms. In the first movement, the soprano voice introduces the individual phrases of the cantus firmus, accompanied by free counterpoint in the alto, tenor and bass; each cantus phrase is interrupted by instrumental passages. The overall tonality of the movement is G major, but there are moments—during the cantus firmus statements—when the harmony suggests the Mixolydian mode. The second movement, a recitative, uses the Mixolydian cantus firmus in the context of E minor; phrases of the melody are interspersed with freely-composed material. The third, fourth and fifth movements are not based on the cantus firmus: the third movement is an aria in A minor, the fourth is a recitative which moves from G major to C minor, and the fifth is an aria in E minor. The final movement is a chorale setting of the Mixolydian cantus firmus, again in a harmonic language which merges G-major and G-Mixolydian harmonic idioms. The overall tonal scheme of the cantata is thus G - E - A - G - C - E - G; the emphasis on the submediant and subdominant in this scheme is idiomatic to the Mixolydian mode, and is related organically to the harmonic structures that are developed in the chorale setting. In the following analysis of the opening and final movements, I will focus on the harmonic language that results when Bach integrates a modal melody into a largely tonal context. I will then turn to another setting of the same cantus firmus (BWV 314) which is a distinctly modal harmonization, and which thus helps us to distinguish between Bach's "tonal" and "modal" harmonic treatments of a Mixolydian melody.

I shall begin with a few comments about the opening movement, to consider how the cantus firmus is integrated into the otherwise tonal work. Given the larger G-major backdrop, it is interesting to consider how the harmony is influenced by the Mixolydian melodic fragments. Since the melody is never heard in a complete continuous presentation, but only in interrupted phrases, and since the remaining counterpoint in the instruments and voices is not derived from the melody, the cantus firmus does not have the impact on the movement that was felt, for example, in the opening movement of BWV 38.

The movement begins with G-major scale passages in the oboes and strings and a G pedal in the timpani and continuo parts. This is a Christmas cantata, with all the fanfare that is associated with the celebration.[16] When the first phrase of the cantus enters in m. 13, G major has been well defined as a modern tonic. In the harmonization of the cantus firmus entries, however, there are subtle features that invoke the Mixolydian mode. Example 46 provides a harmonic reduction of the continuo and voice parts for each phrase entry; the lowest line combines the bass voice and the continuo line.[17] Below the harmonic reduction, an additional staff provides the part for the timpani; they are tuned to D and G, and thus have a limited function, but their participation in the harmony is significant.

A prominent feature of Bach's Mixolydian chorales is the emphasis on the subdominant. Earlier, I identified the resolution of the dominant *through* the subdominant harmony to the tonic as an idiomatic Mixolydian cadence. The opening movement of BWV 91 features such resolutions on a number of occasions. In the first phrase of the cantus, the dominant harmony in m. 15 resolves to vi, which then moves through a V_2^4 of IV to IV_6. From there, the phrase cadences on a tonicized A minor. The V - vi - IV progression avoids the continuation to tonic that is expected in Mixolydian, but in the next phrase, the same progression occurs, this time continuing to a final tonic resolution. The dominant harmony arrives at the end of m. 25, then resolves to the tonic through the progression vi - V_5^6/IV - IV - I. The final vocal phrase in mm. 55–61 features once again a plagal resolution to the tonic. This vocal entry is harmonically prepared by an instrumental V_2^4 of C in m. 54; C is then prolonged through m. 56, resolving to G in m. 57, which is then prolonged while the soprano sustains the final G of the cantus firmus for several measures. A notable harmonic twist concludes this vocal entry: in the final measure of the sustained G, the continuo introduces F in the bass against the G harmony, thus repeating the V_2^4 of C that was heard in m. 54.

---

[16]For the interested reader, a complete copy of the text of cantata 91 and a translation by Z. Philip Ambrose is provided in Appendix 5.

[17]The musical text of Example 46 is based on *NBA* I/2, pp. 133–50.

Example 46: "Gelobet seist du, Jesu Christ," BWV 91/1, harmonic reduction of vocal phrases

Example 46, cont.

One might be tempted to analyze the final vocal cadence in C major, but Bach clarifies that G, and not C, is the tonic. As the C harmony in m. 56 resolves to G in m. 57, the oboe moves from F-sharp to G, creating a leading tone-tonic resolution. In addition, the timpani prolongs G in the lowest register throughout the entire plagal progression: the G pedal begins in m. 54 beneath the V_2^4 of C; in the timpani part, G is sustained until m. 60, where it moves to D; it then returns to G in m. 61 beneath the V_2^4 of C. Thus, C is clarified as a subdominant within the larger prolongation of G. Following the final vocal phrase, an instrumental conclusion moves directly from the V_2^4 of C, through V_7 of A, to A minor; this A is heard as ii and is followed by the final V - I resolutions in G.

The broader context of this movement is tonal, though Bach does allow the Mixolydian modal identity of the cantus firmus to emerge, through subtle harmonic details, such as the plagal resolutions discussed above. The final movement of the cantata is a homophonic setting of the cantus firmus which is comparable to the first movement in its merging of tonal and modal idioms.

The final movement of BWV 91 (B & H, Nr. 51) is reproduced in Example 47.[18] I commented briefly on this chorale in the Introduction as one of the settings of "Gelobet seist du" that Schenker reproduced in his *Kontrapunkt*. My comments focused on the prevalence of F-sharp in BWV 91/6 as compared with the other settings by Bach (BWV 64/2) and Bellermann in Schenker's example. Indeed, the one-sharp key signature of BWV 91 suggests a modern

---

[18]The musical text in Example 47 is based on *NBA* I/2, p. 163. (©1957 Bärenreiter. Used by permission.) This example appeared in Burns, "J. S. Bach's Mixolydian Chorale Harmonizations," *Music Theory Spectrum* 15/2 (Fall, 1993), pp. 166–67.

G-major tonic for this Mixolydian melody. Also contributing to a G-major interpretation of BWV 91 are the accompanying instruments—the oboes and strings simply double the SATB voices, but the two horns, written independently, are in G and the timpani (as in the first movement) are tuned to G and D.

The harmonic language of this setting merges tonal and modal idioms in such a way that a decision in favor of G major versus G Mixolydian is difficult. If one studies the voice and continuo parts alone, the final cadence comprises a Mixolydian plagal progression—V - V_7/IV - IV - I. (This is the progression identified earlier as MX-P1.) Its strength as a plagal cadence is undermined, however, by the horns and timpani. Although the dominant D of m. 9 is resolved in the continuo and the bass voice through the plagal formula, it is resolved in the timpani immediately to G. The timpani then retains G^2 in the final two measures as a tonic pedal to the plagal progression. The G^2 in the timpani is not, however, the lowest sounding pitch throughout m. 10; rather, the continuo leaps from C^3 to C^2 just before the final tonic harmony. This might serve to strengthen the plagal progression as the fundamental harmonic movement. However, the horns undermine the plagal progression by embellishing it with a statement of the G-major scale: the first horn ascends from B^4 to G^5 through the passing tones of the G-major scale. As C resolves to G in the bass, the F-sharp resolves as a leading tone to G in the first horn.

The horns and timpani do not completely undermine the final plagal progression. After all, if Bach wished to resolve a D-major dominant to a G-major tonic it would have been possible for him to do so. Perhaps it is best to think of BWV 91 as a composition which incorporates modal as well as tonal features. The first movement, with its surrounding tonal framework for the Mixolydian chorale, certainly provides a context that would support such an interpretation.

While it is easy to say that the chorale merges modal and tonal idioms, it is more difficult to decide at what level of structure these modal and tonal events take place. An analytic sketch of BWV 91/6 is provided in Example 48.[19] The final cadence is analyzed as a dominant-tonic resolution with a plagal embellishment. Thus, the *Ursatz* does not demonstrate any uniquely Mixolydian characteristics; the *Urlinie* descends from $\hat{3}$ to $\hat{1}$,

---

[19]The musical text in Example 48 is based on *NBA* I/2, p. 163. (©1957 Bärenreiter. Used by permission.) This example appeared in Burns, "J. S. Bach's Mixolydian Chorale Harmonizations," pp. 164–65.

supported by a I - V - I arpeggiation in the bass. I favor this traditional reading over the alternative, a Mixolydian interpretation that would incorporate a Mixolydian plagal formula in the bass. This choice is based not only on the details of the final cadential progression, but on the compositional details of the entire chorale. While the chorale does blend modal and tonal idioms, its harmonic identity is closer to modern G major than G Mixolydian; the *Ursatz* thus reflects that identity.

At the beginning of the chorale, the leading tone F-sharp suggests a G-major, rather than a G-Mixolydian, tonic. The initial triad on G is prolonged by a progression to IV_6 and back, which might be considered as an MX-VI ($^6_3$) progression, but which is colored by the use of the descending as well as ascending passing tone F-sharp in the bass. In mm. 2–3, however, some Mixolydian features of the chorale emerge. The dominant on the third beat of m. 1 moves to vi, which in turn moves to C major for a cadence in that key. The next phrase begins with a progression from E minor to C major that recalls the harmonic connection over the barline of m. 2. Thereafter, the progressions are traditional dominant-tonic resolutions in G. The middleground and background sketches analyze the larger progression over mm. 1–4, G - E - C - G, as a Mixolydian arpeggiation (MX-ARP). The C-major cadence in measure 2 would be conceivable in a traditional tonal piece; indeed, given the melodic phrase of the chorale, a cadence on C major or A minor is almost inevitable, and one could argue that Bach does as little as possible to tonicize C major under the circumstances. Only the passing F-natural at the last minute provides any hint of local C major as opposed to G major. But given the Mixolydian identity of the cantus firmus, the Mixolydian plagal gesture that concludes the chorale as well as the Mixolydian plagal progressions that were explored in the opening movement to the cantata, it seems reasonable to interpret the middleground-level MX-ARP over mm. 1–4.

The third phrase has a very strong tonal, rather than modal, character. The foreground analysis of the bass in m. 5 shows that G^2 is prolonged first by a third-progression harmonized as I_6 - vii°$_6$ - I, and then by a fifth-progression harmonized as I - I_6 - V. The dominant is then tonicized in a perfect cadence, V - I, in D. During the fourth phrase the harmony returns from D major to G major: on beat 3 of m. 7, a passing C-natural in the bass creates a dominant seventh ($^4_2$) in G that resolves to I_6. At the middleground level, the bass progression over mm. 7–9 is analyzed as a descending fifth-progression from D to G, which then returns to D for a half cadence in G.

Example 47: "Gelobet seist du, Jesu Christ," BWV 91/6 (B & H, Nr. 51), full score

Example 47, cont.

Example 48: "Gelobet seist du, Jesu Christ," BWV 91/6 (B & H, Nr. 51) and sketch

Example 48, cont.

If one were to consider only this setting of "Gelobet seist du" it would be possible to overlook its Mixolydian characteristics, and instead to hear the chorale as a tonal piece. But if one is familiar with the Mixolydian tradition of harmonizing this cantus firmus, one will recognize the Mixolydian features that Bach incorporates into his setting. A chorale that provides a useful comparison in this regard is his BWV 314 (B & H, Nr. 288), as a setting which brings out the Mixolydian identity of the cantus firmus to a greater extent than BWV 91/6.

Example 49 reproduces BWV 314 and my analysis of it.[20] The opening three chords, E - G₆ - C, pose a puzzle for the listener who is hearing the piece for the first time. In this progression, labeled X in the score, it is difficult to identify which harmony is being prolonged. The fourth-progression from B to E in the alto suggests a prolongation of E minor, but in that interpretation, how would we analyze the movement from E to C? In order to hear C as the prolonged harmony, the alto's first note B would have to be analyzed as an appoggiatura to the C that immediately follows, but in that interpretation, one would question why Bach wrote E minor in the first place. And if G is the prolonged harmony, then how does the bass E function in relation to the G tonic? In other words, how do the three harmonies—E minor, G major and C major—function in relation to one another? There is no obvious tonal interpretation. In the context of the Mixolydian mode, however, the chord connection is logical as part of a Mixolydian arpeggiation that is thematic to this chorale. The background sketch analyzes the opening E-minor harmony and the C-major triad that follows as the beginning of the MX-ARP; the C within the arpeggiation is prolonged through the cadence in m. 2, and arrives on G at the beginning of m. 3. In contrast to this opening, BWV 91/6 also began with a background-level MX-ARP, but the foreground realization of that arpeggiation had tonal, that is, G-major, characteristics.

Thematically related to the opening progression of BWV 314 is the final cadential resolution. In mm. 9–10, the three chords that began the chorale are presented again—E - G₆ - C. This time, they are approached

[20]The chorale in Example 49 has been transposed from A (with a two–sharp signature) to G (with no sharps). The transposition will make it easier to compare this Mixolydian chorale to another setting of the same cantus firmus. The transposition will also help us to relate the chorale to the abstract theoretical formulas and principles defined for G Mixolydian. The transposition is thus offered for the purpose of theoretical study and is not to be imagined as the composition itself. The musical text in Example 49 is based on Ms. R 18. The two F–naturals marked with an asterisk are written as F–sharp in the *BG* edition. This example appeared in Burns, "J. S. Bach's Mixolydian Chorale Harmonizations," pp. 158–59.

from the minor dominant and lead to the final G-major triad. The foreground sketch analyzes this cadential progression as a Mixolydian plagal formula (MX-P2). The plagal progression appears at the *Ursatz* level as support for the final descent from $\hat{2}$ to $\hat{1}$. An alternative analysis would interpret the plagal resolution as a mere embellishment to an overriding progression from V to I, much as the final plagal progression of BWV 91/6 was analyzed. However, in BWV 314, it makes more sense to hear the final cadence as a distinctly Mixolydian gesture rather than an embellished tonal resolution. The MX-P2 final cadence is organically connected to the Mixolydian arpeggiation of the opening phrase and to other Mixolydian features of the chorale.

The progression labeled X takes on a motivic role in this chorale, occurring in m. 1, in mm. 9–10, and in modified form in m. 5, where it is once again heard as part of a Mixolydian arpeggiation. The background sketch indicates how the MX-ARP begins from the tonic cadence on G in m. 4: G moves through C and E to a first-inversion G triad. In the music, the movement from E to G_6 is labeled X, though the continuation to C major is not carried through as it was in m. 1 and m. 10—the bass in m. 5 does move on to C, but this is heard as a passing tone and the C-major harmony is avoided; rather, the G_6 moves on to D, which is then tonicized at the cadence in m. 6 and prolonged until m. 9.

The prolongation of D as a secondary tonal area is another means by which the Mixolydian mode asserts itself in this setting. In BWV 91/6, D was prolonged as D major, within the higher-level tonic of G major. In BWV 314, however, the prolongation of D has modal characteristics. In mm. 6–7, D is tonicized in the context of D major, with C-sharp and F-sharp as leading tone and major third, but in mm. 8–9 these chromaticisms are replaced by the diatonic degrees C-natural and F-natural to create a Dorian context, as befits the Mixolydian mode. The foreground sketch indicates how A is prolonged in the soprano by means of a third-progression (A - B - C), which returns (C - B - A), while the bass moves stepwise from D^3 to A^2 and back. D is thus prolonged by an A-minor chord, and it is through this A-minor chord that the dominant is transformed from a D-major to a D-minor sonority. The alto in m. 5 of the background sketch establishes F-sharp as the third of D major. When the harmony moves from D (m. 6) to A minor (m. 8) the background F-sharp rises through G-sharp to A. The A returns through G-natural to F-natural as the harmony moves from A minor to D minor (m. 9). The linear progression C - B - A, harmonized by a progression from A minor to

Example 49: "Gelobet seist du, Jesu Christ," BWV 314 (B & H, Nr. 288) and sketch [original tonic: A]

Example 49, cont.

D minor, is characteristic of the Dorian mode. So is its envelope, C - A over A minor - D minor.[21]

Given the degree of overlap that occurs between G Mixolydian and G major, it would be imprecise to assert that these chorales (BWV 91/6 and BWV 314) represent one or the other. In BWV 91/6, Bach explores the modern tonal potential of the cantus firmus, though the setting is not strictly tonal. Conversely, BWV 314 has a stronger Mixolydian identity, yet it is difficult to assert that it is a "pure" example of modal writing. But one assertion can be made about both of these chorales: Bach established unequivocally that they are "in G" and not—as Schenker interpreted the cantus firmus in *Kontrapunkt*— "in C" with a dominant ending.

Dies sind die heiligen zehn Gebot

"Dies sind die heiligen Zehn Gebot," BWV 298 (B & H, Nr. 127), is a chorale in which the powerful subdominant almost certainly would have lead Schenker to hear the tonic as C major instead of G Mixolydian. Bach's setting ultimately confirms that G is indeed the tonic; nevertheless, the chorale challenges our perceptions of harmonic directionality and finality. In the following discussion I will analyze BWV 298 in detail, proposing an analytic solution that allows the strong subdominant to influence the highest level of structure. Then, since this is a singly transmitted chorale and has no larger work context, I will analyze a contrapuntal treatment of this tune by Bach in his cantata 77, which confirms—at least in the context of BWV 77—that he understood the chorale as a closed Mixolydian structure.

The cantus firmus is reproduced in Example 50.[22] The chorale melody begins and ends on G^4 and features a motivic stepwise ascent from G^4 to C^5, which is marked with square brackets on the example. Following the cadences on C in phrases 1 and 2, the cadence on F in the third phrase is a departure, but the fourth phrase returns to the motivic ascending fourth-progression and cadences once again on C. In the penultimate phrase, the emphasized C gives way to B-flat, a chromaticism which contradicts a possible C-major interpretation of the melody—B-natural might be heard as the leading tone in C, but B-flat clearly leads downward, preparing the final descent to G in the

---

[21]The melodic gesture A - C - A will be defined in chapter 4 as a Dorian upper neighbor (DOR–UN).

[22]The musical text in Example 50 is based on *BG* 39, Nr. 45.

last phrase. This striking B-flat is unusual as a chromaticism in Mixolydian, but it is not peculiar to Bach's setting.[23] The B-flat might be considered an indication of a G-Dorian modality, but in his harmonization Bach uses the B-flat sparingly; the more frequent use of B-natural throughout the chorale, including in the ultimate cadence, suggests that the local reference to G Dorian in m. 8 is a brief instance of modal mixture. In my analysis, I will demonstrate that B-flat carries an interesting function in the chorale—it actually helps to define G rather than C as the modal final.

Example 50: Soprano from "Dies sind die heiligen Zehn Gebot," BWV 298 (B & H, Nr. 127)

Bach's setting, BWV 298, and my reductive sketch are provided in Example 51.[24] The chorale begins with a phrase in which the harmony simply rocks back and forth between G major and C major. Although a tonal analyst would undoubtedly analyze G as dominant and C as tonic, these functions are contradicted by the end of the chorale, which confirms G as tonic and C as subdominant. Based on the context of the entire composition, the opening G-major harmony might be analyzed as an initial tonic. One would then look for a possible *Kopfton* in G, a $\hat{3}$ or a $\hat{5}$. However, the cadences on C in m. 2 and m. 4 emphasize C in such a way that it would be hard to hear a B or a D prolonged throughout this passage. Indeed, the melodic pitch that is prolonged from m. 1 until m. 7 is C. Given that context, the opening G harmony might then be analyzed as a dominant to C.

---

[23]For instance, the settings in Scheidt's *Görlitzer Tablaturbuch* (1650) and Telemann's *Evangelisch–Musikalisches Lieder–Buch* (1730) both introduce B-flat at the end of the chorale.

[24]The musical text in Example 51 is based on *BG* 39, Nr. 45. This example appeared in Burns, "J. S. Bach's Mixolydian Chorale Harmonizations," pp. 168–69.

The harmonies on G and C in the Mixolydian mode have a double function that is comparable to the functions of E and A in Phrygian: G is prolonged by its subdominant C, and when C is prolonged as a secondary degree, it is prolonged by its dominant G. An analyst must determine in which capacity the harmony functions, dependent on both the immediate and the higher-level contexts. In my background sketch of mm. 1–7, C is analyzed as a structural subdominant in G (labeled MX-IV), and during its prolongation, G is analyzed as a dominant. Thus, at the background level, the opening G harmony functions as a dominant upbeat to C, which is established in m. 2. However, since this is ultimately a G-Mixolydian composition, I have attempted with my foreground sketch to project the double functions of G and C. That is, even though G is analyzed at a higher level as a dominant to C, the foreground sketch analyzes the opening G - C - G progression (mm. 1–2) as an MX-IV gesture, in which G is heard as the prolonged harmony. Perhaps this seems like a case of over-interpretation. Such an excruciating attempt to manipulate the compositional details is only necessary, however, when one wishes to commit to an analytic sketch, which by nature must show the absolute function of each and every chord. This is one of the limitations of reductive analysis. That is, my hearing of the chorale—encompassing both local and long-range hearing—engages the subtle interplay between G and C, but my sketch may not adequately reflect that interplay since it forces me to draw unambiguous conclusions about each instance of G and C.

The strong melodic and harmonic emphasis on C in mm. 1–7 emerges at the deepest level of structure—the *Ursatz* begins with the subdominant harmony as support for $\hat{4}$ in the *Urlinie*. This $\hat{4}$ is not analyzed as a mere neighbor to a *Kopfton* $\hat{3}$ which follows, but rather is itself the *Kopfton*. I believe that the compositional weight ascribed to the subdominant merits its integration into the *Ursatz*. Rather than saying that "the piece begins in C and ends in G," or that "the piece is in C, but ends on the dominant," or even that "the piece is in G, but begins with a seven-measure prolongation of a neighboring C harmony," I am asserting that the structural emphasis on C is an integral part of the composition, as a means of prolonging the Mixolydian final. In addition to the opening MX-IV, the final cadential formula which supports the *Urlinie* descent—a Mixolydian plagal progression (MX-P1)—also integrates the subdominant into the *Baßbrechung*.

In mm. 5–7 the function of C as a possible tonic is weakened and its role as a subdominant is confirmed by the cadence on G in m. 8. In m. 5. the soprano leaps from the *Kopfton*, C^5, to G^4, which will eventually return to C^5 through an ascending fourth-progression in mm. 6–7. But first G^4 supported by C major is prolonged in an unconventional progression. At the foreground level, the C^3 in the bass in mm. 5–6 (which supports the G^4 in the soprano) is embellished by its upper neighbor D^3, which is itself embellished by a lower neighbor C-sharp^3 and tonicized at the cadence in m. 6. The tonicized D-minor triad returns abruptly to C major at the beginning of phrase 4. The juxtaposition of C major and D minor cannot be understood in conventional C major. In order for the C major chord at the end of m. 6 to make sense tonally, an interpolated harmony that would define the function of C would be necessary between D minor and C major, that is, as tonic, or as dominant of F. Instead, however, D minor returns immediately to C-major. During the D-minor tonicization there is an event which foreshadows the ultimate yielding of C major to the modal final of the chorale, G. The event to which I refer is the B-flat in mm. 5 and 6 in the tenor, which is the means by which C^4 is pulled down to A^3 as the fifth of D minor. In the penultimate phrase, the B-flat in the soprano similarly forces the *Kopfton* C^5 down to A^4, again as support for a D-minor triad, but one which now functions as the minor dominant of G. From there, the Mixolydian plagal cadence closes the chorale.

BWV 298 is a singly transmitted chorale, with no extant larger-work context. There is, however, a cantata movement that can shed light on Bach's handling of the cantus firmus. Cantata 77 begins with a contrapuntal treatment of the Mixolydian melody which asserts the function of G as tonic. My purpose in looking at this cantata is not merely to illuminate Bach's treatment of the Mixolydian cantus firmus in BWV 298. It is worthy of our consideration in its own right, as a cantata which explores an overall tonal structure that is Mixolydian, and as a cantata which concludes with yet another modal chorale that explores fifth relations in a way that is significantly different from the Phrygian and Mixolydian chorales examined thus far. I will say more about the final chorale of BWV 77 later; for now, I would like to focus on the first movement.

The opening movement of cantata 77, for voices, strings, continuo and high trumpet (*tromba da tirarsi*), is a setting of Luke 10:27, the text of the second commandment: "Thou shalt love the Lord thy

Example 51: "Dies sind die heiligen Zehn Gebot," BWV 298 (B & H, Nr. 127) and sketch

Example 51, cont.

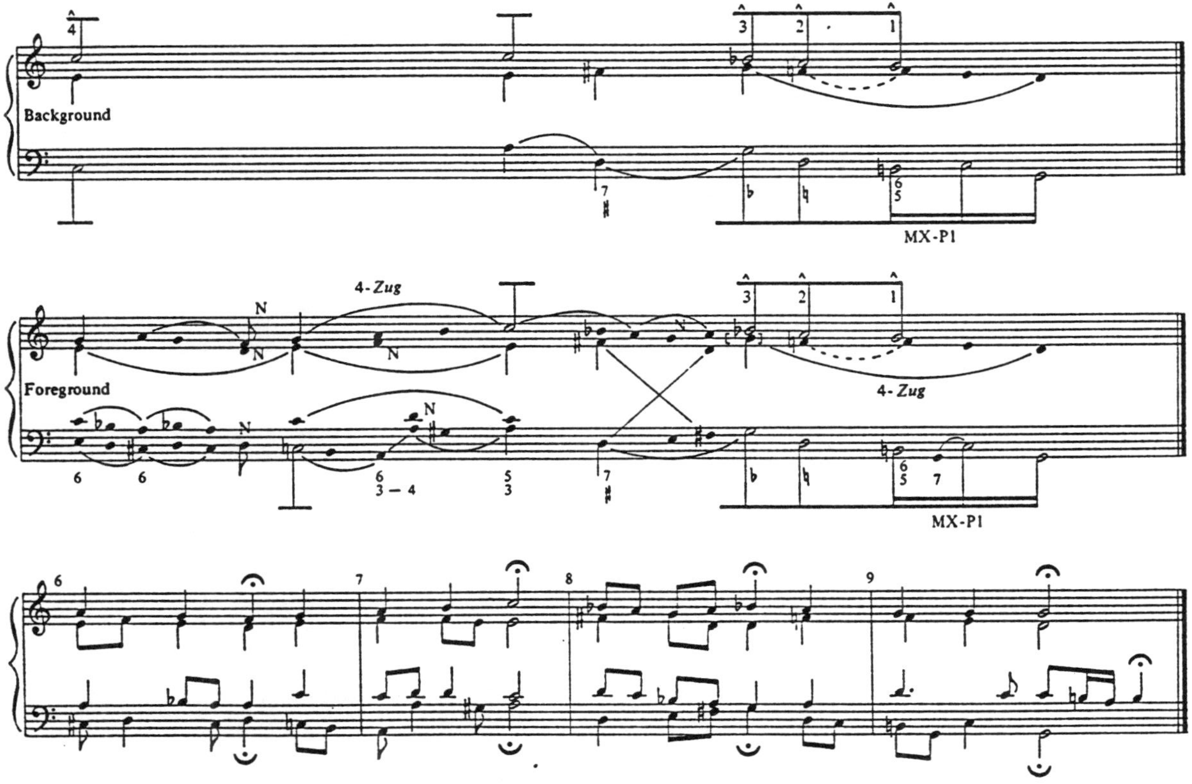

God with all thy heart, and with all thy soul, and with all thy strength, and with all thy mind; and thy neighbor as thyself."[25] Bach chooses to accompany this text with the Lutheran chorale melody on the ten commandments, "Dies sind die heiligen Zehn Gebot." The cantus firmus appears in augmentation in the low register of the continuo (organ). The cantus phrase entries are not presented continuously, but rather are interrupted by a freely-composed bass line which is also played by continuo, but which is distinguished by its registral placement one to two octaves higher than the cantus firmus entries, and by its more active rhythmic texture. In addition to the entries in the organ, there are imitative entries in the high trumpet. The trumpet does not present each phrase of the cantus in order, but rather repeats, and occasionally transposes, individual phrases (the trumpet lines are heard in G, D, or C Mixolydian), in counterpoint to the organ's presentation in G Mixolydian. However, at the very end of the movement, against the sustained final low G^2 of the cantus firmus, the trumpet performs a D-Mixolydian version of the melody in a continuous, complete presentation.[26]

I have already discussed the cantus firmus, but will mention once again its motivic rising fourth-progression from G to C. In my analysis of BWV 298, I asserted that the emphasis on C was idiomatic to Mixolydian and thus did not detract from the chorale's Mixolydian tonal center. Although in BWV 298, the tonal analyst might hear the final progression from C to G as I to V in C, Bach creates a setting in BWV 77/1 which does not leave open the question of finality—it is unambiguously in G. He accomplishes this by manipulating the tonal function of the motivic rising fourth-progression in the cantus firmus; while he affirms the *modal* (Mixolydian) identity of the cantus by defining G as the tonic of the movement, he also explores its *tonal* potential by invoking the dominant-tonic harmonic implications in the rising fourth-progression.

---

[25][Du sollt Gott, deinen Herren, lieben von ganzem Herzen, von ganzer Seele, von allen Kräften und von ganzem Gemüte und deinen Nächsten als dich selbst.] Trans. Gerhard Herz, in "Thoughts on the First Movement of Johann Sebastian Bach's Cantata No. 77 "Du sollt Gott, deinen Herren, lieben," *Essays on J. S. Bach* (Ann Arbor: UMI Research Press, 1985), p. 206.

[26]Gerhard Herz discusses Bach's symbolic use of the number 10 in this 10-Commandment chorale setting in "Thoughts on the First Movement of Johann Sebastian Bach's Cantata No. 77."

Example 52 is a reduced score of BWV 77/1, comprising the continuo and trumpet parts; the cantus firmus entries are labeled according to the phrase and the given mode.[27] I have also indicated where
the voices enter and cadence. The cantus phrases are clearly
delineated throughout the movement, separated by free material in
the instruments and voices. The trumpet introduces each phrase in D
Mixolydian shortly before the organ enters in G Mixolydian; then the
trumpet returns to the first phrase in D, G or C Mixolydian as a
counterpoint to the organ's entry. Bach thus emphasizes the first
phrase of the cantus, with its emblematic fourth-progression. This
fourth progression is already emphasized within the cantus firmus itself, as it is integrated into the first, second, and fourth phrases.

The free counterpoint in the instruments and voices also brings
out the rising tetrachord motive. Example 53 reproduces mm. 1–15 of
the movement.[28] In m. 1 the second violin begins with a rising fourth-
progression from G to C that is imitated in the first violin from C to F.
The voices enter in m. 8, with the basses moving from D to G, the
tenors and then the sopranos from G to C, and the altos from C to F.
Throughout the movement the voices continue to enter with the
motivic ascending tetrachord.

Bach manipulates the first phrase of the cantus to expose its dual
potential as a tonic-subdominant fourth-progression and/or a
dominant-tonic fourth-progression. For instance, the trumpet introduces the first phrase with the rising tetrachord from D to G, heard
above the sustained G in the organ; the linear progression D - E - F-
sharp - G suggests a dominant-tonic resolution in G, while the pedal
G confirms the role of G as a tonic in the G-Mixolydian organ statement. However, by the end of the organ statement, when G rises to C
in mm. 12–13, the harmony moves toward C major; this harmony is
confirmed when the sustained C in mm. 13–15 is heard as a tonic
pedal beneath a vocal cadence from G7 to C in mm. 14–15.

Another trumpet entry (mm. 15–17), this time in C Mixolydian,
dovetails with the organ's presentation. The harmonic support for the
rising tetrachord from C to F demonstrates once again the dual function of the fourth-progression. As C is repeated in mm. 15–16, the

---

[27]Example 52 is based on the edition of the cantata in *NBA* I/21, pp. 3–13. I have not
provided complete figures for the continuo line in this example.

[28]The musical text in Example 53 is based on *NBA* I/21, pp. 3–4. (©1958 Bärenreiter.
Used by permission.)

harmony invokes F major, through dominant-tonic resolutions and the chromaticism B-flat. But as the tetrachord rises to F in m. 17, the bass moves to B-natural and the harmony suggests a V_5^6 in C. Bach thus plays on the $\hat{5}$ - $\hat{1}$ versus $\hat{1}$ - $\hat{4}$ interpretation of the tetrachord here: at first we believe the C - F gesture will receive F-major support, allowing us to ascribe the motive a $\hat{5}$ - $\hat{1}$ function, but ultimately the harmony moves to C, which develops the $\hat{1}$ - $\hat{4}$ potential inherent in the motive as well. Bach explores both implications.

In Example 52 I have indicated the strongest vocal cadences throughout the movement; these tend to coincide with the beginnings or endings of the organ cantus firmus statements. To begin, the harmony centers on C, with V - I cadences in m. 15, m. 28, and m. 41. The focus shifts to G toward the end of the movement, with a V - i cadence in m. 54; the shift in harmonic emphasis begins with the cadence on F in m. 47 and the subsequent modal change to minor immediately thereafter. It is in the final cantus entry that the tonic is confirmed as G. Bach manipulates the cantus firmus to confirm G as a tonal center by combining an organ statement of the final phrase in G Mixolydian, against the trumpet's complete statement in D-Mixolydian. In the latter, the repeated motive D - E - F-sharp - G in the cantus reiterates the dominant-tonic function in G, while the organ holds G as a long pedal tone. The remaining instruments and voices reiterate dominant-tonic function progressions in G.

Bach's treatment of the cantus firmus in this movement demonstrates that he heard the melody not in C, but in G. While the tonal analyst might hear the motivic rising tetrachord exclusively as a $\hat{5}$ to $\hat{1}$ gesture, Bach exploits its dual potential as $\hat{5}$ to $\hat{1}$ and/or $\hat{1}$ to $\hat{4}$.

Example 52: "Du sollt gott, deinen Herren lieben," BWV 77/1, mm 1–15, continuo and trumpet parts

Example 52, cont.

Example 52, cont.

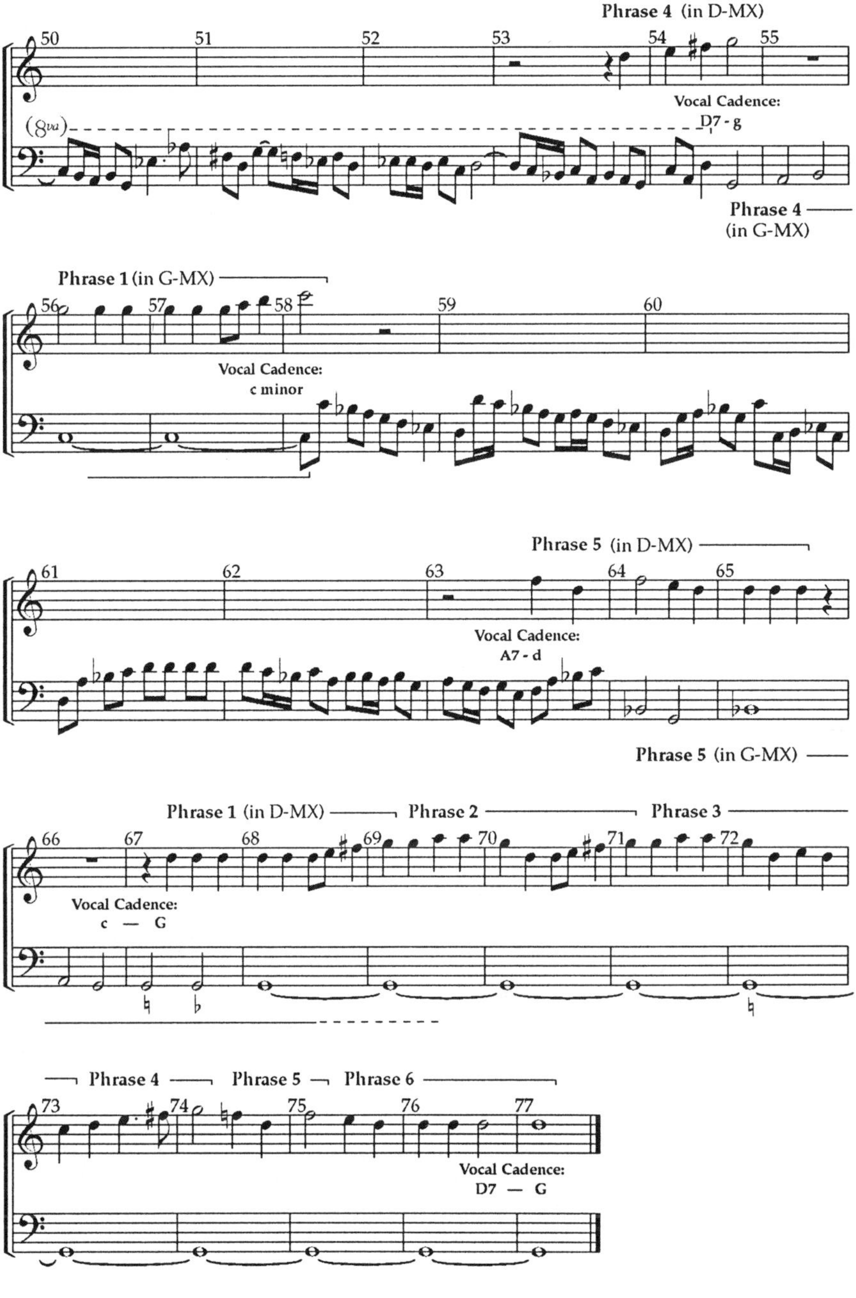

Example 53: "Du sollt Gott, deinen Herren lieben," BWV 77/1, mm. 1–15

Example 53, cont.

Example 53, cont.

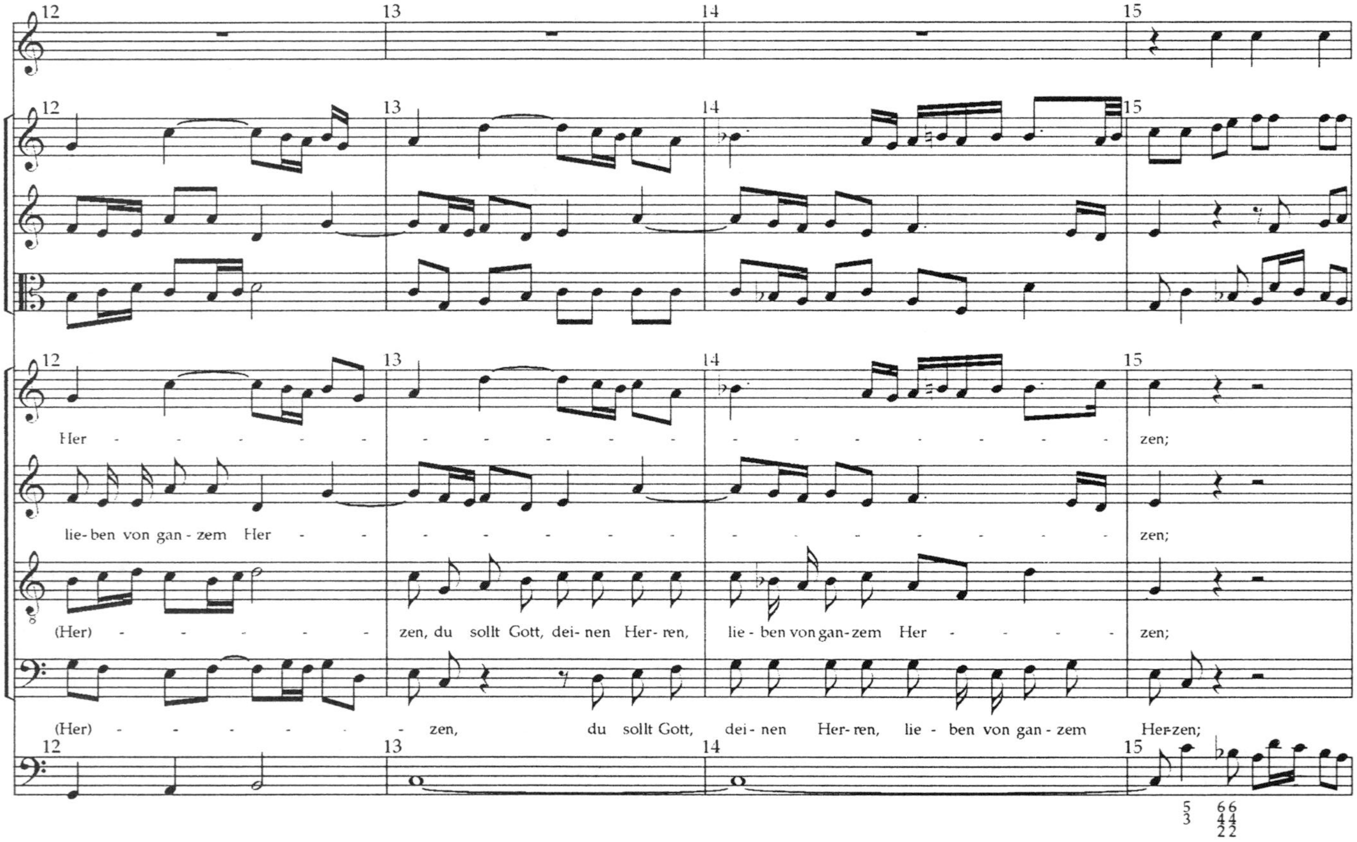

The larger tonal scheme of the cantata reflects the Mixolydian influence in the first movement. The recitative and aria pair that follow this movement are in C major and A minor respectively. The third movement recitative begins in E minor and moves through B minor to end in G major. The fourth movement aria is in D minor, and the final chorale begins in G minor, but closes on the dominant, D. Example 54 illustrates this scheme in linear notation: the connection from movements 1 through 4 might be understood as a Mixolydian arpeggiation G - C - E - G. The use of the minor dominant in the fifth movement is also in keeping with the Mixolydian mode. The sixth movement is in G minor, which recalls the mode shift from major to minor that was heard at the end of the first movement, and closes on the dominant. My interpretation of this chorale as a dominant ending is worthy of our detailed consideration below. Before launching into that discussion, however, I would like to review briefly the text of this cantata, since it sheds light on the overall tonal scheme.[29]

Example 54: Tonal plan, BWV 77

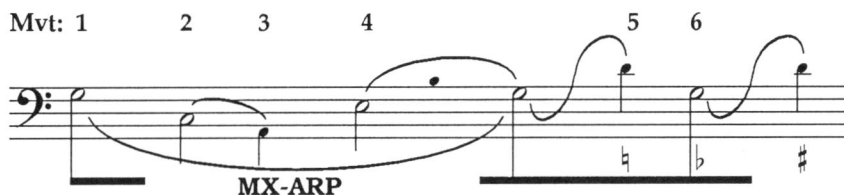

The first movement is a recitation of the commandment to love God and thy neighbor as thyself; this dogmatic assertion is set in G Mixolydian, which tonal center then continues to function as a strong reference point throughout the cantata. The remaining cantata movements explore the sentiment that one must learn to love unconditionally in order to be loved by God. The second movement is a recitative in C major which declares that we must love God completely in order to gain His grace; it functions as a statement of devotion, beginning with "So muß es sein." The third movement, in A minor, casts a shadow of doubt over this mutual devotion, and suggests that humankind needs the reassurance of God's love in order to understand the law and to learn how to love in return. The fourth move-

[29]For the interested reader, the entire text of cantata 77 and a translation by Z. Philip Ambrose is provided in Appendix 5.

ment is a recitative which subdivides into two sections of text. The first part asks again for God's help to learn how to empathize with our neighbors, to provide them with help in time of need; the second part asks for God's help to learn how to be unselfish, in order to be granted the happiness that comes from God's mercy. This recitative begins in E minor, and at the moment when the text refers to over-looking the neighbor in need (*vorübergeh*), the harmony abruptly abandons a dominant of E and moves instead to a vii°$_7$ of B minor, in which key it cadences firmly. After the momentary tonicization of B, the harmony turns toward G—the key of the first movement's com-mandment—at the optimistic expression that God will grant happi-ness (if we learn to live by the commandment). The fifth movement, in D minor, despairingly expresses our inability to fulfill the com-mandments because of our inherent imperfection (*Unvollkommen-heit*). Despite the pleas for help, we have not yet learned how to live by God's laws. When the final chorale text pleads again for a stronger faith and an ability to serve others, the key returns to the opening tonic, G, but now in minor.[30] At the end of the chorale, set to the melody "Ach Gott, vom Himmel sieh darein," the harmony turns toward D as dominant, which is left musically unresolved. The return to D is symbolically associated with the D-minor key of the fifth movement, which expresses our *Unvollkommenheit*. This final gesture symbolizes humankind's everlasting weakness in the face of God's power, a sentiment that is fundamental to the Christian faith.[31]

---

[30]Bach left the final chorale untexted, but the text is assumed to be the eighth strophe of David Denicke's hymn "O Gottes Sohn, Herr Jesu Christ," which begins "Herr, durch den Glauben wohn in mir." See *NBA* I/21, *Kritischer Bericht*, pp. 11–13.

[31]An alternate interpretation is provided by Eric Chafe in his *Tonal Allegory in the Vocal Music of J.S. Bach* (Berkeley: University of California Press, 1991). Chafe understands the overall tonal progression in this cantata as G - C - A - D, which analyzes the progression differently than I do in Example 54, and which understands the final chorale in D minor. This scheme presents a falling fifth progression, which Chafe refers to as "tonal catabasis" and which symbolizes for him, "mankind's awareness of the human condition and the need to submit to God's will" (pp. 201–2). The close on D in the final chorale is interpreted as a symbol of hope: "although the tonal allegory of this cantata conveys our remaining in the imperfect sphere of human existence, there are nevertheless indications of ultimate hope: the ascent of the bass on the last line of the final chorale is one such" (p. 206).

Ach Gott vom Himmel sieh darein

The cantus firmus "Ach Gott vom Himmel sieh darein" is frequently attributed to the Phrygian mode, but I will analyze Bach's setting in BWV 77/6 (B & H, Nr. 253) as Aeolian, with a dominant ending. Such an interpretation may be received with skepticism after my own refusal to analyze Phrygian and Mixolydian chorales as dominant endings, but based on the melodic organization of the cantus itself as well as Bach's handling of the melody, I believe the dominant ending analysis is warranted.

In an example that is fraught with difficulties, Kirnberger uses the melody to illustrate the correct handling of the Phrygian mode. His example, reproduced in Example 55, provides a G-major and an E-Phrygian setting of the tune; the former is described as "insipid and disgusting," and the latter as "expressive and admirable."[32] Kirnberger has chosen an unusual cantus firmus to demonstrate the Phrygian mode. On its own, this melody does not justify an E-Phrygian analysis; rather, with its cadences on B and the introduction of F-sharp in the third phrase, it might well be analyzed as a transposed Phrygian melody, having B as final. However, Kirnberger's E-Phrygian setting of the melody treats the final note as $\hat{5}$ of E. Bach set this melody several times, also assigning the melody an E final, or its transpositional equivalent.[33]

---

[32]Kirnberger, *The Art of Strict Musical Composition*. Example 55 appears on pp. 320–21.

[33]In Chapter 1, I reproduced his setting BWV 153/1 (B & H, Nr. 3) and quoted Lester's remarks about it. Bach also uses the melody in BWV 2 (B & H, Nr. 262). It is possible to find earlier settings which are similar. Schein accompanies the melody at the fifth below in his *Cantional* (Johann Hermann Schein, *Cantional*, vol. 1 (1627), p. 135.) Schütz does the same in his *Die Psalmen Davids* (Heinrich Schütz, *Der Psalter nach Cornelius Beckers Dichtungen* (Freiburg: Georg Hoffman, 1628), ed. Walter Blankenburg, *Neue Ausgabe sämtlicher Werke*, vol. 6 (Kassel–Basel: Bärenreiter Verlag, 1955), p. 12). There are also, however, earlier settings which do treat the final note of the cantus firmus as the modal final, such as Praetorius's settings of 1610 (Michael Praetorius, *Musae Sioniae* (1610), ed. Friedrich Blume, *Gesamtausgabe der Musikalischer Werke von Michael Praetorius*, vols. 8–9 (Wolfenbüttel-Berlin: Georg Kallmeyer, 1932, 1929). Several settings in vol. 8, Nrs. 91, 92, 93 (pp. 72–73), assign the A-Phrygian melody an A final. In vol. 9, Nrs. 145, 146 and 149 do the same, but Nrs. 147 and 148 (pp. 186–190) assign the A-Phrygian melody a D final.)

Example 55: Kirnberger, "Ach Gott von Himmel sieh darein" (1776)

It is curious that Kirnberger illustrates the correct handling of the Phrygian mode with this particular example. The F-sharp in the third phrase prevents a diatonic E-Phrygian setting: the accompaniment of that phrase frequently introduces the B-major triad, a harmony that is foreign to the E-Phrygian mode. Elsewhere, Kirnberger avoids F-sharp, doing what he can to create an E-Phrygian accompaniment. Indeed, with the exception of the third phrase, he exploits the plagal relationship A - E, which is idiomatic to Phrygian.

The accidentals that were considered problematic for an E-Phrygian analysis in Kirnberger's example are equally problematic for a D-Phrygian analysis of Bach's setting, reproduced in Example 56. That is, D is prolonged through its dominant, with the chromaticisms E-natural and C-sharp, at the upbeat to m. 1, and again in m. 11. Bach's final cadence also thwarts the Phrygian mode, inserting the diminished seventh chord on C-sharp as the penultimate harmony. In sum, Bach's setting of "Ach Gott, vom Himmel sieh darein," BWV 77/6, is not easily heard in D Phrygian. Neither the cantus firmus nor its harmonization defines D as a modal final.

In contrast with Kirnberger's Phrygian interpretation, Daniel Gottlob Türk understands the melody as "Aeolian ending on the dominant."[34] Example 57 reproduces the melody as it appeared in its original form, beginning on A.[35] The melody certainly does nothing to reinforce a Phrygian final—in this transposition level—of D. The only time there is a descent to D^4, in Phrase 3, it is approached by E-natural, and immediately returns to cadence on A^4. The cadences alternate between A and G, in an antecedent/consequent relationship that appears to be left unresolved. The first phrase on A is antecedent to the consequent on G at the double bar. The question/answer relationship of the two phrases is reinforced by the motivic connections between them—the A - B-flat - A - G incipit is

---

[34]Türk, *Ein Beytrag zur Verbesserung*, p. 68. He also identifies the following melodies which end on the dominant: "O großer Gott von macht," "Durch Adams Fall," "Es woll' uns Gott genädig sein." There is much theoretical support for the argument that some chorales do end on the dominant or confinal. I have written on this subject in "Irregular Endings in Two Chorales by Bach," *JMT* 38/1 (Spring, 1994), pp. 43–77. Bernhard Meier discusses the topic extensively in his *Die Tonarten der klassischen Vokalpolyphonie, nach den Quellen dargestellt* (Utrecht: Oostök, Scheltema & Holkema, 1974), trans. Ellen S. Beebe as *The Modes of Classical Vocal Polyphony* (New York: Broude Brothers, 1988).

[35]Example 57 is based on Zahn's entry 4431, which derives from the Erfurt *Enchiridion* of 1524, p. 24.

Example 56: BWV 77/6 (B & H, Nr. 253) and sketch

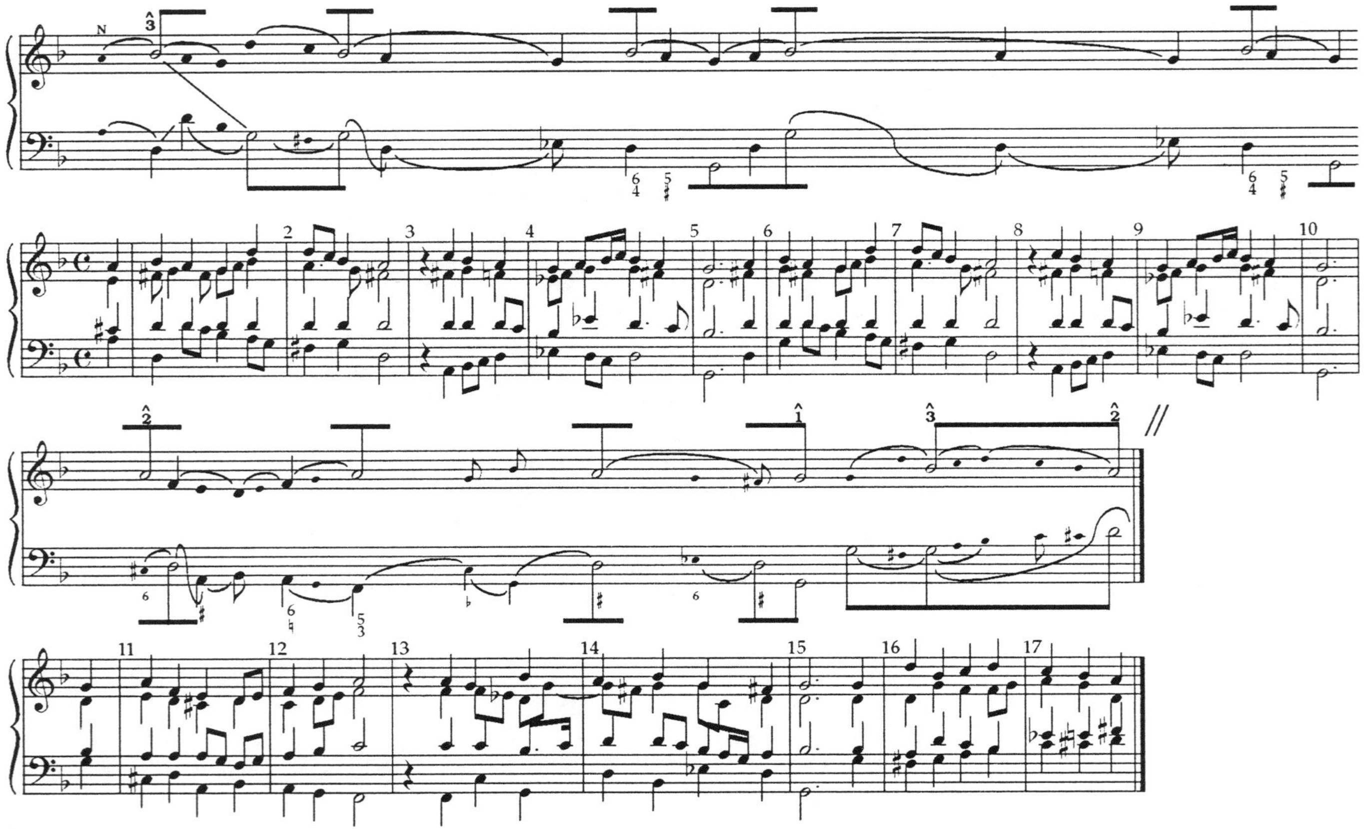

common to both, the first one continuing to cadence on A, the second one resolving to G. The next two phrases repeat the pattern of cadencing on A and then G, once again with a motivic connection—the third phrase begins and ends with the melodic gesture G - A, which is answered by the fourth phrase incipit F - G and cadence F-sharp - G, the F-sharp leading tone appearing to firmly establish G as tonic. The final phrase begins with an outline of the triad on G (G - D - B-flat), but continues to cadence on A; this phrase is related to the opening phrase in its rising-fifth leap from G to D and its descent from D to A at the cadence. When we hear the final phrase, we expect a continuation that is similar to the second phrase, but this previously established antecedent/consequent relationship is left unresolved at the end of the chorale.

Bach's harmonization in BWV 77/6 supports Türk's interpretation that the melody is Aeolian, ending on the dominant. My sketch of the chorale is provided in Example 56.[36] Throughout the chorale, G minor is defined as the tonic in V - i progressions. The *Urlinie* is a $\hat{3}$-line supported by a i - V - i arpeggiation, with the final descent taking place in m. 15. Following that closure, however, the final phrase reintroduces the tonic harmony and *Kopfton* $\hat{3}$, which then descends to $\hat{2}$ supported by the dominant. I have borrowed Schenker's symbol for interruption ("), since the final dominant is left unresolved.

Example 57: "Ach Gott vom Himmel sieh darein," cantus firmus, Erfurt

---

[36]The musical text in Example 56 is based on *NBA* I/21, p. 22. (©1988 Bärenreiter. Used by permission.)

Summary

These analytic studies illuminate the rich variety of Bach's Phrygian and Mixolydian cantus firmus treatment. In each example, Bach blends modal and tonal languages, though the extent to which this is apparent is unique to the individual composition. In his cantata on the cantus firmus "Aus tiefer Not," the Phrygian harmony of the first and last movements is contrasted with the tonal language of the internal movements, but these movements are connected by a large-scale harmonic scheme that expresses the Phrygian mode. In one of the internal movements Bach places the cantus firmus within a tonal context, to explore its potential as a tonal continuo line. The most compelling harmonic issue that is explored during the Phrygian movements is the fifth-relation from A to E. The expectations created by this modal fifth-relation are explored in the remaining movements and in the larger tonal scheme of the cantata.

In Cantata BWV 91, Bach merges modal and tonal harmonic languages using the cantus firmus "Gelobet seist du, Jesu Christ." Here, Mixolydian idioms are overshadowed by a modern G-major tonic. In contrast to his conflated tonal/modal idiom in BWV 91, stands the Mixolydian treatment of the same cantus firmus in BWV 314. In this chorale, the Mixolydian subdominant-tonic relationship C - G, and the diatonic seventh degree F-natural, are allowed to emerge without higher-level G-major implications. The Mixolydian chorale "Dies sind die heiligen Zehn Gebot," BWV 298, emphasizes the subdominant to such an extent that one might be tempted to assign C, rather than G, the role of tonic. But Bach's contrapuntal setting of this melody in his cantata 77 demonstrates unequivocally that Bach heard the melody in G and not in C.

I have consistently interpreted the rising fifth-relations in Phrygian and Mixolydian as IV - I, but Bach does occasionally invoke a structural rising fifth-relation as I - V. The final chorale of cantata 77, a setting of "Ach Gott vom Himmel sieh darein" demonstrates that such a dominant ending is possible even at the close of a multi-movement vocal work.

In all of the analyses above, I hope to have demonstrated the importance of a contest-based interpretation. In order to capture the diversity of Bach's Phrygian and Mixolydian modal language it is vital that the harmonic and melodic gestures that are unique to these modes be allowed to emerge, even if the analyst has to learn to hear such interpretations without a tonal bias.

CHAPTER 4

An Original Analytic Model for Bach's
Dorian and Aeolian Chorales

Although the analytic issues that arise when one interprets chorales in the "minor" modes are not as controversial as the debate over tonal function in Phrygian or Mixolydian, the Dorian and Aeolian modes certainly deserve our close consideration. Indeed, the characteristic patterns in these modes engage *subtle* compositional details—such as the melodic treatment of scale degree $\hat{7}$—yet these details can affect the compositional structure at the deepest analytic levels. Dorian and Aeolian *Ursätze* comprise melodic and harmonic structures which reflect the modal cantus firmi themselves, and which depart significantly from the tonal models proposed by Schenker in *Free Composition*. Indeed, in that theoretical work, Schenker does not address adequately the possible structures in the minor mode, but rather sees the major mode as the norm, in which he demonstrates most of his examples.[1]

With this in mind, I shall propose here an analytic model that accommodates the unique structures of the Dorian and Aeolian modes; I shall then demonstrate the advantages of my analytic model through some detailed chorale analyses.

The Dorian and Aeolian modes are very similar in intervallic structure and this translates into a close connection between their melodic and harmonic profiles. The distinctions between Dorian and Aeolian arise from the treatment of the sixth scale degree. There is, of course, the possibility of modal *mixture* between Dorian and

---

[1] I discussed Schenker's theoretical preference for major earlier, in footnotes 20–21 of Chapter 1.

Aeolian, but the diatonic form of the sixth degree is favored in a composition—the natural sixth degree in Dorian is a major sixth above the
final, symbolized as sharp-$\hat{6}$ and the natural sixth degree in Aeolian is
a minor sixth above the final, symbolized as flat-$\hat{6}$. Modal mixture can
occur in melodic and harmonic contexts, sometimes blurring the line
that separates these two modes.

Earlier theorists recognized the problem of a clear Dorian versus
Aeolian identity. For instance, Kirnberger attempts to show the difference between Dorian and Aeolian with a pair of examples,
reproduced in Example 58. His comparison focuses on the treatment
of the sixth degree:

> Example [58a] is Dorian, because B, as the major sixth of the main tone,
> is used throughout, except for the first B-flat in measure [one]. In spite of
> the fact that the melody in the principal voice is the same, the second ex-
> ample [58b] is Aeolian, because the minor sixth of the main tone is used
> throughout.[2]

Even though he has advised his readers to avoid B-flat in Dorian
melodic composition, Kirnberger introduces it in Example 58a. Elsewhere in this Dorian example, however, the sixth degree is diatonic
(B-natural). The B-flat is introduced only the one time (m. 1) above F
in the bass, to avoid an augmented fourth between the outer voices.
This is a good example of how chromatic alteration is necessary at
times to avoid false relations. The linear context of the B-flat is also
significant—the lowered sixth degree in the neighbor pattern $\hat{5}$ - flat
$\hat{6}$ - $\hat{5}$ is idiomatic.

While Kirnberger has attempted to distinguish Dorian from
Aeolian by using the diatonic sixth degree in each mode, he has not
distinguished these modes successfully from modern minor. Examples
58a and b do not demonstrate the progressions, unique to Dorian and
Aeolian, which incorporate the natural seventh degree, C-natural. Indeed, it is hard to see how these passages are anything but reasonable
examples of modern minor. For instance, the B-natural in m. 3 of Example 58a, which is supposed to define this passage as Dorian, simply
leads up to the leading tone C-sharp in the idiomatic rising form of
the modern minor scale.

---

[2]Kirnberger, *The Art of Strict Musical Composition*. Example 58 is based on
Kirnberger's example on p. 62 of the original treatise; it is given as Examples 2.11 and
2.12 in the translation (p. 332).

Example 58: Kirnberger (1776), example of Dorian (a) and Aeolian, transposed down a fifth (b)

Kirnberger also attempts to demonstrate that a choice between Dorian and Aeolian is sometimes not possible, introducing a problem of modal ambiguity within the literature of chorale melodies:

> It must be noted that among the old hymns there are a few of doubtful mode, so that one cannot immediately tell at first glance from which note they proceed. In such a case one need only look at the digressions to find the main mode and to organize the harmonies accordingly. However, if the modulations are of such a nature that they can belong to two modes, then both are valid, and one selects the one that corresponds most closely to the expression of the piece. Thus the melody of the hymn *Nun kommt der Heyden Heyland* is Dorian as well as Aeolian; likewise the chorale *Auf meinen lieben Gott*.[3]

The two melodies to which he refers are given in Example 59 as they appear in Bach's chorale repertoire.[4] The source of the modal ambiguity is obvious: there are no instances of $\hat{6}$ in either melody; harmonizations could successfully be written in Dorian or Aeolian.

---

[3]Ibid., p. 331.

[4]Examples 59a and b reproduce the soprano voices from "Nun komm, der Heiden Heiland," BWV 36/8 (B & H, Nr. 28) and "Auf meinen lieben Gott," BWV 5/7 (B & H, Nr. 304), respectively. The musical texts in Examples 59a and b are based on *NBA* I/1, p. 74, and *BG* 1, p. 150.

Example 59:

a) Soprano from "Nun komm, der Heiden Heiland," BWV 36/8 (B & H, Nr. 28)

b) Soprano from "Auf meinen lieben Gott," BWV 5/7 (B & H, Nr. 304)

As I explore the characteristic melodic and harmonic formulas of the Dorian and Aeolian modes, I will address issues of overlap and differentiation between them. In this regard it will be helpful here to consider first some representative cantus firmi in each mode.

Dorian and Aeolian Cantus Firmi

Example 60 reproduces some Dorian melodies that are harmonized by Bach. One way in which the Dorian character of these melodies emerges is through the idiomatic descending third-progression C - B-natural - A; this progression is marked by a bracket where it occurs throughout Example 60. B-flat occurs more rarely, as for example in m. 1 of Example 60b and m. 7 of Example 60d. In these cases, the sixth degree is heard as an upper neighbor to $\hat{5}$ in the melodic pattern A - B-flat - A, and it avoids an augmented fourth outline from B-natural to F. This flat $\hat{6}$ in Dorian might be interpreted as an Aeolian reference, or as a mixture with Aeolian, but it does not necessarily impugn the Dorian identity.

Example 60: Dorian Cantus Firmi

a) "Christ lag in Todesbanden," BWV 4/8 (B & H, Nr. 184) [Original tonic: E]

b) "Als Jesus Christus in der Nacht," BWV 265 (B & H, Nr. 180)

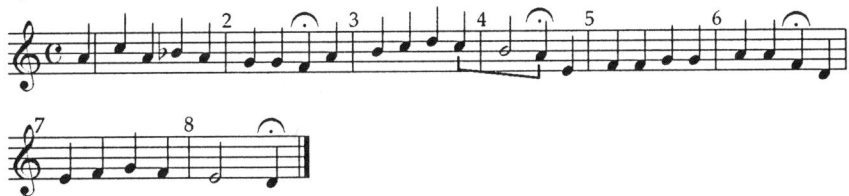

c) "Mit Fried und Freud ich fahr dahin," BWV 382 (B & H, Nr. 49)

d) "Jesu, meine Freude," BWV 227/7 (B & H, Nr. 283) [Original tonic: E]

e) "Erschienen ist der herrlich Tag," BWV 145/5 (B & H, Nr. 17) [Original tonic: F♯]

Similarly, it is not unusual to find instances of the raised sixth degree in Aeolian compositions. Again, this sharp-$\hat{6}$ might be considered as a modal mixture with Dorian, without impugning the Aeolian identity. Example 61 reproduces the cantus firmi of some Aeolian chorales by Bach. One characteristic gesture that can distinguish Aeolian from Dorian is the inflection of the minor sixth degree as a neighbor to $\hat{5}$ in the pattern (E) - F - E. Instances of the idiomatic ($\hat{5}$) - flat $\hat{6}$ - $\hat{5}$ succession are bracketed throughout the example.[5]

[5]The melody "Von Gott will ich nicht lassen" in Example 61d appears to have a clear Aeolian identity, although it was not consistently recognized as Aeolian by the historical theorists. It is instead classified as a plagal Dorian melody. (In Appendix 2, it will be found in the Hypodorian lists of Matthaei, Walther, Sorge, and Knecht.) The cantus firmus does have a plagal range, spanning the octave from E^4 to E^5, with A^4 as final. In its original transposition level, the melody concluded on G, a common Hypodorian final. The original melody also had a different melodic contour at the asterisk (*) in mm. 10–11 which suggested a Dorian identity—the last phrase began $\hat{5}$ - sharp $\hat{6}$, instead of flat $\hat{6}$ - $\hat{5}$ as it does in Bach's setting. In Bach's settings of this tune the last phrase consistently begins with some form of the Aeolian gesture flat $\hat{6}$ - $\hat{5}$. His four settings are listed here: BWV 73/5 (B & H, Nr. 191); BWV 417 (B & H, Nr. 364); BWV 418 (B & H, Nr. 332); BWV 419 (B & H, Nr. 114).

The melody given as Example 61e, "Was mein Gott will, das gescheh allzeit," appears not to have an Aeolian, but rather a Dorian identity, because of the sixth scale degree, which is inflected as F-sharp in mm. 7 and 10. It was classified as Hypodorian in historical writings. (In Appendix 2, it will be found in the Hypodorian lists of Walther and Knecht.) There are good reasons for this classification—the melody has a plagal range (E^4 - D^5, with final A^4) and its original transposition level was G. The original melody also introduced the raised sixth degree, but only once, as a leading tone to $\hat{7}$ at the cadence in m. 7. Since such leading-tone inflections are to be expected at cadences, this sharp $\hat{6}$ does not in itself contradict a possible Aeolian final. However, Bach also introduces a passing sharp $\hat{6}$ in m. 10 where the original melody had skipped from $\hat{5}$ to $\hat{7}$ in imitation of the opening gesture. This F-sharp does seem to contradict the Aeolian final. Yet Bach's own treatment is varied — in other settings, he uses the passing tone F-natural in both mm. 1 and 10. His setting BWV 65/7 (B & H, Nr. 41) will be analyzed later as an *Aeolian* composition, in which the melody is chromatically altered.

Example 61: Aeolian Cantus Firmi

a) "Allein zu dir, Herr Jesu Christ," BWV 261 (B & H, Nr. 259) [Original tonic: B]

b) "Ich ruf zu dir, Herr Jesu Christ," BWV 177/5 (B & H, Nr. 71) [Original tonic: G]

c) "Meine Seel erhebt den Herren," BWV 10/7 (B & H, Nr. 358) [Original tonic: G]

d) "Von Gott will ich nicht lassen," BWV 73/5 (B & H, Nr. 191)

e) "Was mein Gott will, das g'sceh allzeit," BWV 65/7 (B & H, Nr. 41)

The Diatonic Seventh Degree in Dorian—Upper Neighbor Figure

Dorian cantus firmi are strongly characterized by melodic progressions which emphasize $\hat{5}$ (A) and $\hat{7}$ (C). This emphasis is often realized in a construction which will be called the Dorian upper neighbor (DOR-UN), shown symbolically in Example 62. Here the C is flagged; it is not a harmonic interval from the A, an expression of the third A - C, but rather a melodic embellishment of the A, in the manner of a *neighbor note* figure.[6] Various of its harmonic guises, as treated by Bach, are shown in the example.[7] In Example 62a, the *Kopfton* A^4 is prolonged by the DOR-UN—there is a movement away from A^4 to C^5 followed by a return to A^4. The C^5 is harmonized by a first-inversion triad on C which resolves as dominant to an F-major triad that supports the second A^4. (The annotation DOR-M under the bass F—for Dorian mediant—will be discussed later.) In Examples 62b through d, the skip from C^5 down to A^4 is filled in by a passing-tone. In Example 62b, the chromatic passing tone B-flat—an example of mixture with Aeolian—is the seventh for the dominant harmony of F, and thus reinforces the F-*Stufe*. This chromatic alteration of the DOR-UN figure is certainly possible, but it is not all that common in Bach's Dorian chorale practice. In Example 62c, the diatonic Dorian scale governs the stepwise descent from C^5 to A^4; each of the scale degrees in the C - B-natural - A melodic progression is given consonant support as a 3-*Zug* in A minor, harmonized as i - V - i.

---

[6]Edward Phillips has discussed neighbor relationships at the interval of a third in his article "Pitch Structures in a Selected Repertoire of Early German Chorale Melodies," *Music Theory Spectrum* 3 (1981), pp. 98–116. His general purpose is not to identify and classify melodic gestures as modal determinants, but rather to "search for melodic patterns in the genre of German chorale melody with the aim of creating a system of categories for these melodies on the basis of melodic types" (p. 98). He identifies the interval of a third as an important characteristic of melodic organization in the chorale. In his discussion, the concept of neighbor note "is expanded to allow the ornamental pitch to be a distance of a second *or* a third from the principal pitch, either above or below. As with the conventional auxiliary at a second, the neighbor motion at a third can be incomplete" (p. 100). Phillips examines several melodies in which C acts as an upper neighbor to A. The neighbor-note configuration A - C - A can be presented in its pure form, or the motion from C to A can be filled in with a passing tone B. The third-related neighbor construction can function at different levels of structure.

[7]The point cannot be overemphasized, that these are not simply abstract possibilities; rather they symbolize procedures that I believe are audible in the harmonic practice of Bach, as he harmonized pertinent melodic features of the chorale melodies.

Example 62: Dorian upper neighbor (DOR-UN)

An unusual setting of the DOR-UN is given in Example 62d: the diatonic Dorian scale again governs the descent from C to A. As in Example 62b, the harmonic support for the melodic progression C - B - A is C major moving to F major, but now the B-natural denies our perception of F as a traditional tonic. The B-natural forms a dissonant major seventh with the bass note C and an augmented fourth with the root of the following F-triad. An instance of this unusual DOR-UN setting is found in mm. 27–28 of Bach's chorale "Wir glauben all an einen Gott," BWV 437 (B & H, Nr. 133). Example 63 reproduces the pertinent measures of the chorale.[8] The cantus firmus cadences on D^4 in m. 26, then rises from F^4 to C^5 maintaining the diatonic Dorian scale, with B-natural instead of B-flat. From C^5 the cantus descends to a cadence on A^4, again stepping through a passing tone B-natural. The C - B - A descent is harmonized by C major moving to F, with B-natural sounding as a dissonant major seventh against C in the bass.

Example 63: "Wir glauben all an einen Gott," BWV 437 (B & H, Nr. 133), mm. 27–28

---

[8]The musical text in Example 63 is based on *BG* 39, Nr. 184.

Example 64: Aeolian upper neighbor (AOL-UN)

The Diatonic Seventh Degree in Aeolian—Upper Neighbor Figure

Example 64 gives comparable harmonizations of the same construct in the Aeolian mode, a melodic figure in which the fifth degree is embellished by its upper third, identified as an Aeolian upper neighbor (AOL-UN). The AOL-UN is first harmonized in Example 64a, by a movement from the tonic to the mediant. The *Kopfton* E^5 is first supported by A in the bass; E^5 is then embellished by the AOL-UN figure as the bass moves through B to C, suggesting the harmonic progression V_6 - I in C. (The C-major chord is analyzed as an Aeolian mediant (AOL-M), a construct that will be discussed later.) In Example 64b, the AOL-UN figure G^5 - E^5 is filled in by the passing tone F-natural, the diatonic sixth degree in Aeolian. The harmonic support for the pattern is the same as Example 64a, a V_6 - I progression in C. In Example 64c, the AOL-UN figure is filled in by the chromatic passing tone, F-sharp, and is harmonized in the context of E minor. The pattern of Example 64c does not occur with great frequency in the Aeolian mode; the chromatic alteration tends to undermine the Aeolian character by providing a "Dorian" sixth degree. The formula of Example 64c is demonstrated in Bach's Aeolian chorale "Ach, was soll ich Sünder machen," BWV 259 (B & H, Nr. 39), given in Example 65.[9]

Example 65: "Ach was soll ich Sünder machen," BWV 259 (B & H, Nr. 39), mm. 7–10

---

[9]The musical text in Example 65 is based on *BG* 39, Nr. 7.

Examples 64c and 62b demonstrate the mixture or borrowing that can occur between Dorian and Aeolian: the Aeolian formula in Example 64c requires a ficta F-sharp, where its Dorian analog is diatonic; the Dorian formula in Example 62b requires the chromaticism B-flat, where its Aeolian analog is diatonic. Such borrowing is certainly possible, although the diatonic forms of the UN figures are more common. That is, in Dorian, the DOR-UN figure is most commonly heard in the context of Example 62a, where no passing tone occurs between $\hat{7}$ and $\hat{5}$, and Example 62c, where the passing tone is diatonic. Similarly, in Aeolian, the AOL-UN figure is most commonly presented in the settings of Examples 62a and b, where the passing tone, if it does occur, is diatonic.

The Diatonic Seventh Degree in Dorian —Lower Neighbor Figure

The Dorian seventh degree, C-natural, can also prolong $\hat{1}$ in an idiomatic lower neighbor configuration. The Dorian lower neighbor (DOR-LN) is characteristically harmonized by the mediant or the minor dominant. In Example 66a, a i - III - i progression supports the *Kopfton* $\hat{5}$ and the DOR-LN pattern D - C - D. In Example 66b, the DOR-LN is again harmonized by the mediant, but this time the mediant is itself prolonged through a closed harmonic progression, I - V - I, before it returns to the tonic. The F-major prolongation is heard within a larger prolongation of D—F major supports the descent from $\hat{5}$ to $\hat{3}$ of the soprano's fifth-progression in D-minor.[10] In Example 66c, the DOR-LN is again harmonized by the mediant, but here the mediant moves on to the dominant rather than returning to the tonic and the DOR-LN is resolved to D as part of a V $^{6\text{-}5}_{4\text{-}3}$ - i resolution.

Sometimes the DOR-LN returns to the tonic through a chromatic passing tone, C-sharp. In Example 66d, for example, the progression of Example 66a is elaborated by means of passing chords between the tonic and mediant harmonies. The alto moves from D to C-natural as the tonic harmony passes through V_6 of F to F major. The DOR-LN then returns to D through a chromatic passing tone C-sharp as the mediant harmony passes through vii°$_6$ of D to D minor. This hearing of the natural $\hat{7}$ - sharp $\hat{7}$ voice-leading seems at odds with Schenker's tonal exegeses of such passages. Pertinent discussion by Schenker will be examined presently.

---

[10]Schenker makes a similar interpretation of Beethoven's Sonata, Op. 57/1 in *Free Composition* (Figure 154, 4). In that analysis, the descent from $\hat{5}$ to $\hat{3}$ is supported by the progression I - V - I in the mediant key.

Example 66: Dorian lower neighbor (DOR-LN)

The DOR-LN can also be harmonized by the minor dominant, as shown in Example 66e. The DOR-LN is supported by A in a i - v - i progression. The lower neighbor, C-natural, resolves to D through a chromatic passing note C-sharp. In this interpretation, a higher structural value is assigned the C-natural, since it initiates the gesture; hence, the C is flagged as a DOR-LN and C-sharp is slurred as a passing tone.

An unusual instance of the chromatic resolution C - C-sharp - D occurs in Bach's chorale "Als Jesus Christus in der Nacht," BWV 265 (B & H, Nr. 180); mm. 6–8 are reproduced in Example 67.[11] Here, the DOR-LN is supported by A in the bass, which is harmonized as a first-inversion F-major triad. It resolves up to D through the passing note C-sharp, harmonized as a diminished seventh in D. The contrapuntal framework suggests the harmony of F—A - G - F in the soprano against A - E - F in the bass—with a strong convergence on the octave F. The F, however, supports D-minor harmony, and the continuation, V - I in D, confirms D as tonic.

Let us now move on to some analyses and remarks by Schenker, in connection with the direct chromatic succession from natural $\hat{7}$ to sharp $\hat{7}$ (here, C - C-sharp). In *Free Composition*, Schenker discusses the chromatic passing note which functions as a leading tone; in Example 68a, the added third A below the passing C-sharp conceals the chromatic passing tone and creates a stronger root movement of a

---

[11]The musical text in Example 67 is based on *BG* 39, Nr. 13.

Example 67: "Als Jesus Christus in der Nacht," BWV 265 (B & H, Nr. 180) mm. 8–10 and sketch

descending fifth.[12] Schenker later addresses the specific conflict of natural $\hat{7}$ - sharp $\hat{7}$ present in the chord progression i - III - V in minor. He illustrates the abstract progression with Example 68b.[13] Then he refers us to some examples which illustrate the progression in the musical practice. In Example 68c, from Chopin's Etude, Op. 25/11, the i - III - V progression occurs in A minor.[14] The lowered seventh degree G-natural is introduced over the C-major mediant harmony which supports $\hat{3}$ (C) of the descent from $\hat{5}$ (E). As $\hat{3}$ descends to $\hat{2}$ and III moves to V, the G-natural is held, creating a minor dominant, E minor. $\hat{2}$ is then prolonged in the melodic neighbor pattern, B - C - B. The C is harmonized by C major, thus making it "possible to return in an ascending motion to the root of V, which contains the major third G-sharp. Thus the direct succession G-natural - G-sharp is avoided."[15] In other words, the C-major harmonization of the

---

[12]Schenker, *Free Composition*, Figure 112.1 Schenker dicusses the example in §247, p. 90.

[13]Ibid., Figure 113.2. Schenker discusses the example in §248, p. 91. He also discusses the progression I - III - V in major, which is, however, not relevant to our Dorian investigation.

[14]Ibid., Figure 76.3.

[15]Ibid., §247, p. 90.

Example 68: Illustrations from *Free Composition*, Supplement: Musical Examples, by Heinrich Schenker, translated by Ernst Oster (Reprinted with permission of Schirmer Books, an imprint of Simon & Schuster MacMillan, copyright © 1979.)

a)

J.S. Bach, Aria variata (BWV 989)

b)

c)

Chopin, Étude op. 25 no.11

d)

Chopin, Étude op. 25 no.11

neighbor-note C creates an opportunity for the bass to pass from C^4 through D^4 before returning to E, the root of the dominant. The passing note D^4 is then itself harmonized by a ii°$_6$ triad, which allows the G-natural to descend through F-natural to E. The G-natural is thus interpreted as part of a descending scale passage and the leading tone G-sharp is introduced from above, in a descending third-progression B - A - G-sharp. Schenker does not slur the G - F - E succession, but he does indicate the B - A - G-sharp *Zug*. The prolongation of $\hat{2}$ is sketched in more detail in Example 68d, where the G - F - E succession and the B - A - G-sharp progression are actually notated.[16]

Schenker thus preferred not to understand a direct connection between natural $\hat{7}$ and sharp $\hat{7}$. In order to avoid the connection, he asserts a compound melodic structure, in which the lowered seventh degree steps down through flat $\hat{6}$ to $\hat{5}$ while the raised seventh degree is approached from above. In my examples of the DOR-LN, I proposed a different interpretation of the natural $\hat{7}$ - sharp $\hat{7}$ succession: in the Dorian mode, the natural seventh degree can resolve to the tonic through the chromatic passing tone C-sharp. This was shown in Examples 66d and e. The two points of view agree in excluding the direct connection natural $\hat{7}$ - sharp $\hat{7}$ from modern tonal practice. As we have seen elsewhere, Schenker equates modern tonal practice with effective triadic composition. In contrast, I believe that the natural $\hat{7}$ - sharp $\hat{7}$ connection does function effectively within a certain genre of Bach's compositional practice that I am calling Dorian.

The DOR-LN and UN figures can also be heard in the bass, in which case they are elevated to harmonic constructs. In Example 69a, for example, the melodic fifth-progression from A to D is supported by the bass line D - F - C - A - D. On hearing C major immediately following the F-major triad, one might expect it to function as the dominant of F, as in Example 66b, but the C-major triad does not resolve as dominant to an F-major tonic. Rather, C major moves immediately to the dominant of D. The bass gesture C - A is analyzed as a DOR-UN, in which C is understood as an embellishment of the fifth degree, A.

A related paradigm is given in Example 69b. The D-minor tonic once again progresses through F major to a C-major triad which is approached as the dominant of F, but which does not continue as such.

[16]Ibid., Figure 107.

Example 69: Harmonic contexts for DOR-UN and DOR-LN

Rather, C major moves immediately to a D-minor triad. One might hear the progression from C major to D minor as a deceptive resolution, V - vi in F, but F major then vanishes, as the "deceptive" D minor reclaims its tonic role and the 5-*Zug* simply continues its descent from F^4 to D^4 harmonized conventionally in D. Here again, one should not consider the bass C of Example 69b as $\hat{5}$ of F major; rather, in this context it functions as a DOR-LN to D. The "F-major deceptive cadence" is then an overlay of more modern hearing.

Diatonic Seventh Degree in Aeolian—Lower Neighbor Figure

The Aeolian Lower Neighbor (AOL-LN) appears, variously harmonized, in Example 70. Again, these harmonizations are not abstract formulas, but rather are patterns that appear in Bach's chorale practice. I emphasize this because a close comparison of Examples 66 and 70 will reveal that the harmonic situations listed for the DOR-LN and AOL-LN are not identical. It should also be emphasized here that my examples are not intended as a complete listing of all possible harmonizations of the LN figure; these are merely representative patterns of what is found in the chorale literature. One might venture to say that the AOL-LN is more commonly associated with the dominant harmony in that mode, while the DOR-LN is more commonly associated with the mediant harmony. But such a generalization should be made with caution.

In Example 70a, the AOL-LN figure A - G - A appears in the alto voice, beneath a *Kopfton* $\hat{3}$ (C^5), supported in the bass by a movement from the tonic A to the mediant C and back. In Example 70b, the AOL-LN is harmonized by the dominant, resolving to the tonic through the chromatic passing tone G-sharp. Again, such a chromatic gesture is incompatible with Schenker's notion of voice leading, but it is an important part of Bach's Aeolian harmonic practice.

Example 70: Aeolian lower neighbor (AOL-LN)

The AOL-LN is frequently presented in the context of a tonic arpeggiation in the bass. In Example 70c, the alto moves from the tonic A^4 to the AOL-LN G^4 while the soprano prolongs the *Kopfton* C^5 and the bass moves from A to C. G^4 and C^5 are held in the alto and soprano as the bass continues in ascending arpeggiation to E, creating a first-inversion C harmony. C^5 descends to B^4 as the AOL-LN rises to G-sharp; the resulting dominant harmony then resolves to tonic. In Example 70d, the alto again moves from the tonic A^4 to the AOL-LN G^4; this time G^4 is supported by E in the bass. E moves to C through an arpeggiation of the C triad (E - G - C) while the AOL-LN is held. The alto resolves the AOL-LN G^4 directly to the tonic A^4 as the bass falls from C to A, completing the descending arpeggiation of the tonic triad.

Example 70e features another bass arpeggiation, A - C - E - A, as support for an AOL-LN figure in the alto. The bass of Example 70e is the retrograde of Example 70d. In that example I noted the bass arpeggiation of C major within the larger A-minor arpeggiation. Now in Example 70e, the bass again appears to arpeggiate the triad on C. G is approached from C as a dominant, but in its resolution, it functions as an embellishment of the dominant of A. The G - E gesture in the bass is therefore analyzed as an AOL-UN figure. The alto meanwhile introduces the AOL-LN which is supported by the C - G - E bass progression, and resolves through the chromatic passing note G-sharp as the bass moves from E to A.

Example 70f features the AOL-LN as a harmonic construct in the bass. Although G is approached from C, it is not heard in its resolution as a dominant of C, but rather as an embellishment of A.

Dorian Mediant and Aeolian Mediant

The relation between tonic and mediant is frequently an audible harmonic issue in a Dorian or Aeolian chorale, and the mediant does not always function conventionally. In many of the foregoing examples, I have labeled the mediant as a DOR-M or AOL-M and have postponed my discussion of this function until now. The distinction between a Dorian or Aeolian mediant (DOR-M or AOL-M) and a common-practice minor-key mediant (III) depends upon the surrounding melodic and harmonic context. In Example 71a, for instance, F is notated as a DOR-M because it supports the return of a melodic DOR-UN, an idiomatically Dorian (not D-minor) figure. The progression of Example 71a is reduced to that of Example 71b, at a higher structural level; at this level, the mediant no longer has any specifically modal (non-tonal) function. The DOR-UN, in particular, is no longer present on the sketch. Accordingly, on Example 71b, the traditional figure "III" appears beneath the bass F, rather than the special modal symbol "DOR-M."

Example 71a must also be distinguished from Example 71c. In the latter, no distinctly Dorian feature is exposed—the neighbor-note figure A - B-flat - A is tonally consistent with modern D minor, and the supporting mediant is therefore assigned a common-practice "III" function.

Example 71: Dorian mediant (DOR-M)

Another possible context for the modal mediant, this time the AOL-M, is provided in Example 72; here, the AOL-UN figure, G - E, appears in the bass, approached from the mediant, C. As C moves to G, the rising fifth-progression creates an expectation for a subsequent resolution to C, as V - I in C major. However, the G does not function as V of C, but rather as the AOL-UN to E. This paradigm exposes an unusual relationship between the tonic and mediant, which might be heard as a tonal "tension" between the two degrees. However, the tonal tension can be regarded as a symptom of Aeolian modal structuring. Although the bass in Example 72 seems to conflate A-minor and C-major harmony, it is best—for the purposes of an Aeolian interpretation—to understand such a progression as a unified structure in A.

Example 72: Aeolian mediant (AOL-M)

A practical illustration of the DOR-M relation is found in Bach's chorale, "Mit Fried und Freud ich fahr dahin," BWV 382 (B & H, Nr. 49); Example 73 reproduces mm. 6-10 of the chorale.[17] During this passage, the harmony oscillates between D minor and F major. The bass line of mm. 7-9 sums up the situation clearly: the bass moves in stepwise ascent from $\hat{5}$ to $\hat{1}$ in D (m. 7), followed immediately by a similar ascent from $\hat{5}$ to $\hat{1}$ in F (mm. 7–8). Once F is established at the cadence of m. 8, the bass then articulates leading tone - tonic resolutions, first in D (C-sharp - D) and then in F (E - F). While the bass thus rocks back and forth between D and F, the cantus prolongs the F-major triad. Following a melodic descent from A⁴ to C⁴, it arpeggiates F major in the pattern A⁴ - F⁴ - C⁵ - A⁴, and then prolongs A⁴ in the descending and ascending third-progressions A - G - F - G - A. Though the melodic figurations clearly outline the F-major triad, the harmonic support is not equally focused, since it alternates between D and F. Indeed, a structural dissonance exists between the bass D and the melodic C; in addition, the leading tone in D (C-sharp) creates a cross relation against the fifth of F (C-natural).

This conflict is apparent in the foreground sketch. The soprano is analyzed as a prolongation of the *Kopfton* A, which first descends to F in a third-progression that is harmonized in D minor. The melodic F initiates a fourth-progression down to C as the harmony changes from

---

[17]The musical text in Example 73 is based on Ms. R 18, Nr. 51.

Example 73: "Mit Fried und Freud ich fahr dahin," BWV 382 (B & H, Nr. 49), mm. 6–10 and sketch

D minor to F major. C is then prolonged through the F-major arpeggiation, which is harmonized by the parallel V_6 - I progressions, first in D and then in F. The middleground analysis summarizes the progression, and analyzes the melodic C^4 as an inverted DOR-UN to the *Kopfton*. The supporting F-major triad is analyzed as a DOR-M because of its participation in the distinctly Dorian melodic gesture. In the background sketch, the modal character of the mediant is lost, since the melodic figurations that include the C-natural do not appear.

Subdominant-Tonic Relation in Dorian and Aeolian

The harmony on the fourth degree in Dorian is diatonically a major triad, but it is commonly altered through ficta to create a minor harmony, especially in a plagal elaboration of a cadence. The final cadence of "Jesu, meine Freude," BWV 227/7 (B & H, Nr. 283) is given in Example 74.[18] In this example, the structural dominant that supports $\hat{2}$ is a minor harmony (m. 12); this dominant resolves to the tonic through a tonicized subdominant. The alto voice in mm. 12–13 descends from D through C-natural and B-flat to A; thus, the natural seventh degree in this instance does resolve downward as a passing tone in the fourth-progression $\hat{8}$ - $\hat{7}$ - $\hat{6}$ - $\hat{5}$, rather than upward as a DOR-LN.

A similar cadential resolution is possible in Aeolian, as demonstrated by Bach's chorale "Meine Seel erhebt den Herren," BWV 10/7 (B & H, Nr. 358), the final cadence of which is provided in Example 75.[19] Once again, the structural dominant as support for $\hat{2}$ in the *Urlinie* is a minor harmony, which resolves through a plagal embellishment to the tonic. The foreground sketch of this complex passage demonstrates how the minor third of the dominant steps down as part of the fourth-progression from $\hat{8}$ to $\hat{5}$. The plagal resolution is not analyzed as a part of the *Ursatz*, as it was in many of the Phrygian and Mixolydian chorales studied in Chapter 3. Such a decision is based on the particulars of the given chorale. In the case of "Meine Seel," the chorale does not otherwise develop subdominant-tonic progressions; therefore, the fourth degree has not been incorporated into the *Ursatz* as an organic feature of the composition.

---

[18]The musical text in Example 74 is based on *NBA* III/1, p. 94. (©1965 Bärenreiter. Used by permission.)

[19]The musical text in Example 75 is based on *BG* 1, p. 303.

Example 74: "Jesu meine Freude," BWV 227/7 (B & H, Nr. 283), mm. 10–13 and sketch

Example 75: "Meine Seel erhebt den Herren, " BWV 10/7 (B & H, Nr. 358), mm. 18–22 and sketch [original tonic: G]

Although the minor subdominant is inflected for plagal cadences in the Dorian mode, the diatonic Dorian subdominant is a major triad, and it appears that way when it is prolonged as a *Stufe*. Example 76, for instance, is a prolongation of the tonic through a i - IV - i progression, which is labeled DOR-IV. In this progression, a false relation exists between the minor third F-natural of the D-minor triad, and the major third B-natural of the G-major triad. The tritone relation F - B could be corrected by a ficta F-sharp or B-flat, or both, but in the symbolized situation Bach will typically project both the diatonic degrees of the mode, and so the false relation results at this level.

Example 76: Dorian subdominant-tonic relation (DOR-IV)

Ursatz Possibilities in Dorian

The most common *Urlinie* in the Dorian mode is the descent from $\hat{5}$. Many possibilities for *Ursatz* harmonization of the $\hat{5}$-line incorporate the harmonic functions of DOR-M, DOR-UN and DOR-LN, described above. The abstract paradigms that will be discussed here are based on the actual *Ursätze* of Dorian chorales by Bach; I have identified the chorales in each example.

The Dorian characteristics of a chorale do not necessarily emerge at the deepest level of structure; rather, a Dorian chorale may project a conventional *Ursatz*. A harmonization of the $\hat{5}$-line familiar to modern ears is given in Example 77. The *Kopfton* is supported by an arpeggiation from D through F to A. The dominant then inverts to a first-inversion dominant seventh as support for $\hat{4}$ and the descent from $\hat{3}$ to $\hat{1}$ is supported by i - V - i.

Example 77: "Mit Fried und Freud ich fahr dahin," BWV 382 (B & H, Nr. 49)

In contrast to Example 77, however, are *Ursätze* which include idiomatic Dorian constructs such as the DOR-LN and DOR-UN. In Example 78, for instance, $\hat{4}$ is harmonized by C major, which is approached as V of F, but not resolved as such. Rather, the C in the bass functions as a DOR-LN to the subsequent D. The support for $\hat{4}$ and $\hat{3}$ in this structural descent is problematic for the Schenkerian analyst. In a recent article, David Gagné explores a similar situation in a Monteverdi composition—*Ohimè dov'è il mio ben*, a duet from the seventh book of madrigals (1619), which is based on the *romanesca*, a ground-bass melody with a G-Dorian structure. The ground-bass pattern that provides the contrapuntal framework for each of the composition's four main parts is reproduced as Example 79a.[20] In G Dorian, the opening B-flat - F - G gesture is a transposition of the F - C - D ges-

[20]David Gagné, "Monteverdi's *Ohimè dov'è il mio ben* and the Romanesca," *Music Forum* IV (Columbia University Press, 1987), p. 62, Example 1. (©1987 David Gagné. Used by Permission.)

Example 78: "Christ lag in Todesbanden," BWV 4/8 (B & H, Nr. 184)

ture in Example 78. The background structure which Gagné derives from Monteverdi's embellishment of the *romanesca* is given in Example 79b.[21] There is an interrupted descent from $\hat{5}$ to $\hat{2}$ followed by a complete descent from $\hat{5}$ to $\hat{1}$. In this analysis, Gagné interprets the supporting bass notes for $\hat{4}$ and $\hat{3}$ (F and G) as subordinate to the larger progression from III (B-flat) to V (D) within the interrupted descent and from III through IV to V within the complete descent:

> ... the F and G in question assume the function, ... of supports for the top-voice tones C and B-flat ($\hat{4}$ and $\hat{3}$). Thus these bass tones are significant on the highest level of structure, yet they are harmonically subservient to the large scale bass motions B-flat - D (III - V) and B-flat - C - D - G (III - IV - V - I).[22]

In this reading, therefore, $\hat{4}$ and $\hat{3}$ are reduced to the role of passing tones between $\hat{5}$ and $\hat{2}$. Even though the support for $\hat{3}$ is the tonic G, in both the interrupted as well as the complete descent this tonic is not beamed, nor is it given any structural significance in the bass progression. In the complete descent, this is very unusual, since the support for $\hat{3}$ (B-flat) is non-structural, but the support for its incomplete neighbor (C) assumes functional significance in the harmonic progression. In the bass, the C (IV) which supports the incomplete neighbor is of a higher structural priority than the G (i) which supports the structural $\hat{3}$. A dissonance is created between the soprano's B-flat ($\hat{3}$) and the bass's C (IV).

In my proposed *Ursatz* in Example 78, we find a structure that is closely related to the *romanesca* pattern. The differences consist in the initial tonic establishment for Example 78 as opposed to the mediant beginning for the *romanesca*, and the contrapuntal context

---

[21]Ibid., p. 90, Example 8c. (©1987 David Gagné. Used by Permission.) This is the background structure for the *quarta parte*, but it is the same for the *prima parte* (his Example 3c) and the *secunda parte* (his Example 5c). The background of the *terza parte* is slightly different.

[22]Ibid., p. 72.

Example 79: David Gagné, analysis of *romanesca* (© 1987 David Gagné. Used by permission.)

a)

b)

for the IV. In Example 78, I have interpreted the bass support for $\hat{4}$ and $\hat{3}$ in the context of the Dorian modality, assigning DOR-M and DOR-LN functions to the support for the $\hat{5}$ - $\hat{4}$ - $\hat{3}$ descent. Thus $\hat{4}$ and $\hat{3}$ are not supported as if mere passing tones between $\hat{5}$ and $\hat{2}$.

In Example 80, $\hat{5}$ is again supported by D moving to F in the bass, and $\hat{4}$ is again supported by C. But this time the C falls to A in the manner of a DOR-UN figure. The C in the bass descends to A while the upper voice descends from G to F. This counterpoint might create an expectation for a first-inversion F-major triad, but instead of that harmony, the A supports a dominant $^{6\text{-}5}_{4\text{-}3}$ resolution in D minor. C major does not, therefore, function as a dominant of F, but rather as a harmonized DOR-UN. F major is thus analyzed as a DOR-M because of its role in the preparation of the DOR-UN figure. In Example 81, scale degree $\hat{4}$ is again supported by C major, but this time C does resolve as a dominant to F in a closed I - V - I progression in that key.

Example 82 gives an *Ursatz* structure which is not based on a descent from $\hat{5}$. In the Dorian octave descent, the passage from $\hat{7}$ to $\hat{6}$ to $\hat{5}$ is harmonized by the progression V $^{6\text{-}5}_{4\text{-}3}$ - I of V. Following that, the tonic moves to the mediant as $\hat{5}$ is held, and the descent from $\hat{4}$ to $\hat{1}$ is harmonized by the progression ii$_6$ - V $^{6\text{-}5}_{4\text{-}3}$ - I.

Example 80: "Christ lag in Todesbanden," BWV 277 (B & H, Nr. 15)

Example 81: "Christ ist erstanden," BWV 276 (B & H, Nr. 197)

Example 82: "Erschienen ist der herrlich Tag," BWV 145/5 (B & H, Nr. 17)

Ursatz Possibilities in Aeolian

As with the Dorian mode, the fundamental structure of an Aeolian chorale is often a conventional tonal paradigm. In such cases, modal features begin to emerge more strongly at lower levels of structure. Example 83 gives an Aeolian *Urlinie* descent from $\hat{3}$, harmonized by the simple progression i - V - i. Example 84 gives two Aeolian *Urlinie* descents from $\hat{5}$ which are also accompanied by conventional bass progressions. Example 84a is the progression i - iv$_6$ - V$_{4-5}^{6-3}$ - i, and Example 84b is a double arpeggiation of the tonic triad i - V - i - V - i. The structures in Example 85 are unconventional in their presentation of the AOL-UN in the structural bass.

Example 83: "Was mein Gott will, das g'scheh allzeit," BWV 65/7 (B & H, Nr. 41)

$$\hat{3} \quad \hat{2} \quad \hat{1}$$

Example 84: a) "Allein zu dir, Herr Jesu Christ," BWV 261 (B & H, Nr. 359)
b) "Ich ruf zu dir, Herr Jesu Christ," BWV 177/5 (B & H, Nr. 71)

$$\text{a)} \quad \hat{5} \quad \hat{4} \quad \hat{3} \quad \hat{2} \quad \hat{1} \qquad \text{b)} \quad \hat{5} \quad \hat{4} \quad \hat{3} \quad \hat{2} \quad \hat{1}$$

6   6   5
     4   ♯

Example 85: a) "Von Gott will ich nicht lassen," BWV 73/5 (B & H, Nr. 191)
b) "Meine Seel erhebt den Herren," BWV 10/7 (B & H, Nr. 358)

$$\text{a)} \quad \hat{3} \quad \hat{2} \quad \hat{1} \qquad \text{b)} \quad \hat{5} \quad \hat{4} \quad \hat{3} \quad \hat{2} \quad \hat{1}$$

AOL-UN   AOL-UN

6   5
4   ♯

AOL-M   AOL-M

CHAPTER 5

Bach's Chorale Harmonizations of Dorian and Aeolian Cantus Firmi

Christ lag in Todesbanden

I will begin my analytical discussion of Bach's Dorian chorales with his setting of "Christ lag in Todesbanden," BWV 277 (B & H, Nr. 15), given in Example 86.[1] (The *Ursatz* of this chorale was provided earlier, in Example 80.) In order to underscore my own efforts to bring out the Dorian characteristics of this chorale, I would like to examine the linear reduction of another Schenkerian, David Neumeyer, given in Example 87.[2] This sketch, though clearly not intended as a detailed foreground analysis, provides a valuable foil to my own interpretation.

The cantus firmus begins on A^4, and tonicizes that degree through its chromatic lower neighbor G-sharp. Following this initial emphasis on A, the cantus steps up to D and then back to A for the cadence. This opening phrase of the melody appears to offer two choices for *Kopfton*—$\hat{5}$ (A^4) or $\hat{8}$ (D^5). And, as I shall demonstrate in the following discussion, this choice significantly influences the degree to which the Dorian identity of the chorale emerges in the analysis. Neumeyer treats the *Ursatz* of the chorale as an octave descent. He connects the *Kopfton*, D^5, at the end of m. 1 to the tonic harmony from the upbeat to that measure. However, the local harmonic support for the melodic D^5 is V $^6_5$ of V, a dissonant neighbor chord. The minor dominant is established on the third beat of m. 1 as support for C^6; it is then embellished in the progression i - V $^6_5$ - i as the bass moves A - G-sharp - A and the soprano C - D - C. Neumeyer's octave de-

---

[1]The musical text in Example 86 is based on *BG* 39, Nr. 25.

[2]David Neumeyer, "The *Urlinie* from $\hat{8}$ as a Middleground Phenomenon," *In Theory Only* 9/5-6 (1987), pp. 3-25. His analysis of "Christ lag in Todesbanden," BWV 277, is found on p. 20. (©1987 *In Theory Only*. Used by permission.)

Example 86: "Christ lag in Todesbanden," BWV 277 (B & H, Nr. 15) and sketch

Example 86, cont.

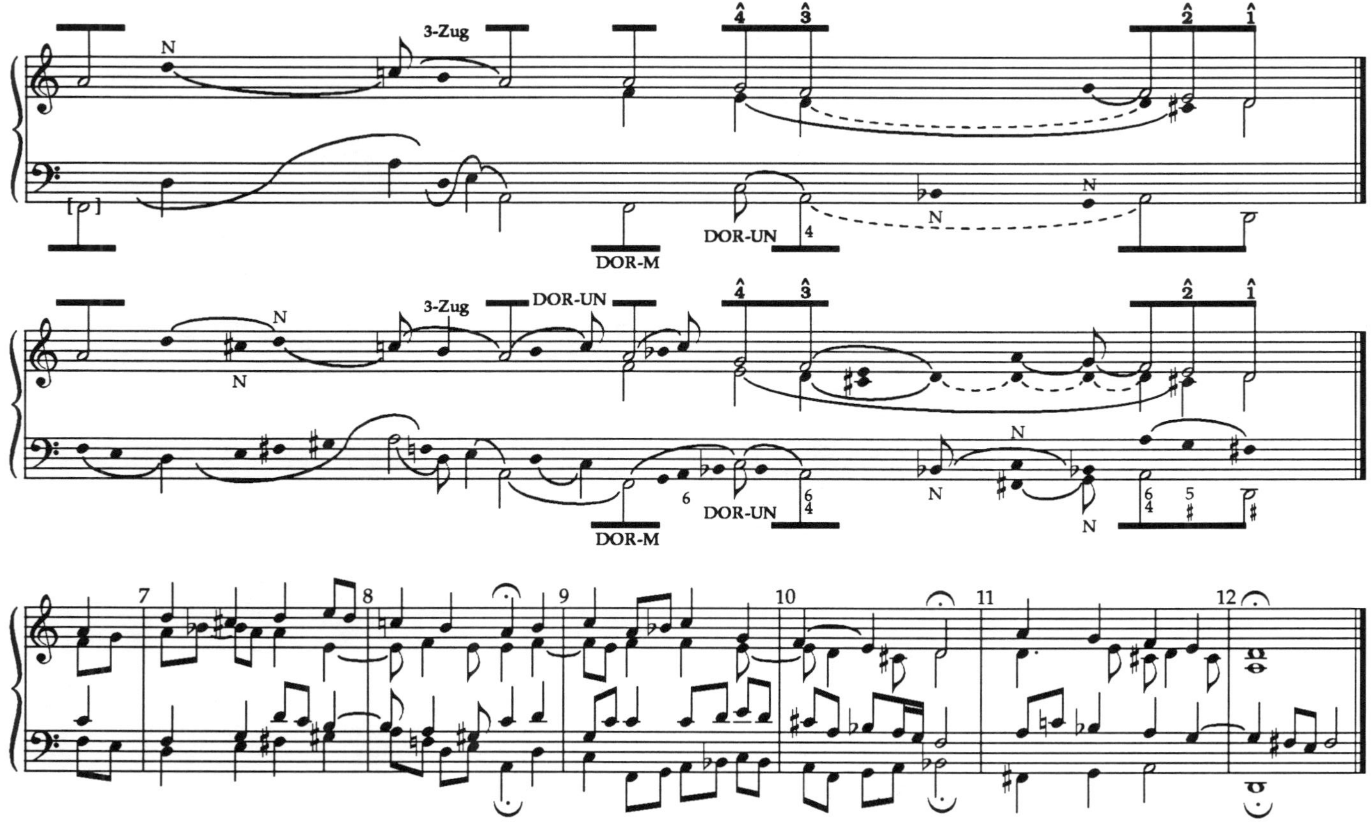

Example 87: David Neumeyer, analysis of "Christ lag in Todesbanden," BWV 277 (©1987 *In Theory Only*. Used by permission.)

scent accounts, abstractly, for the melodic C^5 in mm. 2 and 8: in both instances it is understood as descending from an initial D^5. In contrast, I analyze the chorale as a descent from $\hat{5}$, which is embellished by its upper third in a DOR-UN construct. This allows me to interpret C^5 without depending on an octave descent; that is, the DOR-UN embellishes the *Kopfton* A^4, and does not have to be understood as a passing tone from D.

Example 88 presents the contrapuntal outer-voice structure of mm. 1–2. Bach composes a bass which is motivically connected to the cantus firmus. The soprano begins with motive *a*, A - G-sharp - A, which is accompanied by motive *b*, the stepwise descent from D to A; then motive *b'* is heard in the soprano, accompanied by motive *a'* in the bass. The augmented fourth D - G-sharp between the bass and soprano on the downbeat of m. 1, which results from the combination of *a* and *b*, is answered by the diminished fifth G-sharp - D on the fourth beat during the combination of *a'* and *b'*. Motives *a'* and *b'* receive a shift in metric emphasis—where the D^3 of motive *b* is accented on the downbeat of m. 1, in its transference to the soprano as *b'*, D^5 arrives on an unaccented beat. This interpretation of the motivic contrapuntal structure supports my reading, in which the D^5 functions as a neighbor to the C^5, and is hard to reconcile with Neumeyer's reading in Example 87, in which the D^5 functions as the *Kopfton*. The idea that D^5 neighbors C^5 is also supported by the audible contour inversion of motive *a*, marked *"inv. a"* on the example. As noted there, motive *a* is the low point of the melody, while *inv. a* is the high point of the phrase. That gives rise to a sort of inversion-palindrome: the melodic segment A - G-sharp - A - B - C - D - C

Example 88: Motivic development in "Christ lag in Todesbanden," BWV 277

is its own retrograde-inversion, thereby tightly linking the *Kopfton* A^4 with its Dorian upper accessory tone C^5.

In Neumeyer's sketch, mm. 1-4 comprise an 8-*Zug*, supported by the double arpeggiation, i - V - i - V - i. $\hat{8}$ is reestablished in m. 7, with tonic support held over from m. 4; in m. 8 the tonic moves to the dominant as support for the descent $\hat{7}$ - $\hat{6}$ - $\hat{5}$. The D^5 in m. 7 is indeed harmonized by a D-minor triad, but in my foreground analysis in Example 86, this D-minor triad does not function as a tonic prolonged from m. 4. Rather, the tonic of m. 4 gives way to the mediant *Stufe*, F, which is confirmed at the cadence in m. 6. The harmony then moves to the minor dominant, A, for a cadence in m. 8, before returning to the mediant in m. 9. Thus, the D-minor triad in m. 7 is interpreted as the subdominant of A, and the A-minor harmony is itself heard within the larger prolongation of F. The melodic D^5 in m. 7 is a neighbor note to the C^5 which initiates a third-progression in A. At the middleground level, I analyze the C^5 as a DOR-UN to the *Kopfton* A. Thus, I cannot hear a *Kopfton* $\hat{8}$ prolonged through these measures; rather, I hear the D^5 in m. 7 in a setting that is comparable to the setting in m. 1: D is a neighbor to C, within a local prolongation of A minor.

Further, while the descent from $\hat{8}$ in Neumeyer's sketch theoretically accounts for the C^5s in m. 2 and m. 8, it does not explain the C^5 in m. 9. There, Neumeyer appears to allow the prolongation of A^4, the structural $\hat{5}$, by its upper third, but since his sketch does not provide us with a complete interpretation of his slurs, it is not clear how he accounts for the C, given that his overriding melodic progression here is a descending 5-*Zug* in D. Neumeyer remarks on the emphasis on $\hat{7}$ in the penultimate phrase, which, he feels, obfuscates the final descent.[3] In my analysis, the C^5s in m. 9 are foreground-level DOR-UNs to the *Kopfton* A.

According to Neumeyer's notation, the dominant controls the harmonic material throughout mm. 8–11, giving sole harmonic support at least at the *Ursatz* level for the descent from $\hat{7}$ to $\hat{2}$. In my analysis, the larger *Stufe* that is prolonged from m. 6 to m. 9 is the mediant, F major. As I have already stated, the dominant cadence in m. 8 is nested within the higher-level mediant prolongation. The structural dominant in my interpretation does not arrive until m. 10, and it is approached in a progression that is characteristically Dorian.

---

[3]Ibid., p. 18.

Indeed, the middleground sketch shows how the structural dominant A in the bass is approached by C, in a DOR-UN pattern.

This moment in the chorale—when $\hat{5}$ descends to $\hat{3}$ and the DOR-UN enters the structural bass—is worthy of our close attention. The structural bass D - F - C - A - D appears to juxtapose D minor and F major because of the fifth-relation F - C that is nested within the higher-level fifth-arpeggiation D - A - D. In my theoretical discussion of the DOR-M, I suggested that modern ears might hear this relationship between tonic and mediant as an unresolved "tension." I asserted, however, that such a bass progression should not be interpreted as an unresolved tonal conflict, but rather as a unified structure that derives organically from the natural Dorian scale. In such an interpretation, the C-natural does not need, therefore, to be "resolved," or reduced further in the sketch, but can be part of the fundamental structure. At the lower levels, this tonal "tension" is felt more strongly.

At the foreground level, the F-major triad of m. 9 moves through a first-inversion to its dominant, C major. This dominant does not resolve to an F-major tonic; rather, as the bass passes down from C through B-flat to A (suggesting V - V_2^4 - I_6 of F) and the soprano descends from G to F (suggesting $\hat{2}$ to $\hat{1}$ of F), the harmony changes from the dominant of F to the dominant of D. The harmony which is supported by A in the bass is $V\,^{6\text{-}5}_{4\text{-}3}$ in D. Although the bass appears to express an F-major construct—F - C - A—the A is given a double function, marking the completion of the F-major gesture and the beginning of the return to D.

At the surface of the music, the abrupt shift from F major to D minor in m. 10 is yet more pronounced. As the C in the bass (m. 9) descends through B-flat to A (m. 10), the tenor moves from E (m. 9) through D to C-sharp (m. 10); thus a cross relation occurs between the C in the bass, sounding as the dominant of F, to the C-sharp in the tenor, sounding as leading tone in D. This C-sharp is not even part of the harmony, since the first two beats of m. 10 are analyzed at the foreground level as a $V\,^{6\text{-}5}_{4\text{-}3}$ resolution, with D in the alto on beat 1 resolving to C-sharp on beat 2. The downbeat of m. 10 is further obscured by the suspension of E^4 in the actual alto, which delays D^4. This E was originally approached as leading tone in F, and now will resolve to D in the $V\,^{6\text{-}5}_{4\text{-}3}$ sonority.

Neumeyer avoids the problem of the support for the descent to $\hat{4}$ and $\hat{3}$ in mm. 9–10 by retaining $\hat{5}$ until m. 11, and analyzing the final phrase as the final descent from $\hat{5}$. Indeed, the cantus firmus does descend from A to D in the final phrase, but in my sketch, the descent to $\hat{3}$ has already occurred and this final melodic phrase only articulates the structural descent from that degree. The descent to $\hat{4}$, to my ear, takes place in m. 9, where the melodic phrase emphasizes G^4 through its approaching leap from C^5. I have difficulty hearing $\hat{5}$ (A) prolonged until the final phrase—the deceptive cadence on B-flat in m. 10 does not suggest a continuing prolongation of the melodic A; also, the F-sharp in the bass in m. 11 suggests that this is no longer the structural $\hat{5}$ with tonic support.

Another setting of this chorale by Bach—the final chorale to his well-known cantata based on the cantus firmus "Christ lag in Todesbanden," BWV 4 (B & H, Nr. 184)—provides a different Dorian solution to the structural descent from $\hat{5}$ to $\hat{3}$. MM. 6–12 are provided in Example 89.[4] In this setting the structural bass support for the descent from $\hat{5}$ to $\hat{3}$ is D - F - C - D, a progression which again might suggest a tonal "tension" between D and F, but which is offered here as a unified Dorian structure. The C as support for the melodic $\hat{4}$ is analyzed as a DOR-LN to the Dorian final, D.

As was the case in BWV 277, the surrounding context for the descent from $\hat{4}$ to $\hat{3}$ juxtaposes F-major and D-minor harmony. In m. 9, when F major moves to C major, the B-flats in the bass and tenor suggest the key of F major and a dominant seventh function for the harmony on C. The alto voice takes the leading tone, E. However, as the tenor resolves from B-flat to A, the alto does not resolve, as a leading tone, from E to F; rather E is held against the D-minor chord of m. 10 as a suspension which resolves downward to D. This downward resolution, along with the "deceptive" resolution in the bass from C to D, denies the dominant function of the C-major harmony and instead confirms its function as a DOR-LN to D. The harmony of D is then strongly defined in the harmonic progressions over mm. 10–12.

Bach's organ chorale based on "Christ lag in Todesbanden," BWV 625 provides yet another interesting harmonization of the penultimate phrase. MM. 8–10 of the composition are provided in Example 90.[5] Once again, during the support for the descent from G^4 to F^4 over the barline of m. 9, Bach creates a harmonic tension between

---

[4]The musical text in Example 89 is based on *NBA* I/9, p. 40. (©1985 Bärenreiter. Used by permission.) The example here is transposed to D (from E) for the sake of comparing the different settings. (Incidentally, the Breitkopf & Härtel edition of this melody is transposed to D.) The passing tone marked at the asterisk (*) is a semitone lower in the B & H edition than in the *NBA*; in its transposition level of D-Dorian, this would be a B-flat.

[5]The musical text in Example 90 is based on *BG* 25/2, p. 38.

Example 89: "Christ lag in Todesbanden," BWV 4/8 (B & H, Nr. 184), mm. 6–12 and sketch [original tonic: E]

Example 90: "Christ lag in Todesbanden," BWV 625, mm.8–10.

F major and D minor. The soprano's leap from C to G is harmonized as I to V in F major. The B-flats during the second and fourth beats of m. 9 point to the key of F major, with C functioning as the dominant. However, as G resolves to F in the cantus firmus, the harmony changes from V of F to a cadential $^6_4$ in D. Thus, the C harmony does not resolve as a dominant of F, but rather as a DOR-UN to A, the dominant of D.

The downbeat of m. 10 is not absolutely clear as a cadential $^6_4$. The alto suspends E from the preceding C-major triad, resolving it down to D on the second eighth of the measure. The tenor voice suspends C on the first eighth, but does not resolve it directly. One might hear the alto's D on the second eighth as a resolution of the tenor's C, since it is in the same register, but the resolution is certainly not explicit. Thus, the inner voices contribute to a harmonic ambiguity on the downbeat of m. 10: is it F major in first inversion, as a resolution of the previous chord, or the cadential $^6_4$ in D minor? As the line continues, there is a clear movement to V and then i of D, but at the downbeat of m. 10, Bach allows the ambiguity.

Was mein Gott will das g'scheh allzeit

Another modal chorale which has been analyzed in the Schenkerian literature is "Was mein Gott will das g'scheh allzeit," BWV 65/7 (B & H, Nr. 41), reproduced in Example 91.[6] A sketch by Allen Forte and Stephen Gilbert from the *Instructor's Manual* for the *Introduction to Schenkerian Analysis*, appears as Example 92.[7] Again, this sketch provides a valuable foil for my own analysis. In particular, it is interesting to consider how Forte and Gilbert interpret the natural seventh degree, G, within the context of the A-minor tonic. The opening phrase of the cantus firmus is certainly problematic as an example of conventional A minor. Forte and Gilbert remark on the opening gesture:

> The likelihood that the chorale will first be perceived in C major is already covered in the text instructions; however, it may bear further discussion. The A minor-C major ambiguity is a factor in the opening first-order arpeggiation, which fits the definition in that it leads to the primary tone, although it arpeggiates III rather than I. The setting as a whole is in A minor, with fundamental line $\hat{3}$ - $\hat{2}$ - $\hat{1}$.[8]

The initial arpeggiation of the mediant, mentioned by the authors, is clear in their sketch, from the initial E^4 of the cantus, through G^4 and on to C^5, the *Kopfton*. The bass, meanwhile, moves from A to C, as indicated by the Roman Numeral analysis of I to III. The *Kopfton* is connected by a diagonal line to the initial A in the bass, even though the opening arpeggiation to the C^5 is dissonant against the bass A—the G^4 of the arpeggiation clashes with the initial establishment of the tonic A. This contradiction is never addressed in the discussion, nor is the G logically interpreted in the sketch.

[6]The musical text in Example 91 is based on *NBA* I/5, p. 46. (©1975 Bärenreiter. Used by permission.)

[7]Allen Forte, Stephen E. Gilbert, *Instructor's Manual* for the *Introduction to Schenkerian Analysis* (New York: W. W. Norton and Company, 1982), p. 81. (©1982 W. W. Norton & Co. Used by permission.)

[8]Ibid., p. 80. The chorale is assigned as an exercise in the main text in Chapter 13, "The Harmonized Chorale," where the assignment is qualified with the following remarks: "Although the initial phrase moves immediately toward C major, the home key of this setting is A minor. Your graph should show a fundamental line of $\hat{3}$ - $\hat{2}$ - $\hat{1}$ in that key" (p. 185).

Another noteworthy detail in Forte and Gilbert's sketch is the interpretation of the tonicized G in mm. 6–8. The second line of the sketch gives a large-scale progression of I - VII - III - I, which is further reduced to a prolongation of I. The sketch does not adequately indicate how the harmonies of VII (G) and III (C) relate to and prolong the A-minor tonic. A, G and C are stemmed in the analysis, but it is unclear how G and C function within the larger A-*Stufe*.

In sum, an "A-minor - C-major ambiguity" is identified by the authors, but is not adequately reconciled by their sketch. There are certain progressions, resulting from the Aeolian organization of the cantus firmus, which cannot be explained by conventional Schenkerian analytic methodology. My analysis departs from such conventions in order to ascribe an Aeolian identity to the melodic and harmonic relations of the chorale.[9]

The natural seventh degree is stressed in the cantus firmus, accented at the beginning of Phrase 1 (m. 1) and Phrase 5 (m. 10), and prolonged as a cadential pitch in Phrase 3 (m. 8). Bach develops the inherent emphasis on G in the cantus into a thematic Aeolian lower neighbor (AOL-LN) figure, a melodic motive that emerges clearly in my sketch. It is most apparent in the large-scale prolongation of G major in mm. 6–8. In this passage, G is interpreted at the middleground level as an AOL-LN in the bass: against the rising 3-*Zug* A - B - C in the soprano, the bass articulates the pattern A - G - A.

The AOL-LN resolution is also a prominent feature of the voice-leading over mm. 1–3. The cantus firmus introduces G-natural in m. 1, approached from the E below, and then prolongs it in the neighbor gesture G - A - G. The cantus then leaps up to C, leaving the G—the seventh degree of the scale—unresolved. However, the alto voice picks up the G^4 on the fourth beat of m. 1, sustains it through the C-major cadence in m.

---

[9]I have already discussed the cantus firmus of this chorale and the problems of its modal identity in footnote 5 in Chapter 4. Despite the instances of F-sharp in mm. 7 and 10 of the soprano I consider the chorale to be an example of the Aeolian mode. This decision can be supported by the clear diatonic treatment of the Aeolian final (except for the leading tone G-sharp) in the first two phrases of the chorale where the tonic is defined, and in the last phrase of the chorale where the final cadence occurs. The prominence of the chromatic pitch F-sharp in mm. 6–10 is heard in striking contrast to the diatonic opening and closing passages. In mm. 6–8, F-sharp functions as leading tone to the secondary degree G. In mm. 9–10, sharp $\hat{6}$ (F-sharp) appears in the inner voices in approach to sharp $\hat{7}$ (G-sharp—alto, m. 9, tenor, mm. 9–10) in order to avoid the augmented second from F to G-sharp. In m. 10 the passing tone F-sharp in the cantus is heard within the context of an E-minor prolongation.

2, and then resolves it to A in m. 3 through an embellishing gesture, G - F - G - A. The bass voice echoes this resolution and decorates it further: from the G on the downbeat of m. 3, the bass falls to D, which then rises through the diatonic scale to A (D - E - F - G - A).[10]

The harmonic setting for the AOL-LN in mm. 1-3 is worthy of further consideration. As Forte and Gilbert suggest, the *Kopfton* is established in a context that appears to conflate C major and A minor. After a brief tonic on the anacrusis to m. 1, A minor does not return again until m. 3. The chord that supports the initial $\hat{3}$ (C^5) in the melody is a first-inversion C triad, and C major is then prolonged at the cadence in m. 2. At the beginning of the second phrase, the tonicized C moves to its dominant G. However, G is soon defined not as the dominant of C but as the AOL-LN to A. It is not until the resolution of the AOL-LN in m. 3 that A is clearly stated as support for the *Kopfton*. Further, when the tonic does support the *Kopfton* in m. 3, it is a tonic that has been established through Aeolian harmonic and melodic patterns. The middleground bass over mm. 1–3 especially reflects the Aeolian mode through the integration of the natural seventh degree, G, into the larger prolongation of A: after the initial A^2, the bass moves to E as the fifth of A; E is then heard as part of a C-major arpeggiation E - G - C; G then returns and resolves to A as an AOL-LN. Once the *Kopfton* does receive tonic support in m. 3, the phrase continues in m. 4 with dominant-tonic progressions in A that introduce the ficta G-sharp.

The first two phrases of the cantus firmus are reprised as the final two phrases in mm. 9–12, thus providing an additional setting for the distinctive opening E - G-natural - C melodic arpeggiation. In its harmonization in mm. 1–11, the minor dominant is prolonged as the harmonic support for the melodic incipit E - G - A - G. When the cantus leaps up to C, it is harmonized by A minor, but based on the ensu-

---

[10]It may seem forced to interpret the indirect connection from G major on the first beat to A minor on the fourth beat as an AOL-LN resolution. However, Bach has introduced such embellishing resolutions earlier in the chorale. The first occurs in the tenor when the harmony changes from E minor to C major: the E in the bass and G in the soprano are prolonged through melodic upper neighbor figures (E - F - E and G - A - G); the tenor voice moves from B to C^4 through the embellishing pattern B - A - B - C. In this interpretation, the gesture A - B - C is analyzed as a melodic decoration of the resolution from B to C. The bass voice also projects an embellishing resolution in its neighbor pattern E - F - E: the upper neighbor F does not resolve immediately to E, but rather does so through the melodic decoration C - D - E. These embellished resolutions prepare the resolution of the AOL-LN in m. 3; that is, the patterns G - F - G - A in the alto and G - D - E - F - G - A in the bass are heard in the context of the earlier decorated neighbor resolutions.

Example 91: Was mein Gott will, das g'scheh allzeit," BWV 65/7 (B & H, Nr. 41)

Example 91, cont.

Example 91, cont.

Example 92: Forte/Gilbert, analysis of "Was mein Gott will, das g'scheh allzeit," BWV 65/7 (© 1982 W.W. Norton & Co. Used by permission.)

ing cadential progression, the A-minor triad functions as submediant in C. In m. 12, the C triad returns immediately to A minor to begin the final phrase. The foreground sketch analyzes the G^4 in mm. 10–11 as an AOL-LN which resolves in m. 12 when C major moves directly to A minor. The middleground bass over mm. 10–12 is similar to the middleground bass for mm. 1–3. In both passages the bass moves from A to E; E is then heard within an arpeggiation of the C-major triad, E - G - C. From there, the return to A minor is slightly different: in m. 3 the resolution from C to A occurs through an AOL-LN in the bass and in m. 12, C major moves directly to the A-minor tonic, while the AOL-LN resolution is heard in an inner voice.

"Allein zu dir, Herr Jesu Christ" is an Aeolian cantus firmus that is similar in design to "Was mein Gott will." That is, in both melodies, the interval from G to C is prominent in the first phrase, followed by a stepwise descent from D to A in the second phrase. The first two phrases of Bach's "Allein zu dir," BWV 33/6 (B & H, Nr. 13) and BWV 261 (B & H, Nr. 359) are reproduced in Examples 93a and b.[11] In these chorales, as in "Was mein Gott will," the conflict between C and A is a recurring harmonic issue that results from the emphasis on G in the cantus firmus. In BWV 33/6 the first phrase begins on A, but then moves immediately to C and prolongs C for the remainder of the phrase. The melodic interval from G to C is composed-out as a dominant-tonic relationship. In the second phrase of BWV 33/6, G is redefined as an AOL-LN to A in the bass (m. 4) and in the cantus firmus (mm. 4–5). A is then confirmed as tonic at the cadence in m. 5.

In BWV 261 the conflict between C and A is expressed in a more complex harmonic relationship. The chorale begins on C major, with the soprano's leap from C to G harmonized as I - I_6 in C. Although this opening suggests a tonic of C major, there is a brief tonicization of A minor through the ficta F-sharp and G-sharp in the bass and alto. The A-minor triad in m. 2 is defined, however, as a submediant in C, when the phrase moves toward a cadence in that key. The second phrase begins with a progression from C to G, which suggests that the phrase (and, perhaps, the entire chorale) will continue in C, but G then resolves as an AOL-LN to A and the phrase confirms A in a tonic cadence.

---

[11]The musical text in Example 93a is based on *NBA* I/21, p. 56. (©1958 Bärenreiter. Used by permission.) The musical text of Example 93b is based on *BG* 39, Nr. 9.

Example 93:

a) "Allein zu dir, Herr Jesu Christ," BWV 33/6 (B & H, Nr. 13)

b) "Allein zu dir, Herr Jesu Christ," BWV 261 (B & H, Nr. 359) [Original tonic:B]

In "Allein zu dir" as well as "Was mein Gott will," the harmonic emphasis on the mediant is logically developed from the melodic emphasis on the interval G - C. In each of these chorales, the harmonic tension—or, as Forte and Gilbert identify it, the harmonic "ambiguity"—derives from the dual function of G, which can be heard as the fifth of C, or as the natural seventh degree of the Aeolian scale. A striking aspect of Bach's Aeolian compositional process is the working-out of that "tension" to resolve ultimately in favor of the Aeolian final. Indeed, my background sketch of "Was mein Gott will" is intended to reveal the AOL-LN and the AOL-M as organic features of the composition.

Bach exploits the mediant emphasis in an Aeolian melody to an extreme point in an internal movement of his cantata 92, a cantata that is based on the melody "Was mein Gott will, das g'scheh allzeit." The seventh movement is a chorale and recitative in which the cantus firmus, transposed to B Aeolian, is placed in a harmonic context that assigns the mediant, D major, a tonic role. The final two chorale phrases and the closing recitative section of the movement are reproduced in Example 94.[12] The harmonization of the penultimate chorale phrase predicts the ultimate emphasis on D major. That is, the melodic incipit F-sharp - A - B - A is harmonized by B - D_6 - vii$^{o4}_3$/D - D. Thus, the natural seventh degree of the B-Aeolian scale, A, is not heard within a local context of B, but rather D. When the cantus leaps up to D in m. 27, the B-minor triad returns, but the ensuing harmony clearly defines B as a submediant of D: from B minor at the end of m. 27, the harmony moves through a strong D-major cadential progression (V$^6_5$/V - V - I).

The final phrase of the chorale is harmonized to close in B, as dictated by the melody itself which descends $\hat{3}$ - $\hat{2}$ - $\hat{1}$ in B at the cadence in m. 31. Immediately following the B-minor cadence, however, the recitative returns to D major, in a harmonic progression which recalls the bass line from mm. 27–28 (B - G-sharp - A) and which, in its continuation, clearly defines B as a submediant of D major: in mm. 32–33, A is tonicized as dominant, in mm. 34–35, E minor is tonicized as the supertonic, which returns to the dominant on the third beat of m. 35; this dominant is then prolonged by means of a deceptive resolution, before the final V - I cadence in D. The bass line during the third and fourth beats of m. 35 is particularly interesting given the D major/B minor conflict throughout the movement—as the first-inversion D-major triad moves to the first-inver-

[12]The musical text in Example 94 is based on *NBA* I/7, pp. 74–75. (©1955 Bärenreiter. Used by permission.)

Example 94: BWV 92/7, mm. 26–36

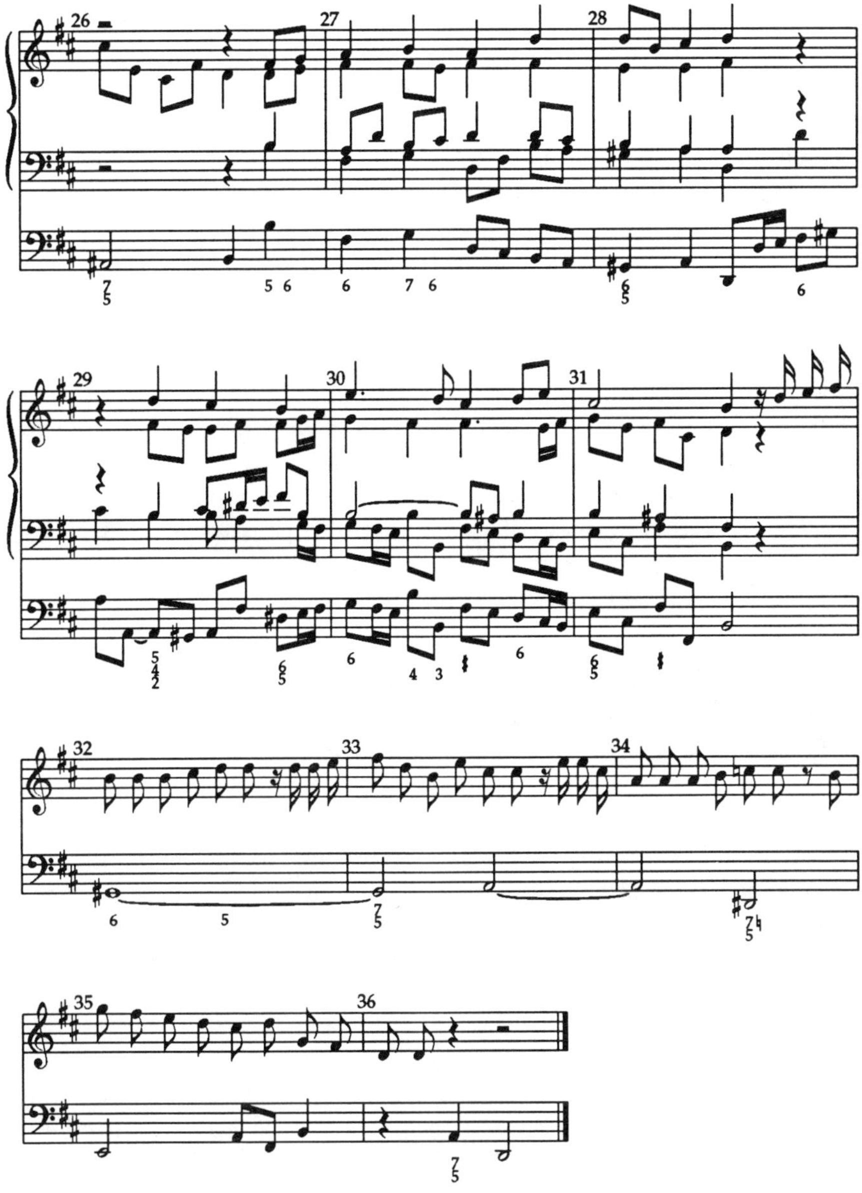

sion G-major triad, the bass gesture is F-sharp - B, alluding to dominant-tonic functions in B minor. However, this bass is harmonized to sound in D, rather than B, and the final cadence of the movement clarifies D as tonic in a strong V - I progression. With this closing recitative passage, Bach works *against* the cantus firmus's tonic of B and provides instead a larger context of D major. He thus develops the existing "tension" between tonic and mediant inherent within the cantus firmus to the extent that the mediant can be heard as a higher-level tonic in this movement.

Erschienen ist der herrlich Tag

Bach's setting of the cantus firmus "Erschienen ist der herrlich Tag," BWV 145/5 (B & H, Nr. 17), reproduced in Example 95, has a strong Dorian identity.[13] (The *Ursatz* of this chorale was provided earlier, in Example 82.) As Knecht suggests with his comparative examples of Dorian and D-minor writing, the Dorian mode is distinguished by the harmonic diversity of its modulations.[14] This chorale is a good example of such harmonic diversity, and it is a good practical illustration of how such non uniformity can actually contribute to a unified Dorian structure.

To begin, the tonic is established by means of a progression that is unique to Dorian, a harmonic relation that I defined earlier as the Dorian subdominant (DOR-IV), i - IV - i in D. This plagal relation is an unusual way to establish the D-minor tonic. Indeed, from the middle of m. 2 through m. 5 there is no audible indication that the chorale might not be in G major. The opening D-minor triad of m. 1 is altered to become D major in m. 2 when the bass moves to F-sharp. It resolves as a leading tone in a V₆ - I progression in G major and then G is prolonged in a cadential I - IV - V - I progression. The second phrase begins by repeating the V₆ - I progression, but continues on to establish D minor when its leading tone, C-sharp, is introduced and resolved in the soprano; the F-

---

[13]The musical text in Example 95 is based on *NBA* I/10, p. 128. The example is based on a transposition of the chorale from F-sharp to D. The alto note in m. 1 (B-natural) is marked with an asterisk (*) because in the *NBA* the accidental is indicated as an editorial accidental above the note.

[14]In Chapter 1, I reproduced an example by Knecht as Example 9, which illustrated the difference between Dorian and D-minor harmonic languages. He suggests that a chorale harmonization which simply moves from tonic to mediant to dominant would be "much too feeble for Church writing," and favors a Dorian harmonic organization that introduces other secondary degrees.

natural in the alto voice in m. 6 at once counters our expectation of F-sharp and recalls the F-natural of the opening D-minor triad.

In the middleground sketch, I have analyzed the D-minor triad in m. 6 as the structural tonic which supports the *Kopfton* D^5. The opening phrase is analyzed as a DOR-IV progression, i - IV - i, beneath a descending third-progression A - G - F in the alto voice of the sketch. The G of that 3-*Zug* is itself prolonged in a descending third-progression B - A - G when G major is tonicized in a I - V - I progression. Throughout this passage, the use of ficta is noteworthy—a false relation occurs between the F-natural of the prolonged D-minor triad and the B-natural of the G-major subdominant. In m. 1 of the foreground sketch the false relation F - B occurs in the outer voices: the B in the upper voice returns as a neighbor note to A; the G in the bass returns as a neighbor note to the third of the triad on D; the third, however, has been transformed into F-sharp, thus "correcting" the false relation. In mm. 3–6 of the middleground sketch, the alto's line A - B - A - G - F—which is analyzed as nested third-progressions (B - A - G within the larger A - G - F)—emphasizes the melodic augmented fourth B - F.

Once D minor is established in m. 6, the harmony quickly modulates again, this time to A minor. The melodic descent C - B - A in the soprano in mm. 7–8 is analyzed as the structural descent from $\hat{7}$ to $\hat{5}$, harmonized by V $^{6-5}_{4-3}$ - I in A minor.

Until this point, the D-minor tonic has appeared only briefly. D minor began the chorale in m. 1, but the harmony moved immediately on to tonicize G major. When it returned in m. 6, its identity as a tonic was a little stronger, as it was approached by the vii°$_6$ harmony at the end of m. 5, but once again it was abandoned in favor of another tonal area, this time A minor. Now D minor returns immediately following the cadence on A (with ficta C-sharp) in m. 8, creating a V - i progression in D. This is the first clear dominant-tonic resolution in D, but it is weakened by the metric placement of the resolving tonic on the third beat, as merely an anacrusis to the next measure which once again moves away from D minor, this time towards the mediant, F. In sum, the harmonic emphasis of the chorale is constantly shifting, to the extent that it might be difficult to determine an unequivocal tonic. Of course, this perception is only based on the experience of listening to the chorale for the first time. At the end of the chorale, when the harmony is resolved in favor of D, the preceding harmonic diversity is understood in the context of the Dorian tonic.

Example 95: "Erschienen ist der herrlich Tag," BWV 145/5 (B & H, Nr. 17) and sketch

Example 95, cont.

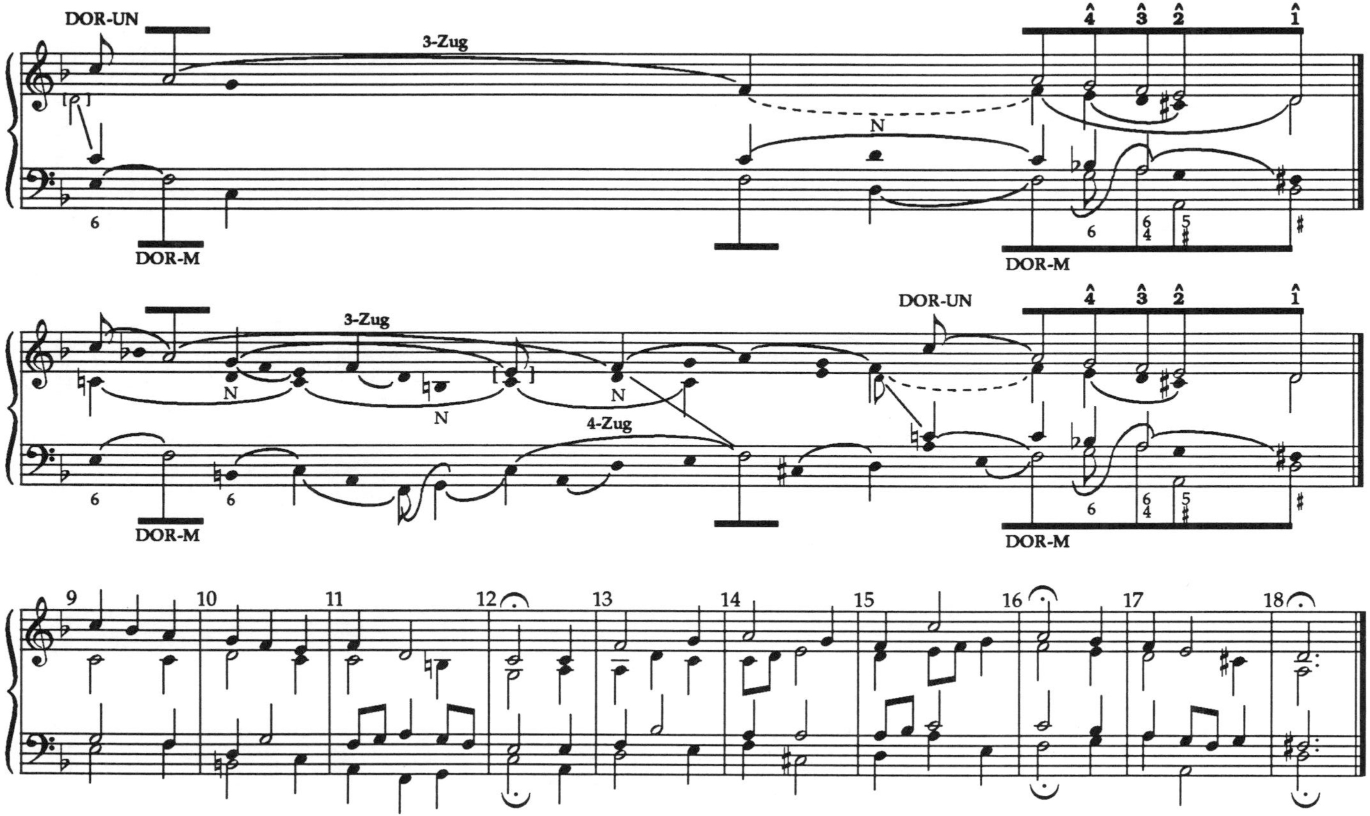

As soon as $\hat{5}$ is established in m. 8, at first with dominant and then with tonic support, the harmony begins to explore the Dorian mediant relationship. The harmonic focus on the mediant is prescribed by the cantus firmus itself, which emphasizes A, C, and F during mm. 9–16: from the A^4 in m. 8 the soprano skips up to C^5, then descends stepwise to cadence on C^4 in m. 12; in the next phrase the soprano works its way back up to C^5 in an outline of F major; at the cadence in m. 16, C^5 skips down to A^4. The foreground sketch analyzes this passage as a prolongation of A^4 ($\hat{5}$), which is supported by the mediant and which is embellished by its upper third, C^5, and lower third, F^4.

During the prolongation of the F-*Stufe* there are references to the D-minor tonic. In the middleground analysis of mm. 9–13, the structural $\hat{5}$ (A) descends to F in a 3-*Zug*, as the harmony prolongs F major in a I - V - I progression. At the foreground level, the third-progression (A^4 - G^4 - F^4) is complicated by a prolongation of the C-major harmony which supports the G^4. Within the higher level 3-*Zug* A - G - F, G^4 is itself prolonged in a 3-*Zug* (G - F - E), as the harmony cadences on C major in m. 12. The resolution of G^4 (m. 10) to F^4 (m. 13) in the middleground-level 3-*Zug*, does not coincide with the resolution of C major as a dominant to F major. The latter resolution is accomplished over the course of mm. 12–14. In the foreground sketch, C in the bass ascends to F, in a 4-*Zug*, (C - D - E - F). The D of the fourth-progression is prefaced by its fifth, A, which emphasizes D. This D in m. 13 is also the actual support for the melodic F^4 of the middleground third-progression; although in the music the soprano's F^4 coincides with the D-minor triad, a diagonal line connects that melodic F with the F^3 in the bass of m. 14.

In mm. 14–15, there is yet a stronger reference to D minor within the F-*Stufe*. At the foreground level, the F-major harmony of m. 14 is followed by a V_6 - i progression in D. The soprano continues here to prolong F^4. D minor moves away to A minor in m. 15, as support for C^5 in the soprano. This C^5 functions as a DOR-UN to $\hat{5}$, thus reestablishing the A^4 in the structural line. The DOR-UN pattern resolves as the harmony moves V_6 - I in F. Thus, the harmonic movement over mm. 14–16 is V_6 - i in D followed by V_6 - I in F. The conflation of D minor and F major over mm. 9–16 is naturally derived from the cantus firmus itself, which emphasizes C, A and F within the context of the melody's higher-level D-minor tonic.

Bach gives this cantus firmus a canonic treatment in his organ chorale prelude BWV 629. The melody thus informs and integrates the structure of the soprano and bass voices. In this setting, the DOR-UN figure emerges as a prominent motive in the soprano and the structural bass voices. Example 96 reproduces the canonic outer voices of the organ prelude and provides a middleground analysis of the voice leading.[15]

In BWV 629, Bach retains the diatonic Dorian scale, avoiding C-sharp in the soprano in m. 5 and the bass in m. 6. In BWV 145/5, the melodic C-sharp helped to secure D^5 as the *Kopfton*, but here the *Urlinie* is best understood as a descent from $\hat{5}$ as there is no adequately supported D^5. The D^5 in m. 6 is harmonized by vii°_6 of A minor, in a local tonicization of A.

In my discussion of BWV 145/5, I identified an interesting conflation of D minor and F major in the latter half of the chorale. The canonic treatment of the organ setting concentrates this relationship, particularly in the final two phrases of the cantus firmus. The penultimate phrase of the melody outlines F major, while the ultimate phrase resolves to the tonic D in stepwise descent. When these two melodic phrases are presented in canon, the resulting contrapuntal structure focuses the mediant-tonic harmonic conflict. That is, the F-major emphasis in the penultimate phrase of the cantus firmus is heard first in the upper voice; then, when that voice moves on to resolve the melody in favor of D, the bass voice presents the F-major material of the penultimate phrase. The penultimate phrase in the soprano in m. 12 begins with a leap from C^4 to F^4; F^4 steps up through an ascending third-progression to A^4 and then returns through a descending third-progression, A^4 - G - F; the final melodic gesture of that phrase is a melodic skip from C^5 to A^4. Because the supporting bass is a full measure behind, the falling third C - A in the soprano in mm. 15–16 is supported by the descending third-progression A - G - F in the bass, thus creating a harmonic cadence on F. Then, while the soprano continues on to the final phrase with its clear D-minor descent from A to D, the bass remains preoccupied with the penultimate phrase cadence, the outline of the F-major triad, F - C - A. As a result of this canon, the structural soprano descent A - G - F ($\hat{5}$ - $\hat{4}$ - $\hat{3}$) is supported by the arpeggiation F - C - A in the bass. This contrapuntal structure suggests an F-major cadence; however, the A in the bass and F in the soprano (m. 17) are not harmonized by F major, but rather by a cadential $^6_4$ in D, which then resolves in D. In my middleground analysis, I have indicated how this counterpoint is interpreted in the

---

[15]The musical text in Example 96 is based on *BG* 25/2, p. 45.

Example 96: "Erschienen ist der herrlich Tag," BWV 629, outer voices and sketch context of the Dorian mode. The falling C^5 - A^4 gesture in the soprano is analyzed as a DOR-UN to the *Kopfton* A^4, supported by the DOR-M. The falling C^3 - A^2 gesture in the bass is similarly analyzed as a DOR-UN to the structural dominant in the *Baßbrechung*. At this level, the DOR-M and DOR-UN are integrated into a unified Dorian contrapuntal structure.

Von Gott will ich nicht lassen

In the foregoing analyses, I have investigated in great detail the harmonic relationship between tonic and mediant in the Dorian and Aeolian modes. I would like now to focus on the role of the dominant in these modes, in particular its treatment as a minor harmony and the melodic treatment of its minor third as the natural seventh degree of the mode.

The Aeolian cantus firmus "Von Gott will ich nicht lassen" strongly implies a harmonic emphasis on the dominant. Bach's setting BWV 73/5 (B & H, Nr. 191) is given in Example 97.[16] (The *Ursatz* of this chorale was provided earlier in Example 85a.) In mm. 1–2, the soprano outlines the G-major triad with a descending arpeggiation D - B - G; the second phrase outlines E minor in the melodic gesture G - A - B - E; G major is invoked again when the melody composes out the D - B - G arpeggiation, beginning in m. 8 with the falling third D - B, and then moving stepwise toward the next cadence which descends B - A - G. Bach harmonizes the melodic cadences on G in phrases 1 and 5 as the third of E-minor, the minor dominant, and the cadence on B in phrase 4 as the third of G major, the subtonic harmony. The prolongations of E minor and G major in this chorale contribute to its distinctly Aeolian identity. These harmonies support AOL-LN and AOL-UN constructs, and participate in patterns that are idiomatic to the Aeolian mode.

The chorale begins with a prolongation of the Aeolian final in a i - V_6 - i progression with ficta G-sharp, a gesture which does not necessarily foreshadow the diatonic Aeolian treatment to come in this first phrase. In m. 2, the leading tone G-sharp disappears and is replaced by the natural seventh G, at first as the root of G major, which is tonicized at the beginning of m. 2 and then as the third of E minor, which is tonicized at the cadence. In the next phrase, the ficta G-sharp returns, for the perfect cadence in mm. 3–4.

---

[16] The musical text in Example 97 is based on *BG* 18, p. 104.

In order to sketch this chorale, one must determine the linear function of the cadential G-naturals in mm. 2 and 10 of the melody. Based on Schenker's analyses of similar passages, given earlier in Example 68, he would likely interpret G as a passing tone from A on its way down through F-natural to E; G-sharp would then appear above the dominant E and would then resolve up to A. However, the foreground details of this chorale do not support such an interpretation. Rather, the G-naturals in the cantus firmus function as AOL-LNs, harmonized by the dominant, which resolve to A through the chromatic passing tone G-sharp. And the G-naturals that occur in the bass in mm. 2 and 8 function as AOL-UNs to the dominant E.

At the middleground level in m. 2, the falling third in the bass G - E supports a descending third in the soprano B - G. The soprano's B is part of a descending third-progression from the *Kopfton*, C - B - A, the C and B of which are prolonged by means of unfolded thirds A - C, then B - G. The higher-level harmonic support for the melodic B - G third is the dominant, which is elaborated by an AOL-UN figure. The middleground sketch then shows the G-natural of the cantus firmus, supported by the dominant, resolving to A at the cadence through a passing tone G-sharp. In the music, however, there is no direct connection from G to G-sharp. There is a clear resolution from G-sharp to A, but this occurs in the bass, not in the alto as the sketch indicates. The sketch also shows that the overriding soprano line over mm. 1–4 is a melodic third-progression C - B - A. In the music, however, the soprano leaps down from B to E at the cadence. The resolution from B to A is thus implied and not stated directly. This analysis of the soprano voice is not likely to seem contentious, as such interpretations are common to Schenkerian analysis. However, my interpretation of how the dominant harmony and the cantus's G-natural are prolonged is sure to raise some questions, so let us consider this passage in greater detail.

In the foreground sketch, the melodic skip B - G in m. 2 is followed by a stepwise return to B. As the soprano steps up from G to A, the bass rises from E to F. This F is analyzed as a complete upper neighbor to E, even though its return to E is not explicit in the music. That is, the bass does not articulate the resolution from F to E, but rather falls from F to D, then leaps down to G-sharp. It is possible to analyze the bass G-sharp as a sub-posed inner voice, beneath the expected E in the tenor voice. However, the connection F - E is still not clear since the tenor's E is approached from F-sharp. The voice-leading function of the F-sharp and its supporting D in the bass is indeed curious, since a fundamental bass progression D - E would create parallel fifths against the soprano's A - B. Perhaps my sketch does not adequately deal with the D-major triad, but nevertheless I hear the F - E neighbor resolution. When the dominant does return at the end of m. 3, it is a major harmony, with ficta G-sharp. The sketch analyzes G-sharp as an inner-voice passing tone between G and A. By analyzing the G-sharp as a passing tone, or subsidiary tone to G, I am asserting the higher-level function of the G as the third of the prolonged dominant, thereby allowing the Aeolian character of the composition to emerge.

This passage causes certain analytic difficulties, but the final measures of the chorale are an elaboration of the same melodic and harmonic content and thus help us to sort out the voice leading and the structural functions of G and E. That is, the cantus firmus in mm. 7–12 and Bach's setting of it are closely related to mm. 1–4: the melodic skip from D to B with G-major support at the barline of m. 2 recurs at the cadence of m. 8; and the skip from B to G with E-minor support at the cadence of m. 2 is composed-out as a melodic third-progression B - A - G over the course of mm. 9–10. The middleground sketch brings out the similarities between these two passages. The bass G in m. 8 is analyzed as an AOL-UN to the E in m. 10, but this time the G - E gesture is composed-out as a third-progression G - F - E to support the melodic third-progression B - A - G. The dominant is thus established in m. 10 as support for an AOL-LN, which is prolonged by its upper neighbor A before it resolves through a passing tone G-sharp to the tonic. Although the connection from G to G-sharp seems clear in the middleground sketch, it is once again obscured at the surface of the music. That is, from the melodic cadence on G in m. 10, the soprano steps down through F to E, which makes possible the analytic interpretation that Schenker would likely choose, which would understand the G as leading down, rather than up to A. However, as I have indicated in the foreground sketch, I hear the G sustained through the downbeat of m. 11, at which point it rises to G-sharp through the upper neighbor A, and ultimately resolves to A at the cadence. The connection from G to A that I hear so strongly is articulated by the tenor voice in m. 11.

Example 97: "Von Gott will ich nicht lassen," BWV 73/5 (B & H, Nr. 191) and sketch

Example 97, cont.

Mit Fried und Freud ich fahr dahin

Another chorale in which the minor dominant and LN emerge prominently is Bach's setting of the Dorian melody, "Mit Fried und Freud ich fahr dahin," BWV 382 (B & H, Nr. 49). The chorale is reproduced in Example 98.[17] I discussed phrases 4 and 5 of this chorale earlier in connection with Example 73. Here, I would like mainly to comment on the role of the minor dominant and DOR-LN. The final phrase emphasizes the natural seventh degree, C, which is harmonized by the structural dominant of the chorale.

In the middleground sketch, the structural $\hat{2}$ supported by the dominant arrives in m. 11; the alto of the sketch descends to C^4, which resolves as a DOR-LN to D^4, through a chromatic passing tone C-sharp. The foreground sketch demonstrates how this DOR-LN is introduced. In m. 11 of the foreground analysis, $\hat{2}$ is extended first through an unfolding of the third C - E, and then through an unfolding of the third E - C-sharp. Within the unfolded thirds from E, C-natural is assigned a higher structural value than C-sharp because of its strong articulation in the cantus firmus. In the music, the soprano moves directly from D^4 to C^4 on the downbeat of m. 11. From C^4 the soprano leaps to F^4, and then descends in stepwise motion to C-sharp. The alto and soprano cross at this point, obscuring the structural voice leading. In the foreground sketch of m. 11, the soprano's C^4 moves to the alto's C-sharp. F^4 in the soprano on beat 2 of m. 11 is analyzed as a suspension from the preceding measure. As it resolves, the alto and soprano merge on a unison E, the structural $\hat{2}$.

The DOR-LN progression in m. 11 is prepared, in the chorale, by a similar progression in m. 1, this time involving the natural seventh degree and leading tone of A, the dominant. Indeed, the progression on the first and second beats of m. 11 is a tonal transformation of the third and fourth beats of m. 1. In m. 1, the cantus firmus moves from A^4 to G^4, just as in m. 11 it moves from D^4 to C^4. The G^4 is harmonized by the minor dominant of A, E minor. The soprano's G-natural is displaced by the alto's F-sharp and G-sharp which function as the raised sixth and seventh degrees in A and resolve to A on the downbeat of m. 2. Meanwhile the soprano of m. 1 reaches over to D^5 against the alto's F-sharp - G-sharp and resolves, as a neighbor, to C^5. The G - A resolution is labeled AOL-LN.

---

[17]The musical text in Example 98 is based on Ms. R 18, Nr. 51. There are a few minor discrepancies with *BG* 39, Nr. 129. For instance, at the asterisk (*) in m. 3, the alto leaps from A to C in Ms. R 18, but retains A as a quarter note in *BG* 39.

The effect of this progression in the opening measure of the chorale has a distinctly "modal" character—we do not understand how the Aeolian tonic and the AOL-LN function within the context of the opening D-minor triad. When this progression recurs in m. 11, tonally altered and transposed, we have considerably more context on which to base our interpretation. The downbeat of m. 11 establishes the minor dominant of D in the identical voicing to that of the minor dominant of A in m. 1. The soprano's C-natural is likewise displaced by the alto's C-sharp, approached from B-natural, which function as the raised sixth and seventh degrees in D. Against the C-sharp, the soprano reaches over and articulates F-natural as a neighbor to E, the fifth of the dominant harmony. If this were a straightforward transposition of the progression in m. 1, the soprano would reach over to G as a neighbor to F, the third of the tonic; however, the larger harmony that is being prolonged is the dominant rather than the tonic of D.

The chorales "Von Gott will ich nicht lassen" and "Mit Fried und Freud ich fahr dahin" demonstrate how the modal lower neighbor can be harmonized by the structural dominant. By asserting that the major third is heard only as a chromatic passing tone from the natural seventh degree, I am assigning the LN figure a higher structural priority. This requires one to hear a different kind of harmonic directionality: the dominant with its minor third is the structural dissonance that requires resolution to the tonic. Such an analytic interpretation is based on the larger context of the chorale, in which the LN figure is an organic feature of the composition. In both chorales studied here, the natural seventh is indeed a thematic element of the chorale and of the original source of the composition, the cantus firmus.

Summary

The analytic model proposed in this study makes a strong case for the unique treatment of modal versus modern tonal harmony. I hope to have demonstrated that not only should this broader distinction be made, but also distinctions among the individual modes, and at an even more specific level, among the structures that might be possible within a single mode. The lack of uniformity among the modes and the modern scales necessarily leads to a pluralistic analytic approach. Yet this pluralism does not manifest itself in chaos—my analytic model is intended to present the possibilities in such a way that certain common precepts are clear.

Example 98: "Mit Fried und Freud ich fahr dahin," BWV 382 (B & H, Nr. 49) and sketch

Example 98, cont.

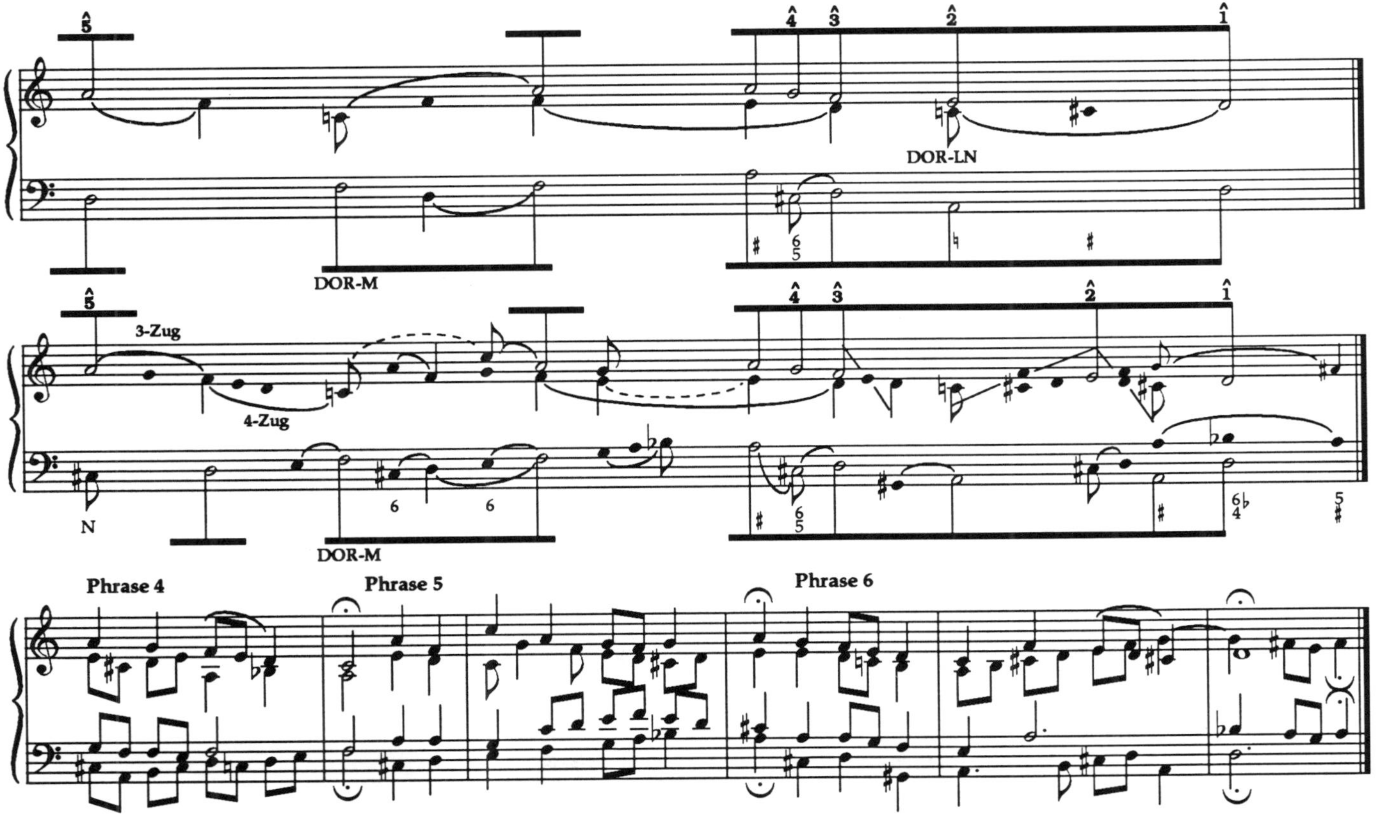

Throughout this study, I have identified general distinctions and correspondences between the modes and modern keys. An obvious distinction exists in the fundamental structures that are possible: many of the background structures I assert for the individual modes are distinguishable from Schenker's tonal models. Emphasis on the fourth and sixth degrees as opposed to the tonic triadic degrees is one obvious case in point. Another is the appearance of the diatonic lower neighbor and upper neighbor figures into the structural bass progressions. Mode-defining progressions occur not only at the structural level, but also at the surface of the music. I explored many such local harmonic progressions that might be heard as modal determinants. The main challenge that my analytic method presents to the tonal theorist is how to appreciate a different kind of harmonic coherence. It is undeniable that the chorales studied here are organically unified, although the unifying structures are unique to the individual compositions.

I believe my analytic model has implications for further study. Although built around Bach's chorales, similar analytic studies are needed for other modal repertoires. It is also possible that future scholars may find ways to apply my Dorian and Aeolian analytic models to an investigation of modern minor, in order to improve our understanding of minor harmonic/contrapuntal practice as distinct from major. Finally, this analytic study should yield a refined understanding of Bach's musical style. His chorale-based compositions are used as the basis of tonal harmonic and contrapuntal structure in music theory classrooms, yet very little has been written on the subject of their modal content. A closer examination of this repertoire should contribute to a better understanding of Bach's harmonic practice and also to an improved pedagogical application of that practice.

APPENDIX 1

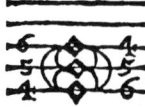

Modal Cadence Systems in Historical Theory

My theory of modality in the Bach chorales and my analytic methods were conceived in a context sensitive to historical modal theory. In the following discussion I will review how certain historical theorists dealt with the unique harmonic identity of each individual mode. Although the theorists to be cited date from the sixteenth through the eighteenth centuries, the discussion is not offered as a thorough historical survey. Rather, this brief essay is intended to provide the interested reader with a historical context for the modal harmonic paradigms presented in Chapters 2 and 4.

In writing on the modes, historical theorists explored modal identity according to a variety of criteria. Such criteria include the final, the octave division (harmonic or arithmetic), the species of fourth and fifth and the placement of tones and semitones within the octave, the modal affect, the *repercussio* or reciting tone (dominant), and the cadence endings, both regular and irregular. I will focus here primarily on their treatment of modal harmonic procedures and modal degree emphasis—that is, to the weight allotted to specific scale degrees through definitions of the *repercussio* and the cadence systems. The theoretical discussions and examples to be reviewed below provide a wealth of material from which to draw insights into modal functional hearing.

Seventeenth-century German writers inherited a tradition of modal theory from **Gioseffo Zarlino**; in particular, they were influenced by his classification of the modes according to the quality—major or minor—of the third above the final, as well as the identification of the regular cadence points with the root, fifth and third degrees of the mode. Zarlino defines regular and irregular cadences as follows:

> It will suffice to say here, once and for all, that there are two sorts of cadences, namely, regular and irregular. The regular cadences are those which are always made on the extreme sounds of notes of the modes, and

on the median note by which the diapason is mediated or divided harmonically or arithmetically. These are the extreme notes of the diapente
and the diatessaron. The regular cadences are also made on the median
note by which the diapente is divided into a ditone and a semiditone. In
other words, the regular cadences are made on the true and natural initial
tones of each mode, and the cadences that are made on all the other notes
are called irregular. The regular cadences of the first mode, then, are
those which are made on the notes D, F, a and d; the irregular cadences
are those which are made on the other notes.[1]

Zarlino thus standardizes the regular cadences into a $\hat{1}$ - $\hat{5}$ - $\hat{3}$
schema for all twelve modes. The regular and irregular cadence points for
each mode are presented in Example A-1. In not attempting to define a
unique cadence system for each mode, Zarlino risks assigning cadential
weight to pitches that are not actually stressed in a given mode. For instance, although B has a false fifth in the diatonic modal system, it is given
cadential emphasis in his modes 3 and 4 (Phrygian and Hypophrygian)
and modes 7 and 8 (Mixolydian and Hypomixolydian):

> It should be noted that in [the third] mode, as in the fourth, seventh, and
> eighth modes, cadences are regularly made on the note b-natural, and
> since this note does not have a corresponding fifth above or fourth below,
> it sounds somewhat hard. Yet this hardness is tolerated in compositions
> written for more than two voices, because then the voices are kept in such
> an order that they produce a good effect. . . .[2]

The traditionally accepted reciting tones or *repercussio* of the
Phrygian and Hypophrygian modes (A and C, respectively) and the
Hypomixolydian mode (C) are not granted cadential status within the
theoretical schema. Zarlino does, however, recognize the emphasis on
these pitches and attempts to accommodate it by invoking the
theoretical concept of mixture: "If the third mode [Phrygian] were not
mixed with the ninth mode [Aeolian], and were heard by itself, its harmony would be somewhat hard, but because it is tempered by the
diapente of the ninth mode and by the cadence made on a, which is

---

[1]Gioseffo Zarlino, *Le Istitutioni harmoniche IV* (Venice, 1558), trans. Vered Cohen,
On the Modes (New Haven: Yale University Press, 1983), p. 55. Zarlino's theory of the
modes changed and developed over the course of his career. The second edition of this
treatise was published in 1573. He also discussed the modes in his *Dimostrationi* of
1571. The renumbering of the modes is the most striking change in this development.
It is not my intent here to trace the development of his modal theory, and the issue of
modal ordering is not of immediate concern. My discussion is therefore based on the
original 1558 treatise.

[2]Ibid., pp. 62–63.

Example A-1: Regular and Irregular Cadences, Zarlino (1558)

Mode	Regular	Irregular
1	D F a d	any other
2	a F D A	"
3	E G b e	"
4	B E G b	"
5	F a c f	"
6	c a F C	"
7	G b d g	"
8	d b G D	"
9	A C E a	"
10	e c a E	"
11	C E G c	"
12	g e c G	"

very much in use in it, some have been of the opinion that the third mode moves one to weeping."[3] Similarly, he recognizes that the fourth mode (Hypophrygian) is mixed with the tenth (Hypoaeolian).[4] And later, he identifies the mixture of the third mode (Phrygian) with the tenth (Hypoaeolian).[5] The mixture of modes 3 and 10 is possible because each is based on the octave species E - e. In the Phrygian mode, the octave is divided harmonically at the fifth, B, while in the Hypoaeolian mode, the octave is divided arithmetically at the fourth, A. The former has regular cadences on E, G and B, the latter on A, C and E. If a composition closes on E, but articulates cadences on A, C, and E, it is judged to be Phrygian mixed with Hypoaeolian, and the only reason to consider the Phrygian mode at all is the final. It is not possible to consider such a composition as simple Phrygian, since the cadential emphasis does not correspond to the $\hat{1}$ - $\hat{5}$ - $\hat{3}$ theoretical schema. The practical result of this theoretical interpretation would be to deny the existence of the simple Phrygian mode, since Phrygian compositions do not adhere to Zarlino's abstract model. Similarly, the eighth mode (Hypomixolydian) is mixed with the eleventh mode (Ionian).[6]

---

[3]Ibid., pp. 63–64.
[4]Ibid., p. 64.
[5]Ibid., pp. 89–91.
[6]Ibid., p. 89.

Example A-2: Cadential Degrees, Dahlhaus (1968)

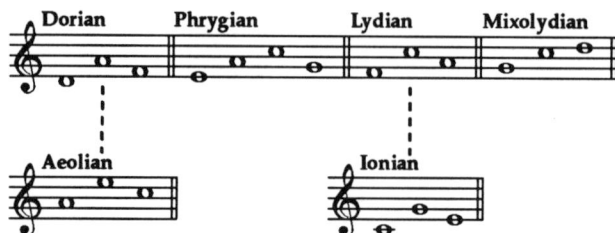

Carl Dahlhaus criticizes Zarlino's $\hat{1}$ - $\hat{5}$ - $\hat{3}$ schema for its speculative rather than empirical basis, which results in its being "too rigid to do justice to musical reality."[7] Dahlhaus holds that the normalization of the modes into such a theoretical system had ill effects on subsequent theorists, hindering them from accurately representing musical practice.[8] Thus opposed to Zarlino's $\hat{1}$ - $\hat{5}$ - $\hat{3}$ schema, Dahlhaus asserts that the individual modes are characterized by different arrangements of cadential degrees. His norms for the dispositions of clausulas are reproduced in Example A-2.[9]

Indeed, during the seventeenth and eighteenth centuries, certain theorists developed Zarlino's notion of the $\hat{1}$ - $\hat{5}$ - $\hat{3}$ cadence system, adhering to it rigorously and thus ignoring the unique properties of the individual modes. Others, however, developed the abstract concept of the primary - secondary - tertiary schema by assigning these functions to the degrees suitable to a given mode, thus allowing or exploiting differences among the modes. Yet other theorists, in defining their cadential schema, were non-systematic in their approach and based their theoretical observations upon empirical evidence.

Johann Andreas Herbst's interest in the unique properties of the modes is evident in his explication of the modal *repercussio*. In *Musica poëtica* (Nürnberg, 1643), he gives *repercussiones* for all twelve modes, designating the emphasized pitches by their hexachord syllables. Example

[7]Dahlhaus, *Studies on the Origin of Harmonic Tonality*, p. 220.

[8]Ibid., p. 225.

[9]Ibid., p. 220. As support for his asserted modal cadential norms, Dahlhaus cites similar findings in the following studies which are based upon the analysis of Renaissance music: R. O. Morris, *Contrapuntal Technique in the Sixteenth Century*, 7th ed. (Oxford, 1958), p. 15; Georg Reichert, "Kirchentonart als Formfaktor in der mehrstimmigen Musik des 15. und 16. Jahrhunderts," *Musikforschung* 4 (1951), pp. 35–48; Siegfried Hermelinck, *Dispositiones modorum. Die Tonarten in der Musik Palestrinas und seiner Zeitgenossen* (Tutzing, 1960).

Example A-3: *Repercussiones*, Herbst (1643)

re   la   re   fa   mi   fa   mi   la   fa   fa   fa   la

ut   sol   ut   fa   re   la   re   fa   ut   sol   fa   la

A-3 translates these syllables into pitch notation. In addition to the modal final, the emphasized degrees are either $\hat{3}$, $\hat{4}$, $\hat{5}$, or $\hat{6}$.[10]

Herbst finds an interesting way to retain Zarlino's abstract $\hat{1}$ - $\hat{5}$ - $\hat{3}$ schema for all modes while at the same time emphasizing the degrees suitable to each individual mode. In Example A-4 he systematically presents the *clausula principalis, minus principalis,* and *affinalis* for each mode.[11] In his abstract definition of these cadences, Herbst defines a $\hat{1}$ - $\hat{5}$ - $\hat{3}$ schema:

> There are three places in which cadences are formed, according to the three notes [of the triad]: 1) the first, which is made on the lowest note of the fifth, according to harmonic and arithmetic division, is called *principalis clausula*; 2) the second, however, which is placed on the upper note of the fifth, is called *minus principalis*; 3) the third introduces the third between the fifth, and will be called *affinalis* or *affinalis clausula*....[12]

Herbst's practical realization of the modal cadence formulas translates the $\hat{1}$ - $\hat{5}$ - $\hat{3}$ schema into the degrees upon which the *soprano* cadences within a four-voice harmonic structure.[13] The bass voice does not always cadence

[10]Johann Andreas Herbst, *Musica poëtica* (Nürnberg, 1643). Chapters 6 (pp. 45–57) and 7 (pp. 58–80) are dedicated to the modes and modal cadences.

[11]Example A–4 is based on Herbst's modal cadence formulas, given in *Musica poëtica,* pp. 58–80.

[12]Ibid., pp. 50–51. Unfortunately Herbst confuses the traditional definitions of *minus principalis* and *affinalis*. The *minus principalis* is usually associated with the third and the *affinalis* is normally associated with the fifth of the triad. Joachim Burmeister does the same in *Musica poetica* (Rostock, 1606, facs. reprint Kassel, 1955), p. 52. Dahlhaus discsusses the terms *affinalis* and *minus principalis* in *Studies on the Origin of Harmonic Tonality,* pp. 229–30.

[13]In his *Musica poëtica,* Herbst adopts the cadence listings of Otto Siegfried Harnisch, *Artis musicae delineatio* (Frankfurt, 1608). Benito Rivera discusses and reproduces Harnisch's cadences in *German Music Theory in the Early Seventeenth Century: The treatises of Johannes Lippius* (Ann Arbor: UMI Press, 1980), pp. 210–215.

on the same degree as the soprano. Thus, Herbst leaves some flexibility within the abstract schema: given the pre-defined soprano pattern he can attempt to find harmonic solutions which characterize the individual mode. In the abstract, Herbst defines two types of formal cadences (*clausula formales*): those with falling-fifth bass progressions and those with falling-fourth bass progressions.[14] In his examples of the modal formulas there is also a third type—the step progression which we would recognize as a "Phrygian" cadence. Thus Herbst explores the harmonic diversity of the modes: first, he specifies for each mode cadential degrees in the bass which do not necessarily follow the $\hat{1}$ - $\hat{5}$ - $\hat{3}$ schema; second, he assigns each of these degrees a unique harmonic progression—"perfect," "plagal," or "Phrygian"—which further defines the harmonic character of the mode.

Herbst's designation *principalis, minus principalis* or *affinalis* appears beneath each cadence in Example A-4. *Principalis* consistently designates the soprano pattern $\hat{1}$ - $\hat{7}$ - $\hat{1}$; *minus principalis* the pattern $\hat{5}$ - $\hat{4}$ - $\hat{5}$; *affinalis* the pattern $\hat{3}$ - $\hat{2}$ - $\hat{3}$. The cadences in the authentic modes are presented in the following order: the soprano cadences on the final, the fifth above the final, the octave above the final and the third above the final. This order symbolizes the authentic division of the octave, followed by the division of the fifth: $\hat{1}$ - $\hat{5}$ - $\hat{8}$ - $\hat{3}$. The cadences in the plagal modes are ordered as follows: the soprano cadences on the fourth below the final, the final, the fifth above the final and the third above. This symbolizes the plagal division of the octave, followed by the division of the fifth: $\hat{5}$ - $\hat{1}$ - $\hat{5}$ - $\hat{3}$.

Beneath Herbst's labels I have indicated with Roman Numerals the scale degree upon which the *bass* cadences. After the mode name, I have classified the schema types exhibited by the individual modes. A quick review of these schemata will demonstrate that despite the formulaic presentation of the cadential soprano pitches, each mode has its own cadential bass emphasis and root motion.

For instance, Herbst finds an unusual way to demonstrate Phrygian harmonic patterns while retaining his soprano cadences on $\hat{1}$, $\hat{5}$, and $\hat{3}$. In Example A-4, his "principal" cadence for Phrygian is a plagal cadence on A, while his "lesser principal" cadence is a plagal cadence on E. Here the tonic and subdominant functions appear to be reversed, but the labels principal and lesser principal refer to the cadential degree in the soprano. He wants to retain the soprano cadential emphasis on $\hat{1}$ and $\hat{5}$, respectively, but he has to cope with the difficulty of cadencing on B within the

---

[14]Herbst, *Music poëtica*, pp. 59–61.

Example A–4: *Clausula Principalis, minus principalis* and *affinalis* in each mode, Herbst (1643)

Example A-4, cont.

V. Lydian [I-V-III]

Clausula principalis   Minus principalis   Principalis   Affinalis
[I   V   I   III]

VI. Hypolydian [I-V-VI]

Claus. minus princ.   Principalis   Minus principalis   Affinalis
[IV   I   V   VI]

VII. Mixolydian [I-V-VI]

Clausula principalis   Minus principalis   Principalis   Affinalis   Assumptae sive peregrinae
[I   V   I   VI]

VII. Hypomixolydian [I-V-VI]

Claus. minus princ.   Principalis   Minus principalis   Affinalis   Assumptae sive peregrinae
[IV   I   V   VI]

Example A-4, cont.

diatonic modal system. His solution is to give the soprano pattern B - A - B a plagal cadence on E, thus avoiding the problematic harmony on B. As a harmonic contrast, he sets the soprano gesture E - D - E with a plagal cadence on A. Then, lest we confuse the functions of A and E because of the labels principal and lesser principal, he firmly establishes E as the modal final by introducing a cadential classification not found in his other modal formulas, the "final" cadence, which is a "Phrygian" cadence on E. The outer voices feature the diatonic seventh degree D resolving up to E, against the diatonic second degree F resolving down to E. (In my analytic model presented in Chapter 2, I assigned these melodic resolutions the labels PH-UN and PH-LN). It is curious that the Hypophrygian mode is treated differently than the Phrygian mode.[15] Here, both the principal and lesser principal cadences are on E, the principal in the progression VI - vii$_6$ - I and the lesser principal in the plagal progression E - a - E.

As in the Phrygian mode, Herbst must find a harmonic solution to the melodic emphasis on B ($\hat{3}$) in Mixolydian. The melodic cadence B - A - B is harmonized by a plagal harmonic gesture E - a - E, thus emphasizing the sixth degree (E) of the Mixolydian scale, rather than the third degree, which cannot support a harmonic triad.

Wolfgang Caspar Printz develops the abstract $\hat{1}$ - $\hat{5}$ - $\hat{3}$ schema into a highly formalized system in his *Phrynis Mitilenaeus, oder Satyrischer Componist* (1676).[16] The degrees $\hat{1}$, $\hat{5}$, and $\hat{3}$ are maintained as the primary, secondary and tertiary degrees upon which cadences can occur in a given mode. These are not, however, simply understood as relationships among scale degrees $\hat{1}$, $\hat{5}$, and $\hat{3}$, but rather, are defined explicitly as interrelationships among the modes, for example, Aeolian as a tonic, Phrygian as a dominant and Ionian as a mediant. In Printz's system, the secondary cadences for Aeolian are the Phrygian primary cadences, and the tertiary cadences for Aeolian are the Ionian primary cadences.

---

[15]Indeed, Herbst does not always treat the authentic and plagal mode pairs the same way; that is, while the Dorian pair and the Aeolian pair share the emphasis on I – V – III, and the Mixolydian pair share the emphasis on I – V – VI, the other mode pairs are not given the same harmonic emphasis. I have mentioned the different treatment of Phrygian (I – IV – III) and Hypophrygian (I – III); in addition, Lydian and Hypolydian are assigned emphasis on I – V – III and I – V – VI, respectively, and Ionian and Hypoionian are assigned I – V – VI and I – V – III, respectively. It is possible that these differences have some basis in musical practice, but I am not able to substantiate his theoretical claim.

[16]Wolfgang Caspar Printz, *Phrynis Mitilenaeus, oder Satyrischer Componist* (Quedlinburg: Christian Okels, 1676; 2d. ed, Dresden–Leipzig, 1696). The modal cadences are discussed in Chapter 8, §§34–42. Chapters 9 and 10 also discuss the modes.

Printz provides, as the primary cadences for a given mode, an extensive list of cadential progressions involving a full vocabulary of chords and cadence types. In so doing, he goes beyond Zarlino's conception of the scale degrees upon which regular and irregular cadences occur. He also goes beyond Herbst's conception of the one particular root progression that is associated with each of the primary, secondary and tertiary degrees.

A cadence (*clausula formalis*) is defined as the place where the melody is inclined toward repose, as it distinguishes the divisions of a text.[17] Printz then classifies the cadences as perfect and reposeful or imperfect and not reposeful. The perfect and imperfect cadence types are subdivided further, generating various forms and inversions. A general distinction can be made between the perfect and imperfect categories: the perfect cadences involve bass motion by fifth, falling or rising, and the imperfect mostly involve bass motion by step. I have reproduced his subdivided categories in Example A-5 and have represented, either with Roman Numerals or with scale degrees, the cadential progression that Printz describes for each of the categories. There are cadences which, in modern terms, would be designated perfect and imperfect, plagal, half, and deceptive.[18] Printz's interpretation of the rising-fifth progression in the category marked *dissecta* (interrupted) is noteworthy, especially considering the tendency of some theorists to interpret a plagal cadence in the Phrygian mode, for instance, as a I - V progression in A. Printz clearly subdivides the rising-fifth progression into two forms: *desiderans* (unresolved) and *acquiescens* (resolved). The unresolved pattern is consistently presented in the modal cadence table as a I - V progression, while the resolved pattern is presented as a IV - I progression. About the former, Printz states that the chord which is required to complete the progression is only implied, whereas in the latter progression (IV - I) the resolving harmony is explicitly stated.[19] Thus, Printz classifies the IV - I resolution as a reposeful (*perfecta*) and resolved (*acquiescens*) progression.

---

[17]Ibid., Chapter 8, §2. This follows Zarlino's definition of cadence in *Istitutione harmoniche III*, trans. Guy A. Marco, *The Art of Counterpoint* (New Haven: Yale University Press, 1968), p. 141.

[18]The different cadential categories that are represented in Example A–5 are defined by Printz in *Satyrischer Componist*, Chapter 8, §§2–32.

[19]Printz, Chapter 8, §§28–31.

Example A-5: Perfect and Imperfect Cadence Types, Printz (1676)

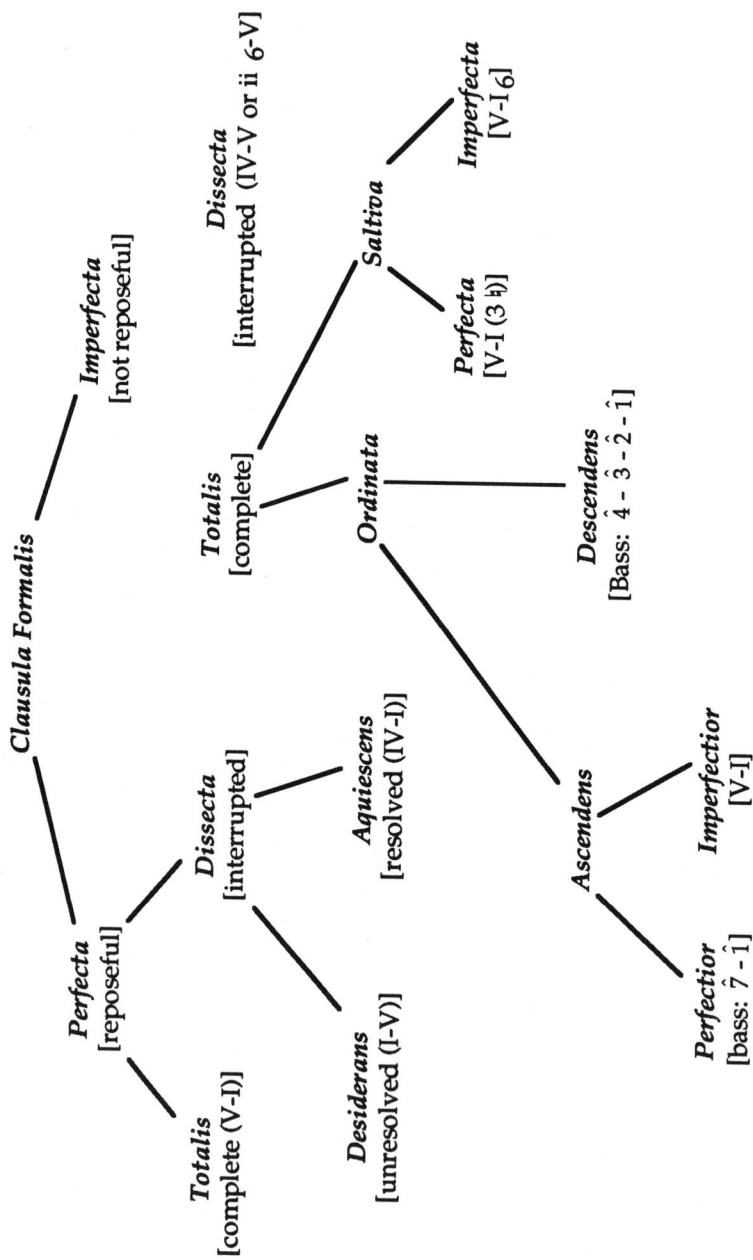

Clausula Formalis

- *Perfecta* [reposeful]
  - *Totalis* [complete (V-I)]
  - *Dissecta* [interrupted]
    - *Desiderans* [unresolved (I-V)]
    - *Aquiescens* [resolved (IV-I)]
- *Imperfecta* [not reposeful]
  - *Totalis* [complete]
    - *Ordinata*
      - *Ascendens*
        - *Perfectior* [bass: 7̂ - 1̂]
        - *Imperfectior* [V-I]
      - *Descendens* [Bass: 4̂ - 3̂ - 2̂ - 1̂]
    - *Saltiva*
      - *Perfecta* [V-I (3♮)]
      - *Imperfecta* [V-I6]
  - *Dissecta* [interrupted (IV-V or ii 6-V)]

After Printz defines the individual cadences in the abstract, he links them with the modes. The cadences of a mode are either *Propriam* (one part of the triad is placed in the harmonic triad of the main mode) or *Peregrinam* (no part of the triad is placed in the harmonic triad of the main mode). The *Propriam* are classified as *Perfectissima* or *Primaria, Perfecta* or *Secundaria, Imperfecta* or *Tertiaria.* The primary cadences are founded on the first degree of the tonic triad. The secondary cadences are based on the dominant, or fifth of the tonic triad, the tertiary cadences on the mediant, or third of the tonic triad. The modal interrelationships expressed by the $\hat{1}$ - $\hat{5}$ - $\hat{3}$ schema are listed in Example A-6.[20] Because of the false fifth on B, the Phrygian mode does not have any secondary cadences, and the Mixolydian does not have any tertiary cadences. The $\hat{1}$ - $\hat{5}$ - $\hat{3}$ pattern therefore falls short of fully accommodating these two modes, but Printz does not suggest an alternative to the pattern. Thus, while he cannot be criticized for forcing the $\hat{1}$ - $\hat{5}$ - $\hat{3}$ schema onto every mode, he can be criticized for not attempting to find those secondary and tertiary cadences that do occur in the Phrygian and Mixolydian modes. That is, he does not stretch his triad-generated theory to encompass the exceptional modes, which are not based on a tonic - dominant - mediant axis.

Example A-6: Primary, Secondary and Tertiary Mode Relationships. Printz (1676)

Primaria	*Secundaria*	*Tertiaria*
Ionian	Mixolydian	Phrygian
Dorian	Aeolian	Lydian
Phrygian	----	Mixolydian
Lydian	Ionian	Aeolian
Mixolydian	Dorian	----
Aeolian	Phrygian	Ionian

---

[20]Example A–6 is based on Printz's illustration, Chapter 8, §§35–36.

Example A-7: Primary Cadences, Printz (1676)

Clausulae Formales Primariae

Example A-7, cont.

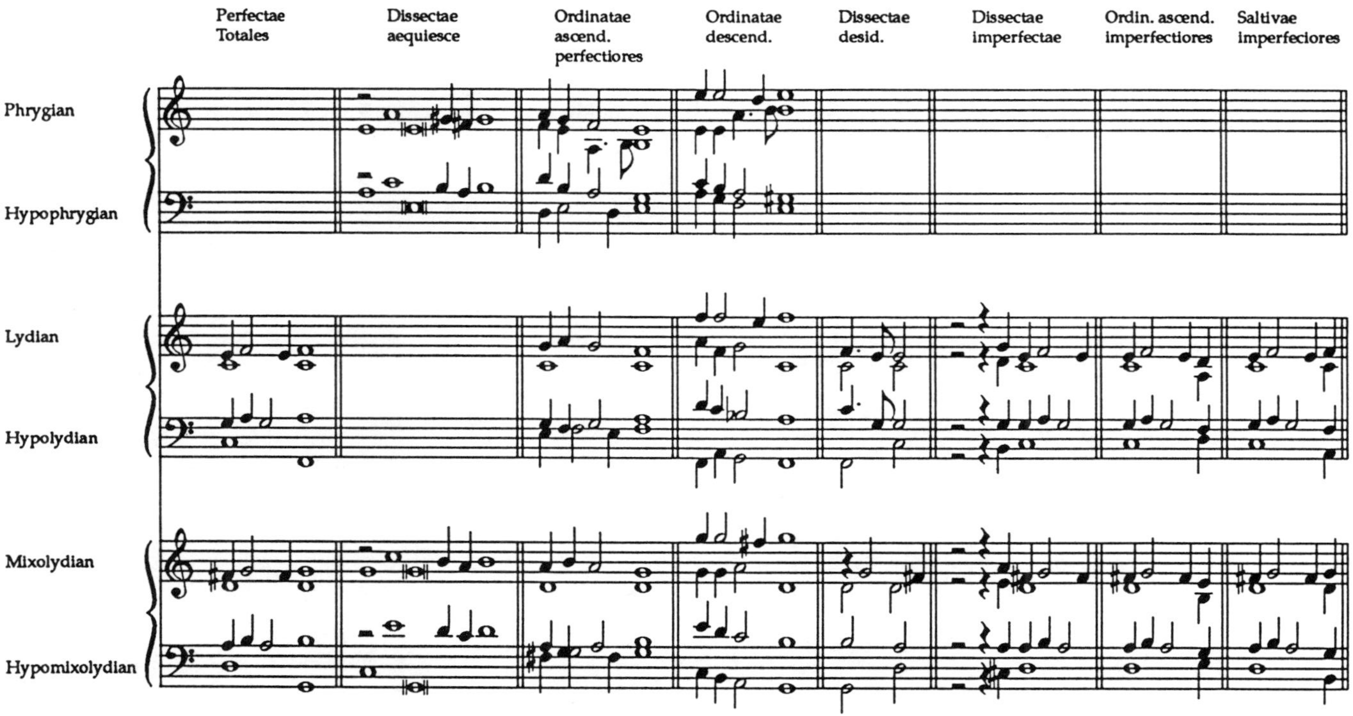

Printz presents the primary cadences for the modes in a large table, which I have reproduced as Example A-7.[21] For the most part, Printz adheres to the diatonic system, applying ficta conventionally. In dominant-tonic cadences, chromaticisms inflect the leading tone of the dominant and the major third of the tonic. B-flat is introduced in one Lydian cadence and in one Dorian cadence; the leading tone to the dominant is applied in one Mixolydian cadence. Elsewhere, Printz adheres to the diatonic system. The chromaticisms can be described as ornamental rather than structural. Printz refuses to use F-sharp in order to get cadences on B in the Phrygian and Mixolydian modes; similarly, he does not use B-flat in the Lydian mode to obtain a IV - I cadence.

In the primary cadences that are given for each mode, there are progressions which approach the final by falling fifth, or rising fifth. Printz describes the rising fifth progression as an interrupted cadence (*clausula dissecta*). The interrupted cadence is twofold: Printz distinguishes between the resolved interrupted cadence (*clausula dissecta acquiescens*), which is realized in a IV - I progression, and the unresolved interrupted cadence (*clausula dissecta desiderans*), which is realized in a I - V progression. The primary cadences do not necessarily resolve to the tonic, as in the I - V progression, and there are even some primary cadences in which the tonic triad is not present, such as the iv - V progression and the deceptive cadence V - VI or V - IV$_6$. In considering these cadential progressions to be primary, Printz departs significantly from earlier definitions of primary cadences.

Johann Gottfried Walther lists modal cadential formulas that are similar to those of Printz.[22] The abstract $\hat{1}$ - $\hat{5}$ - $\hat{3}$ schema is realized in the

---

[21]Example A–7 reproduces the table of cadences found in the first edition of Printz's *Satyrischer Componist* (1676), Chapter 8, §33. In the second edition (1696) some minor changes are made, mostly involving an exchange of parts between alto and tenor, but some which affect the quality of the harmony in a given cadence.

[22]Johann Gottfried Walther discusses the modes and cadential formulas in his *Praecepta der musicalischen Composition* (Ms., 1708), ed. P. Benary (Leipzig: Breitkopf und Härtel, 1960), pp. 288–340. He also discusses the modes in his *Musicalisches Lexicon, oder Musicalische Bibliothec* (Leipzig: Wolffgang Deer, 1732), article "Modus Musicus," pp. 409–15; trans. Joel Lester, *Between Modes and Keys*, Appendix 4 , pp. 211–233. In the *Lexicon*, Walther discusses cadences in the entries under "Clausula," pp. 170–171, where he introduces Printz's terminology, borrows some of his definitions and, when appropriate, matches up his own terms to those of Printz. For instance, under the entry *Clausula ordinata ascendens perfectior* (Printz's term), the definition merely states that this is the same as the *Clausula cantizans* (Walther's term) (*Lexicon*, p. 170). In the *Praecepta* (1708), such borrowing from Printz is not evident.

identification of primary, secondary, and tertiary cadences on the first, fifth and third degrees of each mode. The primary cadences comprise several different tonic-defining harmonic progressions. Like Printz, Walther defines as primary several different cadence types.

Walther's primary cadence formulas are based upon two simple harmonic progressions: the *perfectissima*, which comprises a I - V - I progression, and the *dissecta* (interrupted), which comprises a IV - I progression. The former occurs in different inversions which are theoretically explained as a rearrangement of the voice parts. Since each voice is associated with a specific voice-leading event in the perfect cadence, the inversions are labeled for the voice that is associated with the event taken up by the bass. For example, the cantus is associated with the melodic gesture $\hat{1}$ - $\hat{7}$ - $\hat{1}$; therefore, when the perfect cadence is inverted so that these scale degrees occur in the bass, as in the progression I - V_6 - I, the cadence is named for the cantus and is called *clausula cantizans*. Likewise, the alto voice is associated with the gesture $\hat{5}$ - $\hat{3}$; therefore the progression I - V - I_6 is called *clausula altizans*. The *clausula altizans* is frequently also referred to as the *clausula minus perfecta*. The tenor usually takes the gesture $\hat{3}$ - $\hat{2}$ - $\hat{1}$; the progression I_6 - vii_6 - I is called *clausula tenorizans*. Finally, the bass is associated with the root progression I - V - I, which is the perfect form of the cadence. There are also slight variations on these patterns as will be observed in the summary of Walther's cadences.

The primary cadences, since they have their place in one of the notes of the tonic triad, are called essential (*clausula essentialis*). Walther also provides *affinalis* and *peregrine* cadences. His use of the term *affinalis* is unusual. It is sometimes equated with the dominant or confinal. Here it is used to describe "related" cadences. These are found upon the triads a third and a fifth below the final (VI and IV); they are related through the presence of the final in both of these triads. The *peregrine* or foreign cadences occur on a note which is not found in the tonic triad.

Walther presents the cadence formulas for each mode separately. I have gathered them together in a table given as Example A-8.[23] In order to condense the material, I have provided only the unadorned bass voice of the cadence, allowing figured bass symbols to represent the full harmony. The six modes are aligned according to the cadential categories that are listed at the top of each system.

---

[23]Example A–8 derives from Walther's modal cadences given over pp. 164–179 of the *Praecepta*.

Example A-8: Primary, Secondary and Tertiary Cadences, Walther (1708)

Example A-8, cont.

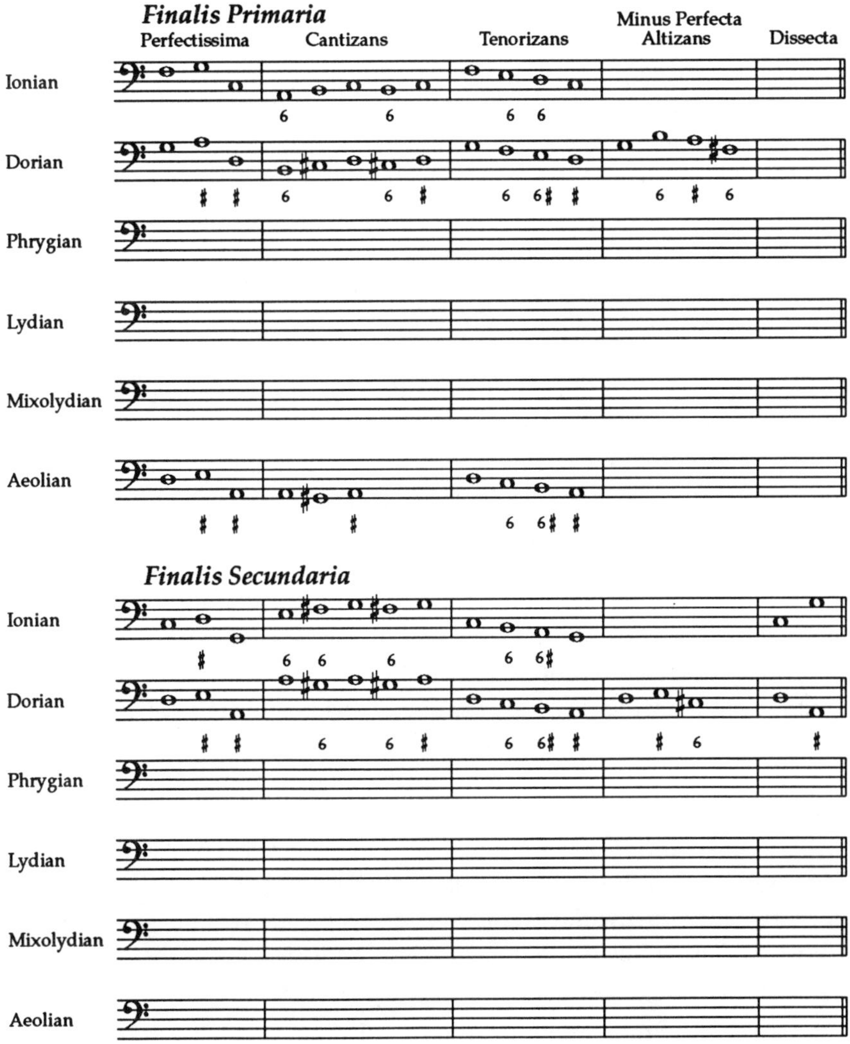

Not only are there primary, secondary, tertiary cadence forms, but also *finalis primaria, finalis secundaria*, and *finalis tertiaria* cadence forms. Walther does not discuss the *"finalis"* cadences, but his examples show that they are slightly more elaborate. For example, the Ionian *primaria perfectissima* is a simple I - V - I progression, and the *finalis primaria perfectissima* is a IV - V - I progression.

It is immediately clear from the blank spaces throughout the table that Walther does not rigorously realize every cadence type for each mode. The Ionian, Dorian and Aeolian modes are well supplied with cadences; the Phrygian, Lydian and Mixolydian, however, are not. As was the case with Printz, most of the blank spaces arise because the I - V - III schema does not fit certain of the modes. The Phrygian mode, for instance, can have no I - V - I cadence, which is the reason for the lack of primary cadences. (With the exception of the interrupted (*dissecta*) cadence, the other primary cadence types are based on the I - V - I progression.) Walther is clearly determined to identify only the falling-fifth root progression as the "perfect" cadence. He does not attempt to accommodate the modes that are not organized according to that harmonic progression. This is evident not only in the small number of primary cadences given for the Phrygian mode, but also in the complete lack of secondary cadences for the Phrygian mode. The pre-defined secondary degree, B, is unusable in this mode, and Walther does not attempt to remedy the problem. He does provide a tertiary cadence for the Phrygian mode—a perfect cadence in G—but his conviction about this is questionable, since he does not classify it further than "tertiary." The small number of cadence forms possible in the Phrygian mode is evident in the Ionian and Aeolian cadence formulas as well. The Phrygian mode is represented in the secondary cadences for the Ionian mode and in the tertiary cadences for the Aeolian mode with only two progressions: the "Phrygian" cadence, d$_6$ - E, which is labeled *perfecta*, and the interrupted (*dissecta*) cadence, a - E.

Like the Phrygian mode, the Mixolydian mode does not conform well to the $\hat{1}$ - $\hat{5}$ - $\hat{3}$ schema. There are no tertiary cadences given for this mode, since B is the third degree. However, this does not explain the scarcity of primary and secondary listings. Walther simply lists the perfect cadence on G as primary, and the perfect cadence on D as secondary, providing no further classification. It is noteworthy that he does not provide an interrupted primary cadence in Mixolydian, IV - I, since in practice that is the common Mixolydian cadence formula.

And he does give the IV - I cadence on G as a possible *finalis secundaria* cadence in Ionian.

Perhaps Walther simply did not intend to provide a rigorous realization of his theoretical $\hat{1}$ - $\hat{5}$ - $\hat{3}$ model. Some of the blank spaces are caused by the inapplicability of the $\hat{1}$ - $\hat{5}$ - $\hat{3}$ schema; there are others, however, that are not so easily explained. In general, a simple overview of the table suggests that the modes that are closest to the modern keys — Ionian, Dorian, Aeolian—are well represented, while the Phrygian, Lydian, and Mixolydian modes have not been well defined.

In developing modal cadence systems, **Johann Philipp Kirnberger** takes a different approach from any of his predecessors.[24] He departs completely from the abstract $\hat{1}$ - $\hat{5}$ - $\hat{3}$ schema, and also from the concomitant threefold concept of primary, secondary and tertiary. Instead of specifying cadences on modal degrees as primary, secondary, tertiary, related, foreign, etc., he simply gives the degrees upon which *primary* and *secondary* cadences can occur, listing them in hierarchical order based on frequency of repose. As well as giving the secondary modal degrees, he provides the appropriate cadential pattern (root progression) that best defines the possible points of repose in each mode. These root progressions include V - I, IV - I and, in the case of the cadence on E, vii$_6$ - I, resolutions. The primary and secondary modal network is presented in a table, reproduced here as Example A-9, which, as the author informs us,

> . . . shows the cadences in each mode to which one can digress from the main mode. By means of longer and shorter note values, it is shown approximately how long one must stay in the secondary modes in such pieces that digress to all the modes indicated. The cadences indicated by quarter notes belong to the more unusual and foreign digressions that are used only in long compositions.[25]

In other words, Kirnberger defines the ideal proportional relationships among the secondary modes and the primary mode within an entire composition. Kirnberger thus creates what may be read as a hierarchical structure of modal organization, or at the very least as some sort of proportional weighting among tonicized degrees in each mode.

---

[24]Johann Philipp Kirnberger discusses the modes in his treatise *Die Kunst des reinen Satzes in der Musik*, vol. 2, part 1 (Berlin–Königsberg: G. J. Decker und G. L. Hartung, 1776; facs. ed., Hildesheim: Georg Olms Verlag, 1988); trans. David Beach and Jürgen Thym, *The Art of Strict Musical Composition* (New Haven: Yale University Press, 1982). The relevant passage on the modes is found in Part 1, Chapter 2 of Vol. II, pp. 314–335 of the translation, pp. 41–67 of the German original.

[25]Kirnberger, *The Art of Strict Musical Composition*, p. 330.

Example A-9: Primary and Secondary Cadences, Kirnberger (1776)

Dorian Mode

Phrygian Mode

Lydian Mode

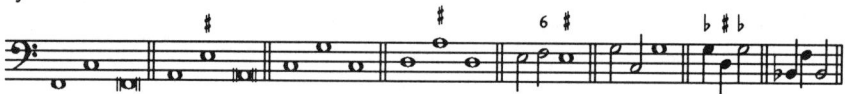

Mixolydian Mode

Aeolian Mode

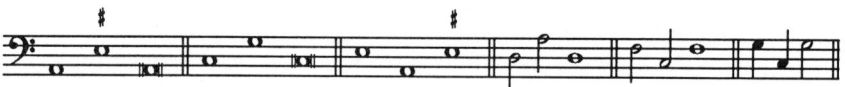

Ionian Mode

Example A-10: Rhythmic Proportions, Kirnberger (1776)

a) b) c) d)

4 : 3 : 2 : 1

There are four possible durational schemes for a cadential pattern: a) two whole notes followed by a breve; b) three whole notes; c) two half notes followed by a whole note; and d) two quarter notes followed by a half note.[26] With his durational values Kirnberger creates a 4 : 3 : 2 : 1 ratio as shown in Example A-10. The relative durations suggest a norm for the relative number of cadences that are idiomatic on each degree within a given mode. For instance, when we look at his paradigms for Phrygian, we see that his symbolic E cadence lasts 4 whole notes, while his symbolic A cadence lasts only 3 whole notes; I interpret this to mean that cadences on A appear in E-Phrygian pieces about three-quarters as often as cadences on E. It is doubtful that a modal composition would fit these proportions exactly, but it is reasonable to suppose that Kirnberger offered his proportions as large statistical generalizations, rather than as assertions about each and every individual piece.

For each mode, the primary and secondary cadence formulas are unique. In the modal network for each mode, a cadence is suggested for every diatonic degree (excluding B) and thus for every possible secondary mode. (Although no mode is assigned a secondary cadence on B, the

---

[26]My reproduction of Kirnberger's table is based on the original 1776 edition (pp. 60–61), since Beach and Thym's version of the table (p. 331) deviates from Kirnberger's original. With one exception, whenever pattern (b) (the three whole notes) appears in the translation, Beach and Thym have substituted pattern (a) (two whole notes followed by a breve). The exception is found in the Lydian table—that is, Beach's fourth cadence in Lydian retains the pattern of three whole notes from the original. All other instances of pattern (b) in the original appear as pattern (a) in the translation. This is especially problematic since the durational values are crucial to Kirnberger's point. Beach and Thym may have assumed that pattern (b) was either arbitrary or a misprint, but I hold that assumption implausible for two reasons. First, pattern (b) occurs frequently; it can be found in the Phrygian, Lydian, Aeolian, and Ionian lists. Second, Kirnberger's table always places pattern (b) between patterns (a) and (c) in the hierarchical order of duration values; thus, in some sense, pattern (b) "mediates" between the other rhythmic patterns.

Dorian and Lydian modes have cadences on B-flat.) A given mode is not always represented by the same cadential formula each time it appears (as either a secondary or primary mode). C and A are represented throughout all modes by perfect cadences. G is represented by both plagal (G - C - G) as well as perfect (g - D - g) cadential formulas in the Dorian and Ionian modes, although only by plagal in Phrygian, Lydian, Mixolydian and Aeolian. Where two possible formulas are given for a secondary degree, they are not necessarily assigned the same proportional weighting—the different cadences on G are not adjacent in the Ionian table; rather, the plagal cadence is shown, by means of the durational symbols, to be equal to the tonic cadence in frequency, but the perfect cadence on G minor is the most remote.

The order in which the secondary degrees appear in the hierarchy is also unique to each mode. This is particularly clear in comparing the Dorian and Aeolian modes, so close in their scalar construction. In Dorian the pattern is I - V - III - VII - II - IV - VI, but in Aeolian it is I - III - V - IV - VI - VII.

Daniel Gottlob Türk advises that the great diversity of the modes is indicated by the different modal cadential formulas. His modal cadences are given in Example A-11.[27] Türk provides only the primary cadences for each mode, that is, only the root progression for the cadences on the final of the mode. Since he does not wish to spend the time discussing secondary closes, he refers us to Kirnberger for a thorough presentation. I am particularly interested in Türk's cadences for Phrygian and Mixolydian. They correspond closely to some of my suggested patterns for those modes. In particular, Türk's d - a - E Phrygian progression is related to the "plagal of plagal" gesture that was discussed in Chapter 2 and illustrated in Example 14d. Also, Türk's second and third Mixolydian cadences resemble my plagal formulas MX-P2 and MX-P1, respectively.

---

[27]Daniel Gottlob Türk, *Von den wichtigsten Pflichten eines Organisten: ein Beytrag zur Verbesserung der musikalischen Liturgie* (Halle, 1787). The modes are discussed on pp. 59–83. The cadential formulas are given on pp. 81–83.

Example A-11: Primary Cadences, Türk (1787)

Ionian (our modern major mode)

Dorian

Lydian

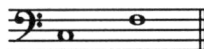

Phrygian

Mixolydian

Aeolian (our modern minor mode)

Justin Heinrich Knecht does not offer a formalized theory of modal cadential formulas in his treatise on the chorale.[28] Although he provides cadential progressions which are common to each mode, he does not classify or rank them in any way. His examples appear to reflect an empirical rather than a theoretical approach. For each mode he provides harmonized scale fragments of different lengths (from three notes to a complete octave), in ascending and descending form; the scale fragments are given one or more harmonizations. Knecht does not interpret the progressions nor does he discuss the context in which they would be heard. Example A-12 reproduces his cadential formulas, reorganizing them for each mode according to the degree upon which the cadences occur. Cadences that were listed for the plagal modes are marked with the symbol (†).

Abbé Vogler defines the appropriate cadence formulas for each mode in his *Choral-System* (1800); these are given in Example A-13.[29] First, he establishes that there are only two cadential classifications: authentic and plagal. The authentic is specifically defined as a falling-fifth progression, from the fifth degree to the first. The plagal is defined more broadly as anything other than a falling-fifth progression. Next, he specifies the characteristic cadences for each of the six modal finals. He does not define cadences on secondary degrees.

Vogler distinguishes the modes according to which type of cadence is taken by the final: Dorian, Lydian, Aeolian and Ionian can close with authentic cadences; Phrygian and Mixolydian, however, can close only with "plagal" cadences. Vogler interprets his modal cadence formulas using tonal functional values and symbols. For instance, the plagal Phrygian cadence is analyzed as a "reversal" of the Aeolian authentic cadence.

---

[28]Justin Heinrich Knecht, *Vollständige Orgelschule für Anfänger und Geübtere*, 3 vols. (Leipzig, 1795–98). While the entire third volume is dedicated to the chorale, the detailed discussions of the modes are found on pp. 8–19, 44–55.

[29]Abbé Georg Joseph Vogler, *Choral–System* (Copenhagen, 1800), Table I. In another publication, *Zwölfe Choräle von Sebastian Bach, umgearbeitet von Vogler, zergliedert von Carl Maria von Weber* (Leipzig, 1810), Vogler and Weber criticize and reharmonize twelve of Bach's chorales. Floyd K. and Margaret G. Grave explore Vogler's theory of harmony in their book, *In Praise of Harmony: The Teachings of Abbé Georg Joseph Vogler* (Nebraska: University of Nebraska Press, 1987), pp. 158–172 cover the modes and chorale harmonization.

Example A-12: Modal Harmonic Progressions, Knecht (1798)
Mixolydian Mode

Example A-12, cont.
Phrygian Mode

Example A-12, cont.
Dorian Mode

Example A-12, cont.
(Dorian Mode)

Cadences on G

Cadences on E

Cadences on B♭

Example A-12, cont.
Aeolian Mode

Cadences on A

Cadences on C

Cadences on E

Example A-13: Modal Cadences, Vogler (1800)

Dorian D♮ — Authentic — V I

Phrygian E♮ — Plagal — V I V — A E

Lydian F — Authentic — V I

Mixolydian G — Plagal Plagal — IV I

Aeolian A♮ — Authentic Plagal — V I I V — D A

Ionian C — Authentic Plagal Plagal — V I IV I F H C / VI VII I

APPENDIX 2

Dorian, Phrygian, Mixolydian and Aeolian Cantus Firmi, as Classified by 17th– and 18th–Century Theorists

Conrad Matthaei, *Kurtzer, oder ausführlicher Bericht von den Modis Musicis* (1652)

Dorian

Vater unser im Himmelreich
Christ der du bist der helle Tag
Christ fuhr den Himmel
Durch Adams Fall ist ganz verderbt
Wir glauben all an einen Gott
Auf meinen lieben Gott
Christ lag in Todes Banden
Christ unser Herr zum Jordan kam

Hypodorian

Christ der du bis Tag und Licht
Kommt her au mir spricht
Nun komm der Heyden Heyland
Von Gott will ich nicht lassen
Was mein Gott will
Dancket dem Herren
Jesus Christus unser Heyland der den
    Tod
Puer natus in Bethlehem
Warum betrübst du dich mein ...

Phrygian

Christus der uns selig macht
O Herre Gott begnade mich
Da Jesus an dem Kreuze stund
Es wollt uns Gott gnädig sein

Hypophrygian

Erbarm dich mein
Mensch wiltu leben
Herr Gott dich loben wir
Mitten wir im Leben sind

Mixolydian

O wir armen Sünder (irregular ending
    in the upper part of the fifth)
Es ist das Heil uns kommen her

Hypomixolydian

Gelobet seist du Jesu Christ
Der du bist Drei in Einigkeit
Dancksagen wir alle
Dies sind die heiligen Zehn Gebot

Aeolian

Meine Seele erhebt den Herren

Ach Gott vom Himmel (irregular
  ending)

Gott hat das Evangelium (irregular
  ending)

Ich ruf zu dir Herr Jesu Christ

Hypoaeolian

Allein zu dir Herr Jesu Christ

Wo Gott der Herr nicht bei uns halt

Wer Gott nicht mit uns diese Zeit

Johann Gottfried Walther, *Praecepta der musicalischen Composition* (1708)

Dorian

Mit Fried und Freud ich fahr dahin

Christ lag in Todesbanden

Christ ist erstanden

Wir glauben all an einen Gott

Vater unser im Himmelreich

Jesus Christus unser Heyland, der von
  uns

Christ unser Herr zum Jordan kam

Durch Adams Fall ist gantz verderbt

Singen wir aus Hertzens Grund

Warum betrübst du dich mein Hertz

Wir Christen Leut, hab jetz und Freud

Auf meinen lieben Gott

Ach Gott thu dich erbarmen

Jesulein, du bist mein, weil ich habe

Hypodorian

Nun kom der Heyden Heyland

Christe der du bist Tag und Licht

Jesus Christus unser Heyland, der den
  Tod

Was mein Gott will das gescheh allzeit

Christ der du bist der helle Tag

Hilff Gott daß mir gelinge

Von Gott will ich nicht laßen

Ach Gott und Herr

Wer nur den lieben Gott läßt walten

Kommt her zu mir spricht Gottes Sohn

Phrygian

Christum wir sollen loben schon

Da Jesus an dem Creutze stund

Aus tiefer Not last uns zu Gott

Es woll uns Gott genädig sein

Mensch wilt du Leben seeliglich

Ach Herr mich armen Sünder

Nimm von uns Herre Gott alle Sünd

Ach Gott vom Himmel sieh därein

O großer Gott von macht

Herr Jesu Christ wahr Mensch und
  Gott

Hypophrygian

Te Deum Laudamus

Erbarm dich mein o Herre Gott

Mitten wir im Leben sind

Mensch wilt du leben seligkeit

O großer Gott von Macht

Mixolydian

Ach wir armen Sünder, unsre Mißethat

Nun schlaff mein liebes Kindelein

Es ist das Heyl uns kommen her

Hypomixolydian

Gelobet seyst du Jesu Christ

Gott sey gelobet und gebenedeyet

Diß sind die heiligen zehn Gebot

Komm Heiliger Geist, erfüll die
  Hertzen

Komm Gott Schöpfer Heiliger Geist

Danck sagen wir alle

Der du bist Drey in Einigkeit

Aeolian

Meine Seele erhebt den Herren

Ich ruf zu dir Herr Jesu Christ

Erhalt uns Herr bey deinem Wort

Gott hat das Evangelium

Ich dancke dem Herrn von gantzen
  Hertzen

Hypoaeolian

Allein zu dir Herr Jesu Christ

Mag ich Unglück nicht wiederstahn

Wär Gott nicht mit uns diese Zeit

Wo Gott der Herr nicht bey uns hält

Von allen Menschen abgewand

Georg Andreas Sorge, *Vorgemach der musikalischen Composition*
  (1745)

Dorian

Wir glauben all an einen Gott

Vater unser im Himmelreich

Jesus Christus unser Heiland, der von
  uns den Gottes Zorn wand...

Hypodorian

Von Gott will ich nicht lassen

Gott Vater der du deine Sohn

Phrygian

Es woll uns Gott genädig sein

Ach Gott vom Himmel sieh darein

Christus der uns selig macht

Da Jesus an dem Kreutze Stund

Ach Herr mich armen Sünder

Hypophrygian

Mitten wir im Leben sind

Erbarm dich mein o Herre Gott

O großer Gott von Macht

Mixolydian

Veni sancte spiritus

Komm heiliger Geist

Danksagen wir alle

Gott unsern Herrn Christo

O Lux beata Trinitas

Der du bist Drei in Einigkeit

Komm Gott Schöpfer heiliger Geist

Gelobet seist du Jesu Christ

Gott sei gelobet und gebenedeiet

Dies sind die heil'gen Zehn Gebot'

Aeolian

Ich ruf' zu dir Herr Jesu Christ

Hypoaeolian

Allein zu dir Herr Jesu Christ

Johann Philipp Kirnberger, *Die Kunst des reinen Satzes in der*
Musik, vol. 2 (1776)

Dorian

Christ unser Herr zum Jordan kam
Durch Adams Fall ist ganz verderbt
Jesus Christus unser Heiland, der von
    uns
Mit Fried und Freud ich fahr dahin
Vater unser im Himmelreich
Wir glauben all' an einen Gott

Phrygian

Ach Gott, vom Himmel sieh' darein
Aus tiefer Not schrei' ich zu dir

Erbarm' dich mein, o Herre Gott
Herzlich tut mich verlangen

Mixolydian

Dies sind die heiligen Zehn Gebot
Gelobet seist du, Jesu Christ
Komm Gott Schöpfer, heiliger Geist

Aeolian

Allein zu dir Herr Jesu Christ
Ich ruf' zu dir Herr Jesu Christ

Daniel Gottlob Türk, *Ein Beytrag zur Verbesserung der musikalische*
Liturgie **(1787)**

Dorian

Wir glauben all' an einen Gott
Durch Adams Fall
Mit Fired und Freud ich fahr dahin
Christ ist erstanden

Phrygian

Ach Herr, mich armen Sünder
Christus der uns seelig macht
Erbarm' dich mein, O Herre Gott
Mitten wir im Leben sind

Mixolydian

Komm Gott Schöpfer heiliger Geist
Dies sind die heiligen Zehn Gebot
Gelobet seist du, Jesu Christ

Aeolian

Allein zu dir, Herr Jesu Christ
Erhalt uns Herr, bey deinem Wort
Ich ruf zu dir, Herr Jesu Christ
Herzliebster Jesu, was hast du
    verbrochen
Es woll' uns Gott genädig sein

Justin Heinrich Knecht, *Vollständige Orgelschule für Anfänger und*
Geübtere, vol. 3, (1798)

Dorian

Ach Gott thu dich erbarmen
Auf meinen lieben Gott, trau ich in
    Angst und Noth
Als Christus geboren war

Christ ist erstanden von der Marter alle
Christ lag in Todesbanden
Jesus Christus unser Heiland, der von
    uns
Jesulein, du bist mein

Mit Fried' und Freud' ich fahr' dahin

Vater unser im Himmelreich

Wir glauben all' an einen Gott

Hypodorian

Gott Vater, der du deine Sonne

Hilf Gott, daß mirs gelinge/Wenn mein Sünd mich kränken

Jesus Christus, unser Heiland, der den Tod

Von Gott will ich nicht lassen/Helf mir Gott's Güte preisen

Was mein Gott will, das gescheh allzeit

Phrygian

Ach Gott von Himmel sieh darein

Ach Herr mich armen Sünder

Aus tiefer Noth, laßt uns zu Gott

Christum, wir sollen loben schon

Christus, der uns selig macht

Da Jesus an dem Kreuze stund

Es woll' uns Gott genädig sein

Herr Jesu Christ wahr'r Mensch und Gott

Hypophrygian

Erbarm dich mein, O Herre Gott

Herr Gott, dich loben wir

Mensch, willt du leben seliglich

Mitten wir im Leben sind mit dem Tod umfangen

O großer Gott von Macht

Mixolydian

Ach wir armen Sünder unsre Missethat

Auf diesen Tag bedenken wir

Es ist das Heil uns kommen her

Hypomixolydian

Dies sind die heiligen zehn Gebot

Gelobet seist du Jesu Christ

Gott sei gelobet

Grates nunc omces reddamus Domino [Danksagen wir alle Gott, unserm herrn Christo]

O Lux beata Trinitas or *Iam sol recedit igneus* [Der du bist drei in Einigkeit]

Veni, Creator Spiritus [Komm Gott Schöpfer, heiliger Geist]

Veni, Sancte Spiritus [Komm, heiliger Geist, erfüll die Herzen]

Aeolian

Erhalt uns Herr, bei deinem Wort

Gott hat das Evangelium

Ich danke dem Herrn von ganzen Herzen

Ich ruf zu dir, Herr Jesu Christ

Magnificat [Meine Seel erhebt den Herren]

Wer nur den lieben Gott läßt walten

Hypoaeolian

Allein zu dir

Mag ich Unglück, nicht widerstahn

Von allen Menschen abgewandt

Wär Gott nicht mit uns diese Zeit

Wo Gott der Herr nicht bei uns hält

APPENDIX 3

Index to the Chorale Examples

The following index provides source information for the chorales that appear in the Examples. Each chorale is identified by its text incipit (organized alphabetically), BWV number, and Breitkopf and Härtel edition number (B & H).[1] Next is provided the catalogue number for the chorale in the *Bach Compendium* (BC), where the chorales are classified under Work Group F.[2] Unless the chorale is singly transmitted, the larger work context of the chorale will be identified along with its catalogue number within the *Bach Compendium*. (The cantatas are given under Work Group A.) Finally, this index provides concordances for the chorale within the following sources: *Bach Gesellschaft* (BG)[3] and *Neue Bach-Ausgabe* (NBA)[4] editions, as well as Ms. Leipzig R 18.[5]

The first collection of Bach's chorales dates from around 1735, a gathering of 149 chorales in a manuscript (Ms. R 18) prepared in Leipzig by Bach's assistant, Johann Ludwig Dietel. F. W. Marpurg, C. P. E. Bach and J. P. Kirnberger were involved in the preparation of

---

[1] *371 vierstimmige Choralgesänge von Johann Sebastian Bach*, Dritte Auflage (Leipzig: Breitkopf und Härtel, 1832); reprint, J. S. Bach, 371 *Four-Part Chorales* (New York: Associated Music Publishers, Inc. [194–]).

[2] Hans–Joachim Schulze and Christoph Wolff, *Bach Compendium. Analytisch–bibliographisches Repertorium der Werke Johann Sebastian Bachs*, vol. I, *Vokalwerke*, parts 1–4 (Leipzig: Edition Peters, 1985–89). For source information concerning the cantus firmus and text, I will refer the reader to this comprehensive catalogue of Bach's vocal works.

[3] *J. S. Bach Werke*. Gesamtausgabe der Bachgesellschaft (Leipzig, 1851–1899; reprint, Ann Arbor, 1947; Farnborough, 1967).

[4] *Johann Sebastian Bach. Neue Ausgabe sämtliche Werke*. (*Neue Bach–Ausgabe*), edited by the Johann–Sebastian–Bach–Institut of Göttingen and by the Bach–Archiv of Leipzig (Kassel and Basel, 1954—). Volumes in preparation are indicated by brackets [ ].

[5] Leipzig Musikbibliothek der Stadt, Ms. R 18. *Vierstimmige / Choräle / von / J. Seb. Bach*. Partiturabschrift of J. L. Dietel, c. 1735. The manuscript will be catalogued in

posthumously published editions during the 1760s and 1780s.[6] Most of the source material for these published editions is unfortunately not preserved. The two-volume edition of 200 chorales published by Birnstiel in 1765 and 1769 was based on a manuscript in Marpurg's possession, one in C. P. E. Bach's possession and one in the publisher's possession.[7] A larger collection was offered by Breitkopf's four-volume edition of 1784-87, which included 371 chorales.[8] The first two volumes (1784, 1785) comprised a reprint of the Birnstiel edition;[9] the last two volumes (1786, 1787) were based on the pre-

---

the *Bach Compendium* under Work Group Z (Z 1); its function as a source for the chorales is described in the context of Work Group F in *BC* I/iv, p. 1288. An edition of the manuscript is forthcoming in *NBA* III/2. Discussions of Ms. R 18 are found in articles by Friedrich Smend, "Zu den ältesten Sammlungen der vierstimmigen Choräle J. S. Bachs," *Bach Jahrbuch* 52 (1966), pp. 5–40 and Hans Joachim Schulze, "150 Stück von den Bachischen Erben. Zur Überlieferung der vierstimmigen Choräle Johann Sebastian Bachs," *Bach Jahrbuch* 69 (1983), pp. 81–100.

[6]Gerd Wachowski reviews the publication history of Bach's chorales in his article "Die vierstimmigen Choräle Johann Sebastian Bachs. Untersuchungen zu den Druckausgaben von 1765 bis 1932 und zur Frage der Authentizität," *Bach Jahrbuch* 69 (1983), pp. 51–79. Wachowski summarizes the contents of the major publications from the eigtheenth to the twentieth century and discusses the sources used for these publications. In this context, see also Schulze, "150 Stück von den Bachischen Erben," pp. 81–84 and Smend, "Zu den ältesten Sammlungen," pp. 5ff. Several of the documents and letters that concern the origins of publication are translated in *The Bach Reader*, edited Hans T. David and Arthur Mendel (New York: W. W. Norton and Co., 1945; revised 1966), pp. 270–274.

[7]*Johann Sebastian Bach's vierstimmige 373 Choralgesänge*, Erster/Zweyter Theil (Berlin and Leipzig: F. W. Birnstiel, 1765, 1769; Reprint, Hildesheim and New York, 1975). Part I (1765) of this edition includes a Preface by C. P. E. Bach (translated in *The Bach Reader*, pp. 270–71) and a list of printing errors. Part II (1769) was edited by Johann Friedrich Agricola to the dissatisfaction of C. P. E. Bach, who published a "Note to the public" denouncing the edition (translated in *The Bach Reader*, p. 271). The lost manuscript sources for this edition are described in the *BC*, pp. 1288–1289: Marpurg [Z 2], C. P. E. Bach [Z 3] and Birnstiel [Z 4].

[8]*Johann Sebastian Bachs vierstimmige Choralgesänge*, Erster–vierter Theil (Leipzig: J. G. I. Breitkopf, 1784–87). This collection was edited by C. P. E. Bach and it includes an updated version of his 1765 Preface (translated in *The Bach Reader*, p. 274). Kirnberger had a significant role in the preparation of this publication but died in 1783 before its completion.

[9]The contents of Birnstiel 1765/69 and Breitkopf 1784–87 are compared in Smend, "Zu den ältesten Sammlungen," Table A, pp. 26–30.

viously mentioned Ms. R 18[10] and a manuscript in the possession of Princess Anna Amalia of Prussia (Am. B. 46).[11]

The Birnstiel and Breitkopf editions served as the foundation for subsequent editions. It is not my purpose here to review the publication history,[12] but I will take a moment to consider the placement of the chorales in the complete works edition of the *Bach Gesellschaft*. Throughout this series the chorales which derive from larger vocal works are published in their original context. Volume 39, edited by Franz Wüllner in 1892, includes 185 singly transmitted chorales (BWV numbers 253-438).[13] Wüllner relied upon only one source for his edition of these 185 chorales—the Breitkopf publication of 1784-87. It is important to establish that there are problems with the transmission of the independent chorales through the printed editions by Birnstiel and Breitkopf. While the prints may serve as the only extant sources for many of the singly transmitted chorales, they are most probably not error-free. In the case of published chorales for which an authentic source *is* available, discrepancies exist between the musical texts of the print and the original source. We can assume that such discrepancies appear also in the chorales for which autograph sources are not extant.

Ms. R 18 is significant as an extant source for Volumes 3 (1786) and 4 (1787) of the Breitkopf edition.[14] It also holds a unique position as the only collection prepared during Bach's lifetime; indeed, one that was prepared by the composer's assistant. Although also not error-free it can be established as a more reliable source than the printed editions—in the case of chorales from extant vocal works which are found in Ms. R 18, the musical text in the manuscript

---

[10]The connection between Ms. R 18 and Bretikopf 1786–87 is discussed in Schulze, "150 Stück von den Bachischen Erben," pp. 84ff. The contents of Ms. R 18, Birnstiel 1765/69, and Breitkopf 1784–87 are compared in Smend, "Zu den ältesten Sammlungen," Table B, pp. 30–34 and discussed on pp. 19–20.

[11]Berlin, Deutsche Staatsbibliothek, Am. B. 46. Collection for Anna Amalia of Prussia, between 1776 and 1783. The manuscript is catalogued in *BC* as Z 6 and is described in connection with Work Group F on p. 1289.

[12]As mentioned earlier, Wachowski reviews the publication history of the Bach chorales. In his discussion he describes the format of the chorale notation, the sources used, and the editing principles.

[13]*J. S. Bach Werke, Gesamtausgabe der Bachgesellschaft*, Vol. 39, ed. Franz Wüllner (Leipzig, 1892; Reprint, Ann Arbor, 1947, Farnborough, 1968), pp. 177–276.

[14]For 41 chorales, Ms. R 18 is the only manuscript source. See Schulze, "150 Stück von den Bachischen Erben," p. 93.

reflects more closely the original source than does the printed version.[15] There is reason to assume that Ms. R 18 is a fairly reliable source for those singly transmitted chorales contained therein. For the singly transmitted chorales, therefore, my musical texts in this study have been based on Ms. R 18, or if the chorale is not found in that source, on the *Bach Gesellschaft* edition (vol. 39) of 1892.

Ach Gott, vom Himmel sieh darein. BWV 153/1 (B & H, Nr. 3)   Ex. 2

    BC F 3; opening chorale of cantata "Schau, lieber   (p. 13)
        Gott, wie meine Feind," BC A 25
    BG 32, p. 43; NBA I/4, p. 201

Ach Gott, vom Himmel sieh darein. BWV 77/6 (B & H, Nr.   Ex. 56
253)

    BC F 3; final chorale of cantata "Du sollt Gott,   (p. 118)
        deinen Herren, lieben," BC A 126
    BG 18, p. 254; NBA I/21, p. 22

Ach, was soll ich Sünder machen. BWV 259 (B & H, Nr. 39)   Ex. 65

    BC F 5; singly transmitted chorale   (p. 130)
    BG 39, Nr. 96; [NBA III/2]

Allein zu dir, Herr Jesu Christ. BWV 33/6 (B & H, Nr. 13)   Ex. 93a

    BC F 11; final chorale of cantata "Allein zu dir, Herr   (p. 167)
        Jesu Christ," BC A 127
    BG 7, p. 114; NBA I/21, p. 56

Allein zu dir, Herr Jesu Christ. BWV 261 (B & H, Nr. 359)   Ex. 93b

    BC F 11; singly transmitted chorale   (p. 167)
    BG 39, Nr. 9; [NBA III/2]

Als Jesus Christus in der Nacht. BWV 265 (B & H, Nr. 180)   Ex. 67

    BC F 14; singly transmitted chorale   (p. 133)
    BG 39, Nr. 13; [NBA III/2]

Aus tiefer Not schrei ich zu dir. BWV 38/6 (B & H, Nr. 10)   Ex. 39

    BC F 22; final chorale of cantata "Aus tiefer Not   (pp. 66–67)
        schrei ich zu dir," BC A 152
    BG 7, p. 300; [NBA I/25]; Ms. R 18, Nr. 94

---

[15]Smend, "Zu den ältesten Sammlungen," pp. 23–24. For instance, based on a comparison of Ms. R 18, the print, and the chorale as it appears in its original context, Smend identifies instances in which the print transposes the chorale, but Ms. R 18 does not, and instances in which the print changes the note values, while Ms. R 18 does not.

Befiehl du deine Wege. BWV 161/6 (B & H, Nr. 270) Ex. 28
BC F 92; final chorale of cantata "Komm, du süße (p. 54)
Todesstunde," BC A 135b
BG 33, pp. 27–28; NBA I/23, pp. 32–33 (1st version),
pp. 63–64 (2nd); Ms. R 18, Nr. 34 (without
obligato instruments)

Christ lag in Todesbanden. BWV 4/8 (B & H, Nr. 184) Ex. 89
BC F 26; final chorale of cantata "Christ lag in Todes (p. 157)
Banden," BC A 54
BG 1, p. 124; NBA I/9, p. 40

Christ lag in Todesbanden. BWV 277 (B & H, Nr. 15) Ex. 86
BC F 26; singly transmitted chorale (pp. 150–151)
BG 39, Nr. 25; [NBA III/2]

Christus, der uns selig macht. BWV 245/21 (B & H, Nr. 81) Ex. 8, 15, 24
BC F 31; first movement, Part II of the St. John Pas- (pp. 29, 45, 51)
sion, BC D 2/15
BG 12/1, p. 43; NBA II/4, p. 51

Der du bist drei in Einigkeit. BWV 293 (B & H, Nr. 154) Ex. 30
BC F 42; singly transmitted chorale (p. 55)
BG 39, Nr. 40; [NBA III/2]

Dies sind die heiligen Zehn Gebot. BWV 298 (B & H, Nr. 127) Ex. 51
BC F 46; singly transmitted chorale (pp. 102–103)
BG 39, Nr. 45; [NBA III/2]

Erschienen ist der herrlich Tag. BWV 145/5 (B & H, Nr. 17) Ex. 95
BC F 16; final chorale of cantata "Ich lebe mein (pp. 172–73)
Herze, zu deinem Ergötzen," BC A 60
BG 30, p. 122; NBA I/10, p. 128

Gelobet seist du, Jesu Christ. BWV 91/6 (B & H, Nr. 51) Ex. 3, 47, 48
BC F 69; final chorale of cantata "Gelobet seist du, (pp. 18, 90–91,
Jesu Christ," BC A 9 92–93)
BG 22, p. 32; NBA I/2, p. 163; Ms. R 18, Nr. 131

Gelobet seist du, Jesu Christ. BWV 314 (B & H, Nr. 288) Ex. 49
BC F 69; singly transmitted chorale (pp. 96–97)
BG 39, Nr. 61; [NBA III/2]; Ms. R 18, Nr. 65

Jesu, meine Freude. BWV 227/7 (B & H, Nr. 283)   Ex. 74

    BC F 116; from motet "Jesu, meine Freude," BC C 5   (p. 142)
    BG 39, pp. 75–76; NBA III/1, p. 94; Ms. R 18, Nr. 21
    33

Komm, Gott Schöpfer, heiliger Geist. BWV 370 (B & H, Nr.   [Ex. 4, 19, 21]
187)

    BC F 125; singly transmitted chorale   (pp. 24, 47, 48)
    BG 39, Nr. 117; [NBA III/2]

Meine Seel erhebt den Herren. BWV 10/7 (B & H, Nr. 358)   Ex. 10, 75

    BC F 140; final chorale of cantata "Meine Seel er-   (pp. 35, 143)
      hebt den Herren," BC A 175
    BG 1, p. 303; [NBA I/28]

Mit Fried und Freud ich fahr dahin. BWV 382 (B & H, Nr. 49) Ex. 73, 98

    BC F 144; singly transmitted chorale   (pp. 140, 184–185)
    BG 39, Nr. 129; [NBA III/2]; Ms. R 18, Nr. 51

Von Gott will ich nicht lassen. BWV 73/5 (B & H, Nr. 191)   Ex. 97

    BC F 185; final chorale of cantata "Herr, wie du   (pp. 180–81)
      willt, so schick's mit mir," BC A 35
    BG 18, p. 104; [NBA I/6]

Was mein Gott will, das g'scheh allzeit. BWV 65/7 (B & H, Nr.   Ex. 91
41)

    BC F 194; final chorale of cantata "Sie werden aus   (pp. 162–164)
      Saba alle kommen," BC A 27
    BG 16, p. 166; NBA I/5, p. 46

Wir glauben all an einen Gott. BWB 437 (B & H, Nr. 133)   Ex. 63

    BC F 211; singly transmitted chorale   (p. 129)
    BG 39, Nr. 184; [NBA III/2]

APPENDIX 4

Representative Modal Chorales by Bach

Dorian

    Als Jesus Christus in der Nacht, BWV 265

    Christ ist erstanden von der Marter alle, BWV 276

    Christ lag in Todesbanden, BWV 4/8, 277

    Erschienen ist der herrlich Tag, BWV 145/5

    Hilf, Gott, laß mirs gelingen, BWV 343

    Jesu, meine Freude, BWV 227/7

    Mit Fried und Freud ich fahr dahin, BWV 83/5, 382

    Wir glauben all an einen Gott, BWV 437

Phrygian

    Aus tiefer Not schrei ich zu dir, BWV 38/6

    Befiehl du deine Wege, BWV 161/6, 270, 271

    Christum wir sollen loben schon, BWV 121/6

    Christus, der uns selig macht, BWV 245/21, 245/65, 283

    Erbarm dich mein, o Herre Gott, BWV 305

    Es woll' uns Gott genädig sein, BWV 311, 312

    Herr Gott, dich loben wir, BWV 328

    Herr, nun laß in Friede, BWV 337

    Herzlich tut mich verlangen, BWV 153/5

    Kyrie, Gott Vater in Ewigkeit, BWV 371

    O Haupt voll Blut und Wunden, BWV 244/72, 248/5

    Mitten wir im Leben sind, BWV 383

Mixolydian

Der du bist drei in Einigkeit, BWV 293
Die Nacht ist kommen, BWV 296
Dies sind die heiligen zehn Gebot, BWV 298
Es ist das Heil uns kommen her, BWV 155/5
Gelobet seist du, Jesu Christ, BWV 64/2, 91/6, 248/28, 314
Komm, Gott Schöpfer, heiliger Geist, BWV 370
Warum sollt ich mich den grämen, BWV 422

Aeolian

Ach lieben Christen seid getröst, BWV 256
Ach was soll ich Sünder machen, BWV 259
Allein zu dir, Herr Jesu Christ, BWV 33/6, 261
Das walt mein Gott, BWV 291
Helft mir Gotts Güte preisen, BWV 16/6, 183
Ich ruf zu dir, Herr Jesu Christ, BWV 177/5
Meine Seel erhebt den Herren, BWV 10/7, 324
Von Gott will ich nicht lassen, BWV 73/5, 418, 419
Wär Gott nicht mit uns diese Zeit, BWV 257
Was mein Gott will, das gescheh allzeit, BWV 65/7
Wer nur den lieben Gott läßt walten, BWV 179

APPENDIX 5

Texts and Translations for Cantatas 38, 77, 91

BWV 38. Aus tiefer Not schrei ich zu dir

Text and translation by Z. Philip Ambrose. © 1984 Hänßler. Used by permission.

1. Coro (Choral)

Aus tiefer Not schrei ich zu dir,
Herr Gott, erhör mein Rufen;
Dein gnädig Ohr neig her zu mir
Und meiner Bitt sie öffne!
Denn so du willst das sehen an,
Was Sünd und Unrecht ist getan,
Wer kann, Herr, vor dir bleiben?

2. Recitativo

In Jesu Gnade wird allein
Der Trost vor uns und die
    Vergebung sein,
Weil durch des Satans Trug und
    List
Der Menschen ganzes Leben
Vor Gott ein Sündengreuel ist.
Was könnte nun
Die Geistesfreudigkeit zu unserm
    Beten geben,
Wo Jesu Geist und Wort nicht
    neue Wunder tun?

3. Aria

Ich höre mitten in den Leiden
Ein Trostwort, so mein Jesus
    spricht.
Drum, o geängstigtes Gemüte,

1. Chorale

In deep distress I cry to thee,
Lord God, hear thou my calling;
Thy gracious ear bend low to me
And open to my crying!
For if thou wilt observance make
Of sin and deed unjustly done,
Who can, Lord, stand before thee?

2. Recitative

In Jesus' mercy will alone
Our comfort be and our
forgiveness rest,
Because through Satan's craft and
guile
Is mankind's whole existence
'Fore God a sinful outrage found.
What could then now
Bring peace and joy of mind to us
in our petitions
If Jesus' Spirit's word did not new
wonders do?

3. Aria

I hear amidst my very suff'ring
This comfort which my Jesus
speaks.
Thus, O most anguished heart and
spirit,

233

Vertraue deines Gottes Güte,	Put trust in this thy God's dear kindness,
Sein Wort besteht und fehlet nicht,	His word shall stand and never fail,
Sein Trost wird niemals von dir scheiden.	His comfort never thee abandon!

4. Recitativo con Choral — **4. Recitative with instrumental chorale**

Ach!	Ah!
Daß mein Glaube noch so schwach,	That my faith is still so frail,
Und daß ich mein Vertrauen	And that all my reliance
Auf feuchtem Grunde muß erbauen!	On soggy ground I must establish!
Wie ofte müssen neue Zeichen	How often must I have new portents
Mein Herz erweichen!	My heart to soften!
Wie? kennst du deinen Helfer nicht,	What? Dost thou know thy helper not,
Der nur ein einzig Trostwort spricht,	Who speaks but one consoling word,
Und gleich erscheint,	And then appears,
Eh deine Schwachheit es vermeint,	Before thy weakness doth perceive,
Die Rettungsstunde.	Salvation's hour.
Vertraue nur der Allmachtshand	Just trust in his almighty hand
und seiner Wahrheit Munde!	and in his mouth so truthful!

5. Aria (Terzetto) — **5. Aria**

Wenn meine Trübsal als mit Ketten	When my despair as though with fetters
Ein Unglück an dem andern hält,	One sorrow to the next doth bind,
So wird mich doch mein Heil erretten,	Yet shall no less my Savior free me,
Daß alles plötzlich von mir fällt.	And all shall sudden from me fall.
Wie bald erscheint des Trostes Morgen	How soon appears the hopeful morning
Auf diese Nacht der Not und Sorgen!	Upon the night of woe and sorrow!

6. Choral — **6. Chorale**

Ob bei uns ist der Sünden viel,	Though with us many sins abound,
Bei Gott ist viel mehr Gnade;	With God is much more mercy;
Sein Hand zu helfen hat kein Ziel,	His hand's assistance hath no end,

Wie groß auch sei der Schade.	However great our wrong be.
Er ist allein der gute Hirt,	He is alone our shepherd true,
Der Israel erlösen wird	Who Israel shall yet set free
Aus seinen Sünden allen.	Of all his sinful doings.

BWV 77. Du sollt Gott, deinen Herren, lieben.

Text and translation by Z. Philip Ambrose. © 1984 Hänßler. Used by permission.

1. Coro con Choral

Du sollt Gott, deinen Herren, lieben von ganzem Herzen, von ganzer Seele, von allen Kräften und von ganzem Gemüte und deinen Nächsten als dich selbst.

1. Chorus with instrumental chorale

Thou shalt thy God and master cherish with all thy bosom, with all thy spirit, with all thy power and with all thine affection, as well thy neighbor as thyself.

2. Recitativo

So muß es sein!
Gott will das Herz vor sich alleine haben.
Man muß den Herrn von ganzer Seele
Zu seiner Lust erwählen
Und sich nicht mehr erfreun,
Als wenn er das Gemüte
Durch seinen Geist entzündt,
Weil wir nur seiner Huld und Güte

Alsdann erst recht versichert sind.

2. Recitative

So must it be!
God would our hearts himself possess completely.
We must the Lord with all our spirit
Elect as he requireth,
And never be content
But when he doth our spirits
Through his own Spirit fire,
For we, of all his grace and kindness,
Are only then completely sure.

3. Aria

Mein Gott, ich liebe dich von Herzen,
Mein ganzes Leben hangt dir an.
Laß mich doch dein Gebot erkennen
Und in Liebe so entbrennen,
Daß ich dich ewig lieben kann.

3. Aria

My God, with all my heart I love thee,
And all my life depends on thee.
But help me thy great law to fathom
And with love to be so kindled
That I thee evermore may love.

4. Recitativo

Gib mir dabei, mein Gott! ein Samariterherz,

4. Recitative

Make me as well, my God,
Samaritan in heart

Daß ich zugleich den Nächsten liebe	That I may both my neighbor cherish
Und mich bei seinem Schmerz Auch über ihn betrübe,	And be amidst his pain For his sake also troubled,
Damit ich nicht bei ihm vorübergeh	That I may never merely pass him by
Und ihn in seiner Not nicht lasse.	And him to his distress abandon.
Gib, daß ich Eigenliebe hasse,	Make me to self–concern contrary,
So wirst du mir dereinst das Freudenleben	For then thou shalt one day the life of gladness
Nach meinem Wunsch, jedoch aus Gnade geben.	That I desire in thy dear mercy grant me.

5. Aria   5. Aria

Ach, es bleibt in meiner Liebe Lauter Unvollkommenheit!	Ah, there bideth in my loving Nought but imperfection still!
Hab ich oftmals gleich den Willen, Was Gott saget, zu erfüllen,	Though I often may be willing God's commandments to accomplish,
Fehlt mir's doch an Möglichkeit.	'Tis beyond my power yet.

6. Choral   6. Chorale

Herr, durch den Glauben wohn in mir,	Lord, through my faith come dwell in me,
Laß ihn sich immer stärken,	Make it grow ever stronger,
Daß er sei fruchtbar für und für	That it be fruitful more and more
Und reich in guten Werken;	And rich in righteous labors;
Daß er sei tätig durch die Lieb,	That it be active in my love,
Mit Freuden und Geduld sich üb,	In gladness and forbearance skilled,
Dem Nächsten fort zu deinen.	My neighbor ever serving.

BWV 91. Gelobet seist du, Jesu Christ.

Text and translation by Z. Philip Ambrose. © 1984 Hänßler. Used by permission.

1. Coro (Choral)   1. Chorus

Gelobet seist du, Jesu Christ,	All glory to thee, Jesus Christ,
Daß du Mensch geboren bist	For thou man today wast born,
Von einer Jungfrau, das ist wahr,	Born of a virgin, that is sure,
Das freuet sich der Engel Schar.	Thus joyful is the angel host.
Kyrie eleis!	Kyrie eleis!

2. Recitativo e Choral

Der Glanz der höchsten
    Herrlichkeit,
Das Ebenbild von Gottes Wesen,
Hat in bestimmter Zeit
Sich einen Wohnplatz auserlesen.

Das ewgen Vaters einigs Kind,
Das ewge Licht von Licht geboren,
Itzt man in der Krippe findt.
O Menschen, schauet an,
Was hier der Liebe Kraft getan!

In unser armes Fleisch und Blut,

(Und war denn dieses nicht
    verflucht, verdammt, verloren?)
Verkleidet sich das ewge Gut.
So wird es ja zum Segen
    auserkoren.

3. Aria

Gott, dem der Erden Kreis zu
    klein,
Den weder Welt noch Himmel
    fassen,
Will in der engen Krippe sein.
Erscheinet uns dies ewge Licht,
So wird hinfüro Gott uns nicht

Als dieses Lichtes Kinder hassen.

4. Recitativo

O Christenheit!
Wohlan, so mache dich bereit,
Bei dir den Schöpfer zu
    empfangen.
Der große Gottessohn
Kömmt als ein Gast zu dir
    gegangen.

2. Recitative and Chorale

The light of highest majesty,

The image of God's very being,
Hath, when the time was full,
Himself a dwelling found and
    chosen.

Th'eternal Father's only child
Th'eternal light of light begotten,
Who now in the crib is found.
Ye mortals, now behold
What here the pow'r of love hath
    done!

Within our wretched flesh and
    blood,
And was this flesh then not
    accursed,condemned, and fallen?)
Doth veil itself eternal good.
Yet is it, yea, for grace and
    blessing chosen.

3. Aria

God, for whom earth's orb is too
    small,
Whom neither world nor heaven
    limits,
Would in the narrow crib now lie.
Revealed to us this lasting light,
Thus henceforth will us God not
    hate,
For of this light we are the
    children.

4. Recitative

O Christian world,
Now rise and get thyself prepared
To thee thy maker now to
    welcome.
The mighty son of God
Comes as a guest to thee
    descended.

Ach, laß dein Herz durch diese Liebe rühren;	Ah, let thy heart by this his love be smitten;
Er kömmt zu dir, um dich vor seinen Thron	He comes to thee, that he before his throne
Durch dieses Jammertal zu führen.	Through this deep vale of tears may lead thee.

5. Aria   5. Aria

Die Armut, so Gott auf sich nimmt,	The weakness which God hath assumed
Hat uns ein ewig Heil bestimmt,	On us eternal health bestowed,
Den Überfluß an Himmelsschätzen.	The richest store of heaven's treasures.
Sein menschlich Wesen machet euch	His mortal nature maketh you
Den Engelsherrlichkeiten gleich,	The angel's glory now to share,
Euch zu der Engel Chor zu setzen.	You to the angels' choir appointeth.

6. Choral   6. Chorale

Das hat er alles uns getan,	All this he hath for us achieved,
Sein groß Lieb zu zeigen an;	His great love to manifest;
Des freu sich alle Christenheit	Rejoice then all Christianity
Und dank ihm des in Ewigkeit.	And thank him for this evermore.
Kyrie eleis!	Kyrie eleis!

BIBLIOGRAPHY

Bach References

1. General References

David, Hans T. and Arthur Mendel. *The Bach Reader. A Life of Johann Sebastian Bach in Letters and Documents.* New York and London: W. W. Norton and Co., 1966.

Emery, Walter, Nicholas Temperley, and Christoph Wolff. "Johann Sebastian Bach." *The New Grove Dictionary of Music and Musicians.* Edited by Stanley Sadie. London: MacMillian Publishers Ltd., 1980. Reprinted in *The New Grove Bach Family.* New York and London: W. W. Norton and Company, 1983, pp. 44–237.

Schmieder, Wolfgang. *Thematisch–systematisches Verzeichnis der musikalischen Werke Johann Sebastian Bachs: Bach–Werke–Verzeichnis.* Leipzig: Breitkopf und Härtel, 1950; 7th reprint edition, 1980.

Schulze, Hans-Joachim, and Christoph Wolff. *Bach Compendium: Analytisch-bibliographisches Repertorium der Werke Johann Sebastian Bachs.* Vol. 1. *Vokalwerke.* Parts 1–4. Leipzig: Edition Peters, 1985–89.

Wolff, Christoph. *Stile antico in der Musik Johann Sebastian Bachs; Studien zu Bachs Spätwerk.* Vol. 6 of *Beihefte zum Archiv für Musikwissenschaft.* Wiesbaden and Steiner, 1968.

_____. *Bach. Essays on His Life and Music.* Cambridge: Harvard University Press, 1991.

2. Editions and Manuscript Sources for the Chorales

J. S. Bach Werke. Gesamtausgabe der Bach–Gesellschaft. Vols. 1–47. Leipzig: Breitkopf und Härtel, 1851–99. Reprint, Ann Arbor, 1947; Farnborough 1968.

J. S. Bach. Neue Ausgabe sämtlicher Werke (Neue Bach–Ausgabe). Edited by the Johann-Sebastian-Bach-Institut of Göttingen and by the Bach-Archiv of Leipzig. Series I–VIII. Kassel and Basel, 1954–.

371 vierstimmige Choralgesänge von Johann Sebastian Bach. Dritte Auflage. Leipzig: Breitkopf und Härtel, 1832. Reprint, J. S. Bach, *371 Four-Part Chorales.* New York: Associated Music Publishers, Inc. [194–].

Leipzig, Bibliothek der Stadt, Ms. R 18. *Vierstimmige Choräle von J. Seb. Bach.* Copied by Johann Ludwig Dietel. Leipzig, c. 1735.

3. Chorale Studies and Analytical Studies

Blankenburg, Walter. "Johann Sebastian Bach und das evangelische Kirchenlied zu seiner Zeit." *Bachiana et alia musicologica. Festschrift Alfred Dürr.* Edited by Wolfgang Rehm. Kassel: Bärenreiter, 1983, pp. 31–38.

Breig, Werner. "Grundzüge einer Geschichte von Bachs vierstimmigem Choralsatz." *Archiv für Musikwissenschaft* 45.3 (1988), pp. 165–185; continued, *AfM* 45.4 (1988), pp. 300–319.

Burns, Lori. "J. S. Bach's Chorale Harmonizations of Modal Cantus Firmi." Ph.D. dissertation, Harvard University, 1991.

————. "J. S Bach's Mixolydian Chorale Harmonizations." *Music Theory Spectrum* 15/2 (Fall, 1993), pp. 144–172.

————. "Modal Identity and Irregular Endings in Two Chorale Harmonizations by J. S. Bach." *Journal of Music Theory* 38/1 (Spring, 1994), pp. 43–77.

Buszin, Walter E. "The Chorale in the Baroque Era and J. S. Bach's Contribution to It." *Studies in Eighteenth-Century Music.* London: George Allen and Unwin, Ltd., 1970. Reprint, New York: Da Capo Press, 1979, pp. 108–116.

Chafe, Eric. *Tonal Allegory in the Vocal Music of J. S. Bach.* Berkeley: University of California Press, 1991.

Dürr, Alfred. "J. S. Bach und das Kirchengesangbuch." *Jahrbuch für Liturgik und Hymnologie* 1 (1955), pp. 120–122.

————. "Melodievarianten in Johann Sebastian Bachs Kirchenliedbearbeitungen." *Wolfenbütteler Forschungen* 31 (1986), pp. 149–163.

Herz, Gerhard. *Essays on J. S. Bach.* Ann Arbor: UMI Research Press, 1985.

Leaver, Robin A. "Bach and Hymnody. The Evidence of the *Orgelbüchlein.*" *Early Music* 13 (1985), pp. 227–235.

Marshall, Robert. "How J. S. Bach Composed Four-Part Chorales." *Musical Quarterly* 56.2 (1970), pp. 198–220.

Neumann, Werner. "Zur Frage der Gesangbücher Johann Sebastian Bachs." *Bach Jahrbuch* 42 (1956), pp. 112–123.

Platen, Emil. "Zur Echtheit einiger Choralsätze Johann Sebastian Bachs." *Bach Jahrbuch* 61 (1975), pp. 50–61.

Renwick, William. "Voice-Leading Patterns in the Fugal Expositions of J. S. Bach's *Well-Tempered Clavier.*" Ph.D. dissertation, City University of New York, 1987.

_____. "Modality, Imitation and Structural Levels: Bach's *Manualiter Kyries* from *Clavierübung III.*" *Music Analysis* 11/1 (1992), pp. 55–74.

_____. *Analyzing Fugue: A Schenkerian Approach.* Stuyvesant, NY: Pendragon Press, 1995.

Schering, Arnold. "Joh. Phil. Kirnberger als Herausgeber Bachscher Choräle." *Bach Jahrbuch* 15 (1918), pp. 141–150.

Schulze, Hans-Joachim. "150 Stück von Bachischen Erben. Zur Überlieferung der vierstimmigen Choräle Johann Sebastian Bachs." *Bach Jahrbuch* 69 (1983), pp. 81–100.

Smend, Friedrich. "Zu den ältesten Sammlungen der vierstimmigen Choräle J. S. Bachs." *Bach Jahrbuch* 52 (1966), pp. 5–40.

Wachowski, Gerd. "Die vierstimmigen Choräle von Johann Sebastian Bachs. Untersuchungen zu den Druckausgaben von 1765 bis 1932 und zur Frage der Authentizität." *Bach-Jahrbuch* 69 (1983), pp. 51–79.

Wolff, Christoph. "Bachs vierstimmige Choräle. Geschichtliche Perspektive im 18. Jahrhundert." *Jahrbuch des Staatlichen Institut für Musikforschung Preußischer Kulturbesitz* 1985/86, pp. 257–263. Translated by the author, "On the Recognition of Bach and 'the Bach Chorale': Eighteenth–Century Perspectives." In *Bach: Essays on his Life and Music.* Cambridge and London: Harvard University Press, 1991, pp. 383–390.

Hymnological References

1. Sources for the Texts and Cantus Firmi

A. F. W. Fischer and W. Tümpel. *Das deutsche evangelische Kirchenlied des 17. Jahrhunderts.* 6 vols. Gütersloh, 1904–16. Reprint, Hildesheim and New York: Georg Olms, 1964.

Wackernagel, Philipp. *Das deutsche Kirchenlied von der ältesten Zeit bis zu Anfang des 17. Jahrhunderts.* 5 vols. Leipzig, 1864–77. Reprint, Hildesheim and New York: Georg Olms, 1964.

Zahn, Johannes. *Die Melodien der deutschen evangelischen Kirchenlieder.* 6 vols. Gütersloh: C. Bertelsmann, 1889–93. Reprint, Hildesheim and New York: Georg Olms, 1963.

2. Historical Chorale Works

Buxtehude, Dietrich. *Sämtliche Orgelwerke.* Edited K. Beckmann. Wiesbaden, 1972.

Haßler, Hans Leo. *Lustgarten Neuer Teutscher Gesäng, Balletti, Gaillarden und Intraden.* Nürnberg, 1601. Edited by Friedrich Zelle. *Gesellschaft für Musikforschung.* Vol. 15. Leipzig: Breitkopf und Härtel, 1887.

Peter, Christoph. *Andachts Zymbeln.* Leipzig, 1682.

Praetorius, Michael. *Musae Sioniae.* Parts 1–9, 1605–1610. *Gesamtausgabe der Musikalischer Werke von Michael Praetorius.* Vols. 1–9. Edited by Friedrich Blume. Wolfenbüttel and Berlin: Georg Kallmeyer, 1928–39.

Scheidt, Samuel. *Das Görlitzer Tablaturbuch vom Jahre 1650.* Edited by Christhard Mahrenholz. Leipzig: Peters, 1940.

Schein, Johann Hermann. *Cantional oder Gesangbuch Augsburgischer Konfession.* 2 vols. [Leipzig], 1627/1645. Edited by Adam Adrio. Kassel: Bärenreiter, 1965/1967.

Schemelli, Georg Christian. *Musicalisches Gesang–Buch, Darinnen 954 geistreiche, sowohl alte als neue Lieder und Arien, mit wohlgesetzten Melodien, in Discant und Bass befindlich sind.* Leipzig: Breitkopf, 1736. Facsimile, Hildesheim and New York: Georg Olms, 1975.

Schütz, Heinrich. *Neue Ausgabe sämtlicher Werke.* Vol. 6. *Der Psalter nach Cornelius Beckers Dichtungen.* Freiburg: Georg Hoffman, 1628. Edited by Walter Blankenburg. Kassel and Basel: Bärenreiter, 1955.

Telemann, Georg Philipp. *Fast allgemeines Evangelisch-Musikalisches Lieder-Buch.* Hamburg: Ludwig Stromer, 1730. Reprint, Hildesheim and New York: Georg Olms, 1977.

Vetter, Daniel. *Musikalischer Kirch- und Haus-Ergötzlichkeit.* Leipzig, 1713.

Vopelius, Gottfried. *Neu Leipziger Gesangbuch.* Leipzig: Breitkopf, 1682.

Walther, Johann Gottfried. *Gesammelte Werke für Orgel.* Vols. 26–27 of *Denkmaler Deutscher Tonkunst.* Edited by Max Sieffert. Wiesbaden: Breitkopf und Härtel, 1958.

Theory and Analysis

1. Theoretical Writings

Adlung, Jacob. *Anleitung zu der Musikalischen Gelahrheit.* Erfurt, 1758. Facsimile edition by Hans Joachim Moser. Kassel and Basel: Bärenreiter, 1953.

Albrecht, Johann Lorenz. *Gründliche Einleitung in die Anfangslehren der Tonkunst.* Langensalza: Johann Christian Martini, 1761.

Atcherson, W. T. "Modal Theory of 16th-Century German Theorists." Ph.D. dissertation, Indiana, 1960.

———. "Theory Accomodates Practice: *Confinalis* Theory in Renaissance Music Treatises." *Journal of the American Musicological Society* 23.2 (1970), pp. 326–330.

———. "Key and Mode in Seventeenth-Century Theory Books." *Journal of Music Theory* 17 (1973), pp. 204–234.

Bellermann, Heinrich. *Der Kontrapunkt.* Berlin, 1861.

Bernhard, Christoph. *Tractatus compositionis augmentatis* (after 1657). Edited by Joseph Müller Blattau. *Die Kompositionslehre Heinrich Schützens in der Fassung seines Schülers Christoph Bernhard.* 2d ed. Kassel: Bärenreiter, 1963. Translated by Walter Hilse in "The Treatises of Christoph Bernhard." *Music Forum* III (1973), pp. 1–196.

Burmeister, Joachim. *Musica poetica.* Rostock, 1606. Facsimile edition, Kassel, 1955.

Calvisius, Sethus. *Melopoeia sive melodiae condendae ratio.* Erfurt, 1592.

———. *Exercitationes musicae duae.* Leipzig, 1600.

———. *Exercitatio musica tertia.* Leipzig, 1611.

Crüger, Johann. *Synopsis musica continens rationem constituendi & componendi melos harmonicum.* Berlin: Johann Kall, 1630.

Dahlhaus, Carl. *Untersuchungen über die Entstehung der harmonischen Tonalität.* Kassel: Bärenreiter, 1968. Translated by Robert O. Gjerdingen as *Studies on the Origin of Harmonic Tonality.* Princeton, 1990.

Fétis, François-Joseph. *Traité complet de la théorie et de la pratique de l'harmonie contenant la doctrine de la science et de l'art.* Paris, 1844.

Fux, Johann Joseph. *Gradus ad Parnassum.* Vienna, 1725. Translated into German by Lorenz Mizler, *Gradus ad Parnassum oder Anführung zur regelmässigen Composition, aus dem Lateinischen ins Deutsch übersetzt.* Leipzig, 1732. Reprint, Hildesheim and New York: Georg Olms, 1984.

Grave, Floyd K. "Abbé Vogler and the Bach Legacy." *Eighteenth-Century Studies* 13.2 (1979–80), pp. 119–41.

Grave, Floyd K. and Margaret G. *In Praise of Harmony: The Teachings of Abbé Georg Joseph Vogler.* Lincoln: University of Nebraska Press, 1987.

Harnisch, Otto Siegfried. *Artis musicae delineatio.* Frankfurt, 1608.

Herbst, Johann Andreas. *Musica poëtica. Das ist: Kurze Anleitung wie man einen Gesang componieren und setzen soll.* Nürnberg, 1643.

Jakoby, Richard. "Untersuchungen über die Klausellehre in deutschen Musiktraktaten des 17. Jahrhunderts." Ph.D. dissertation, Mainz, 1955.

Kirnberger, Johann Philipp. *Die Kunst des reinen Satzes in der Musik.* 2 vols. Berlin, 1771–79. Translated by David Beach and Jürgen Thym as *The Art of Strict Musical Composition.* New Haven: Yale University Press, 1982.

Kittel, Johann Christian. *Der angehende praktische Organist.* 3 vols. Beyer and Maring: Erfurt, 1801, 1803, 1808. Facsimile edition by Peter Williams in vol. 72 of *Bibliotheca Organologica.* Buren: Frits Knuf, 1981.

Knecht, Justin Heinrich. *Vollständige Orgelschule für Anfänger und Geübtere.* 3 vols. Leipzig, 1795–98.

Kollman, August Friedrich Christoph. *An Essay on Musical Harmony.* London, 1776.

Kreitz, Helmut. "Abbé Vogler als Musiktheoretiker. Ein Beitrag zur Geschichte der Musiktheorie im 18. Jahrhundert." Ph.D. dissertation, Saarbrücken, 1957.

Lester, Joel. "Major-Minor Concepts and Modal Theory in Germany, 1592–1680." *Journal of the American Musicological Society* 30 (1977), pp. 208–253.

_____. "The Recognition of Major and Minor Keys in German Theory: 1680–1730." *Journal of Music Theory* 22 (1978), pp. 65–103.

_____. *Between Modes and Keys: German Theory, 1592–1802.* Stuyvesant, NY: Pendragon Press, 1989.

Lippius, Johannes. *Synopsis Musicae Novae.* Anno, 1612. Translated by Benito Rivera as *Synopsis of New Music.* Colorado Springs: Colorado College Music Press, 1977.

Matthaei, Conrad. *Kurzer, doch ausführilicher Bericht von den Modis Musicis, welchen aus den besten, ältesten, berühmtesten und bewerthesten Autoribus der Music zusammengetragen.* Königsberg: Johann Reusner, 1652.

Mattheson, Johann. *Der vollkommene Capellmeister.* Hamburg, 1739. Translated by Ernest C. Harriss as *Johann Mattheson's Der vollkommene Capellmeister.* Ann Arbor: UMI Research Press, 1981.

Meier, Bernhard. "Die Harmonik im c.f.-haltigen Satz des 15. Jahrhunderts. *Archiv für Musikwissenschaft* 10 (1953), pp. 289–310.

_____. *Die Tonarten der klassischen Vokalpolyphonie, nach den Quellen dargestellt.* Utrecht: Oostök, Scheltema & Holkema, 1974. Translated by Ellen S. Beebe as *The Modes of Classical Vocal Polyphony.* New York: Broude Brothers, 1988.

Niedt, Friedrich Erhard. *Musikalishce Handleitung; oder, gründlicher Unterricht.* Vol. 3. *Handlend vom Contra-Punct, Canon, Motetten, Choral, Recitativ-Stylo and Cavaten.* Edited J. Mattheson. Hamburg: Benjamin Schillers Erben, 1717. Translated by Pamela L. Poulin and Irmgard C.

Taylor as *The Musical Guide: Parts I (1700/1710), II (1721), and III (1717)*. Oxford: Clarendon Press; New York: Oxford University Press, 1988.

Printz, Wolfgang Caspar. *Phrynis Mitilenaeus, oder Satyrischer Componist.* Quedlinburg: Christian Okels, 1676; 2d ed., Dresden and Leipzig, 1696.

Rameau, Jean Philipp. *Traité de l'harmonie.* Paris, 1722. Translated by Philip Gossett as *Treatise on Harmony.* New York: Dover Publications, 1971.

Riemann, Hugo. *Grosse Kompositionslehre.* 3 vols. Berlin and Stuttgart, 1902–13.

Rivera, Benito. *German Music Theory in the Early Seventeeth Century: The Treatises of Johannes Lippius.* Ann Arbor: UMI Research Press, 1980.

_____. "The Seventeenth–Century Theory of Triadic Generation and Invertibility and its Application in Contemporaneous Rules of Composition." *Music Theory Spectrum* 6 (1984), pp. 63–78.

Sorge, Georg Andreas. *Vorgemach der Musikalischen Composition.* Lobenstein, 1745. Translated by Allyn Dixon Reilly in "Georg Andreas Sorge's 'Vorgemach der Musikalischen Composition'; A Translation and Commentary." Ph.D. dissertation, Northwestern University, 1980.

_____. *Anleitung zur Fantasie oder zu der schönen Kunst, das Clavier, wie auch andere Instrumente, aus dem Kopfe zu spielen.* Lobenstein, 1767.

Sweelinck. "Kompositionsregeln." [Mss. Vienna and Berlin] Edited by Hermann Gehrmann in *Werken van Jan Pieterszn Sweelinck.* Vol. X. The Hague: Martinus Nijhoff; Leipzig: Breitkopf und Härtel, 1901; reprint edition, Farnborough, England: Gregg International Publishers, 1968. Translated by Victoria G. Mathis as "Introduction and Translation of Jan Pieterszn Sweelinck's *Rules of Composition.*" M.A. thesis, Memphis State University, 1975.

Tolkoff, Lyn. "French Modal Theory before Rameau." *Journal of Music Theory* 17 (1973), pp. 150–163.

Türk, Daniel Gottlob. *Von den wichtigsten Pflichten eines Organisten: ein Beytrag zur Verbesserung der Musikalische Liturgie.* Halle, 1787.

_____. *Kurze Anweisung zum Generalbaß spielen.* Halle and Leipzig, 1791. Translated by Raymond H. Haggh as *School of Clavier Playing.* Lincoln and London: University of Nebraska Press, 1982.

Vogler, Abbé Georg Joseph. *Choral–System.* Copenhagen, 1800.

_____. *Organist-schola.* Stockholm, 1798–99.

Vogler, G. J. and Carl Maria von Weber. *Zwölfe Choräle von Sebastian Bach, umgearbeitet von Vogler, zergliedert von Carl Maria von Weber.* Leipzig, 1810.

Walther, Johann Gottfried. *Praecepta der musicalischen Composition.* Ms., 1708. Edited by P. Benary. Leipzig: Breitkopf und Härtel, 1960.

_____. *Musicalisches Lexicon, oder Musicalische Bibliothek.* Leipzig, 1732. Facsimile edition by Richard Schaal. Kassel: Bärenreiter, 1953, 4/1986.

Werckmeister, Andreas. *Harmonologia musica oder Kurze Anleitung zur Musikalischen Composition.* Frankfurt and Leipzig, 1687. Facsimile edition in Andreas Werckmeister, *Hypomnemata Musica und andere Schriften.* Hildesheim and New York: Georg Olms, 1970.

_____. *Musikalische Paradoxical–Discourse.* Quedlinburg, 1707.

Zarlino, Gioseffo. *Le Istitutione harmoniche III.* Venice, 1558. Translated by Guy A. Marco as *The Art of Counterpoint.* New Haven: Yale University Press, 1968.

_____. *Le Istitutione harmoniche IV.* Venice, 1558. Translated by Vered Cohen as *On the Modes.* New Haven: Yale University Press, 1983.

2. Schenkerian Theory

Forte, Allen and Stephen E. Gilbert. *Introduction to Schenkerian Analysis.* Text and Instructor's Manual. New York: W. W. Norton and Co., 1982.

Neumeyer, David and Susan Tepping. *A Guide to Schenkerian Analysis.* New Jersey: Prentice Hall, 1992.

Schenker, Heinrich. *Von der Stimmführung im Generalbaß .* (Ms. 1917). (Introduction published in "Heinrich Schenker: Von der Stimmführung im Generalbaß ." *Der Dreiklang* 3 (June, 1937), pp. 75–81.) Discussed by Hedi Siegel in "A Source for Schenker's Study of Thorough Bass: His Annotated Copy of J. S. Bach's *Generalbaßbüchlein*." *Schenker Studies.* Edited by Hedi Siegel. Cambridge: Cambridge University Press, 1990, pp. 15–28. Translation forthcoming by Hedi Siegel in *Music Forum* VI/2.

_____. *Funf Urlinie-Tafeln.* New York: David Mannes School and Vienna: Universal Edition, 1932. Reprinted as *Five Graphic Music Analyses,* New York: Dover, 1969.

_____. "J. S. Bach: Matthäuspassion Einleitungschor (Erste Choral–Fantasie)." *Der Tonwille* IV/4 (October, 1924), pp. 3–10.

_____. *Neue musikalische Theorien und Phantasien.* Part 1. *Harmonielehre.* Vienna: Universal Edition, 1906. Edited by Oswald Jonas and translated by Elisabeth Mann Borgese as *Harmony.* Chicago: University of Chicago Press, 1954.

_____. *Neue musikalische Theorien und Phantasien.* Part 2. *Kontrapunkt.* 2 vols. Vienna: Universal Edition, 1910–22. Translated by John Rothgeb and Jürgen Thym as *Counterpoint.* New York: Schirmer Books, A Division of MacMillan, 1987.

_____. *Neue musikalische Theorien und Phantasien.* Part 3. *Der freie Satz.* Vienna: Universal Edition, 1935. Translated and edited by Ernst Oster as *Free Composition.* New York: Longman Inc., 1979.

3. Analytical Writings

Bashour, Frederick J. "Towards a More Rigorous Methodology for the Analysis of the Pre-Tonal Repertory." *College Music Symposium* 19.2 (1979): 140–153.

Beach, David. "The Fundamental Line from Scale Degree $\hat{8}$: Criteria for Evaluation." *Journal of Music Theory* 32/2 (1988), pp. 271–94.

_____. "Apples and Oranges: Neumeyer's Reading of the Octave Line." *In Theory Only* 11/5 (1990), pp. 9–17.

Cook, Nicholas. *A Guide to Musical Analysis.* London: J. M. Dent and Sons, Ltd., 1987.

Gagné, David. "Monteverdi's *Ohimè dov'è il mio ben* and the Romanesca." *Music Forum* VI (1987), pp. 61–91.

Judd, Cristle Collins. "Some Problems of Pre-Baroque Analysis: An Examination of Josquin's *Ave Maria . . . Virgo Serena.*" *Music Analysis* 4 (1985), pp. 201–239.

Leech-Wilkinson, Daniel. "Machaut's *Rose, Lis* and the Problem of Early Music Analysis." *Music Analysis* 3/1 (1984), 9–28.

Mahrt, William Peter. "Guillaume Dufay's Chansons in the Phrygian Mode." *Studies in Music at the University of Western Ontario* 5 (1980), pp. 81–98.

McClary, Susan. "The Transition from Modal to Tonal in the Works of Monteverdi." Ph.D. dissertation, Harvard University, 1976.

Mitchell, William J. "The Prologue to Orlando di Lasso's *Prophetiae Sibyllarum.*" *Music Forum* II (1970), pp. 264–273.

Neumeyer, David. "The Three-Part *Ursatz.*" *In Theory Only* 10/1–2 (1987), pp. 3–27.

_____. "The Ascending *Urlinie.*" *Journal of Music Theory* 31 (1987), pp. 275–303.

_____. "The *Urlinie* from $\hat{8}$ as a Middleground Phenomenon." *In Theory Only* 9/5–6 (1987), pp. 3–25.

_____. "Fragile Octaves, Broken Lines." *In Theory Only* 11/3 (1989), pp. 11–30.

Novack, Saul. "Fusion of Design and Tonal Order in Mass and Motet: Josquin Deprez and Heinrich Isaac." *Music Forum* II (1970), pp. 187–263.

_____. "The Analysis of Pre-Baroque Music." *Aspects of Schenkerian Theory*. Edited by David Beach. New Haven: Yale University Press, 1983, pp. 113–33.

_____. "The Significance of the Phrygian Mode in the History of Tonality." *Miscellanea Musicologica* 9 (1977), pp. 82–127.

_____. "Foreground, Middleground and Background: Their Significance in the History of Tonality." *Schenker Studies*. Edited by Hedi Siegel. Cambridge: Cambridge University Press, 1990.

Philipps, Edward. "Pitch Structures in a Selected Repertoire of Early German Chorale Melodies." *Music Theory Spectrum* 3 (1981), pp. 98–116.

Powers, Harold. "Mode." *The New Grove Dictionary of Music and Musicians*. Edited by Stanley Sadie. London: MacMillan Publishers Ltd., 1980, vol. 12, pp. 376–418 (§§I–III).

_____. "Modal Representation in Polyphonic Offertories." *Early Music History 2: Studies in Medieval and Early Modern Music*. Edited by Iain Fenlon. Cambridge, 1982.

Rivera, Benito. "The Two-Voice Framework and its Harmonization in Arcadelt's First Book of Madrigals." *Music Analysis* 6 (1987), pp. 59–88.

Roig-Francoli, Miguel Angel. "Compositional Theory and Practice in Mid-Sixteenth Century Spanish Instrumental Music: The Arte de Taner Fantasia by Thomas Santa Maria and the Music of Antonio de Cabezon (Sixteenth Century)." Ph.D. Dissertation, Indiana, 1990.

Salzer, Felix. *Structural Hearing.* 2 vols. New York: Charles Boni, 1952.

_____. "Heinrich Schenker and Historical Research: Monteverdi's Madrigal *Oimé, se tanto amate.*" *Aspects of Schenkerian Theory*. Edited by David Beach. New Haven: Yale University Press, 1983, pp. 135–52.

Schmalzriedt, Siegfried. *Heinrich Schütz und andere zeitgenössische Musiker in der Lehre Giovanni Gabrielis; Studien zu ihren Madrigalen.* Neuhausen–Stuttgart: Hänssler, 1972.

Schulenberg, David. "Modes, Prolongation, and Analysis." *Journal of Musicology* 4 (1985–86), pp. 303–329.

Stern, David. "Tonal Organization in Modal Polyphony." *Theory and Practice* 6.2 (1981), pp. 5–39.

_____. "Hidden Uses of Chorale Melodies in Bach's Cantatas." *Trends in Schenkerian Research*. Edited by Allen Cadwallader. New York: Schirmer Books, A Division of MacMillan, 1990, pp. 115–132.

INDEX OF NAMES

Bach, Carl Philipp Emanuel, 224–25

Bellermann, Heinrich, 17, 19–20

Burmeister, Joachim, 191 (fn 12)

Chafe, Eric, 114 (fn 31)

Cook, Nicholas, 16

Dahlhaus, Carl, vii, 9, 13-15, 190, 191 (fn 12)

Dietel, Johann Ludwig, 224

Fétis, François–Joseph, 5

Forte, Allen, 159–60, 161, 165, 168

Gagné, David, 144–46

Gilbert, Stephen, 159–60, 161, 165, 168

Harnisch, Otto Siegfried, 191 (fn 13)

Herbst, Johann Andreas, 190–96, 197

Herz, Gerhard, 104 (fns 25, 26)

Josquin, 42

Kirnberger, Johann Philipp, 3, 21, 22–24, 74, 115–17, 122–23, 207–10, 222, 224–25

Knecht, Justin Heinrich, 30, 34, 126 (fn 5), 170, 212–17, 222–23

Leech–Wilkinson, Daniel, 2

Lester, Joel, 12, 115 (fn 33)

Matthaei, Conrad, 126 (fn 5), 219–20

Mattheson, Johann, 25–28

Marpurg, Friedrich Wilhelm, 224–25

Meier, Bernhard, 117 (fn 34)

Monteverdi, Claudio, 144–46

Neumeyer, David, 15–16, 40, 149, 152–55

Novack, Saul, 3, 64 (fn 20)

Phillips, Edward, 128 (fn 6)

Praetorius, Michael, 115 (fn 48)

Printz, Wolfgang Caspar, 196–202, 203

Rameau, Jean Philipp, 4–5

Renwick, William, 10–11, 53

Rivera, Benito, 191 (fn 13)

Salzer, Felix, 16

Scheidt, Samuel, 99 (fn 23)

Schein, Johann Hermann, 115 (fn 48)

Schenker, Heinrich, vii, 2, 4, 5–7, 16, 17–21, 38, 39, 40, 41, 45, 50, 87, 98, 121, 131, 132–35, 160, 178

Schütz, Heinrich, 115 (fn 48)

Sorge, Georg Andreas, 11, 34, 126 (fn 5), 221

Stern, David, 41–43

Telemann, Georg Philipp, 99 (fn 23)

Tepping, Susan, 15–16

Türk, Daniel Gottlob, 117–19, 210–11

Vogler, Abbé Georg Joseph, 212, 218

Walther, Johann Gottfried, 21–22, 23, 25, 33, 126 (fn 5), 202–7, 220–21

Zarlino, Gioseffo, vii, 28 (fn 51), 41, 187–90, 197